Missing Socrates

Missing Socrates

Problems of Plato's Writing

Jay Farness

The Pennsylvania State University Press
University Park, Pennsylvania

Library of Congress Cataloging-in-Publication Data

Farness, Jay.
   Missing Socrates : problems of Plato's writing / Jay Farness.
      p.   cm.
   Includes bibliographical references and index.
   ISBN 0-271-00722-2
   1. Plato. Dialogues.   2. Plato–Style.   3. Socrates.
4. Criticism   I. Title.
B395.F32   1991
184—dc20   90-37580
                                                                       CIP

Copyright © 1991 The Pennsylvania State University
All rights reserved
Printed in the United States of America

It is the policy of The Pennsylvania State University Press to use acid-free paper for the first printing of all clothbound books. Publications on uncoated stock satisfy the minimum requirements of American National Standard for Information Sciences—Permanence of Paper for Printed Library Materials, ANSI Z39.48–1984.

*For Kay and Ray,
for Peter and Emily*

From these people—springing up of themselves, each drawing inspiration from any chance place, the one thinking the other knows nothing—from these you would never get a *logos* either willingly or unwillingly. But one must take over from these and investigate it as a *problēma* [a "projection," a geometrical problem].

Theodorus
(*Theaetetus* 180B–C)

Means of defense may be divided into antidotes both divine and human and into *problēmata* ["projections," coverings]; *problēmata* into armament for war and into other business; the other business into screens and into protections against winter and heat.

The Stranger from Elea
(*Statesman* 279C)

Contents

Acknowledgments ix

One / A Preface to This Plato 1

Two / Missing Socrates 31

Three / Plato's Architexture 55

Four / Person, Tradition, Text in *Ion* 79

Five / Innocence and Experience in *Charmides* 105

Six / The Reproduction of Socrates in *Phaedrus* 135

Seven / Derrida in the Prescience of Plato 171

Index 197

Acknowledgments

This is a book from beyond the walls, but it does not come from so far beyond the walls that it is altogether shameless about its rusticities. I beg a reader's indulgence for its occasional breach of manners and urge your exoneration from responsibility of all those it approvingly cites, names, or thanks.

And I would like to thank some: the Board of Studies in Literature at the University of California, Santa Cruz, for the opportunity to offer as a guest a graduate proseminar in Plato and Derrida; Henry Hooper and the Organized Research Committee at Northern Arizona University for patient support of this project; Werner Gundersheimer of the Folger Library in Washington, D.C., for fellowship support of a cluster of research projects that surreptitiously included this one; Zeph Stewart of Washington's Center for Hellenic Studies for library privileges during a sabbatical; Seth Schein and his Santa Cruz Plato Conference for prompting my chapter 6; Gerald Bruns for timely recognition and support of my work; Mary-Kay Gamel, who allowed this work its first hearing; and Charles Griswold for welcoming a provincial to town.

And then there are friends and colleagues who have variously encouraged, informed, amused, and restrained me in my study: Paul Mann, Jerrold Hogle, the aforementioned Seth Schein and Mary-Kay Gamel, John Lynch, Michael Miller, Jan Swearingen, Bryan Short, and Jim Simmerman.

And there is Harry Berger, Jr., who shared with me the Santa Cruz proseminar and much else. Perhaps you hold the unassigned and unexpected paper for the long course in Plato I began in 1973 as an auditor of a Berger seminar. I acknowledge here, at least, a substantial debt in order to avoid dragging his good name through innumerable notes and references. I supply enough bibliography, however, to direct my reader to Berger's own texts, where you can better learn and decide how much or how little they have a part in what I write.

And finally I send my gratitude and good wishes to the muses of Minnesota, to the taxpayers of California, and to the critics of Arizona.

Thanks is also owed to the following journals for permission to reprint in revised form articles originally published in their pages: *Philosophy and Rhetoric* for an earlier version of chapter 2; *Arethusa* for an earlier version of chapter 3; and *Philological Quarterly* for an earlier version of chapter 4.

One / A Preface to This Plato

To begin with a far-fetched thought: Socrates, I believe, would not have much interest in what I am trying to do in this book. Laying it aside, he would school me in the familiar way concerning fundamentals that the book assumes, mentions, or bedevils. Imagining such a Socratic response, I suspect that what follows will tax a reader's Socratic loyalties.

Then again, I think that Plato's view of my project would be more encouraging. My sympathy for what Plato is writing should partly account for this far-fetched expectation. At the very least, my writing might be allowed among the activities that a tolerant Academy pursued once philosophical inquiry began missing Socrates in earnest. And so I appeal to a reader's Platonic situation, to the famously uncertain footings from which Socratic loyalties rise, and to the gains and losses implicated in what I term "missing Socrates."

If I could, I surely would lay aside this work and take my seat, and my medicine, opposite a living, questioning, mischievously winning Socrates. But Socrates—the Socrates of the *Phaedo,* for example, who chides Simmias and Cebes for such dependency on him—might very well strive to dispel this longing for his charm, which Plato repeatedly portrays as a very pleasant substitute for the work of philosophy. According to this reproach, my nostalgia, my mourning or missing him, would indeed miss Socrates: Like that of the participants in the *Phaedo*, my desire would miss its object in misrecognizing or misrepresenting it. Like Simmias, Cebes, or Crito, I would be haunted by an *eidōlon*, or shade, or worse by a *mormolukeion*, or bugbear, and stand in need of a "magician" to dispel my fixation on the dead and the dead's fixation on me (*Phaedo* 81C–D, 77E, 115C–D).

I write to demonstrate how such difficulties manifest themselves in Plato's writing and in the way one might read that writing as a complex strategy of "missing Socrates." This strategy finds in the resources of writing a path for philosophy—and for Plato—leading out of an *aporia*, or perplex: philosophy's (and Plato's) profound, self-defeating dependence on the presence of Socrates. My parenthetical inclusion of Plato's name here, however, is imprecise; it cuts against the grain of his writing, which is studiously anonymous, impersonal, open to a host of questions and criticisms and so, like Socrates, strategically self-effacing.[1] These features of the self-effacing author are the textual equivalents of Plato's absence from the *Phaedo*'s prison scene during the inauguration of Socrates' absence, on that day when Plato began missing (i.e., mourning) Socrates by taking ill and missing (i.e., not seeing or meeting) him (*Phaedo* 59B).

I

A number of the difficulties I stir up involve the very untidy logic of textual interpretation and its regard for equivocation, for various tonalities of utterance, for impersonations, for fictive modes of statement, and for literary and rhetorical forms—all of which eclipse the clear light of propositional logic or constative statement and cast a hermeneutical shade over Platonic philosophy. In self-defense one might urge how, in addition to their affection for the logician's acumen, Plato and Socrates seem to glory in the multiple meanings, readings, characters, beginnings, end-

---

1. Ludwig Edelstein, "Platonic Anonymity," *American Journal of Philology* 83 (1962): 1–22.

ings, and points of view that divert the hermeneut from certitudes.[2] And interpretive practice is made still more uncertain, of course, by problems of historical and cultural difference that further diffract Plato's lights.

By way of illustration, consider this well-known problem in interpretation, nearly contemporary to Socrates in its origin: What difference would it make to our study of the ancient drama to know whether or to what extent women regularly attended theatrical performances? Scholars are, in fact, not sure about this, though so simple an item of knowledge would seem to be crucial to our understanding of a drama that features Lysistrata, Praxagora, and *thesmophoriazousai,* as well as Antigone, Alcestis, Medea, Phaedra, Electra, or Clytemnestra. Or take this similar case: What difference would it make to our study to know whether Homer, whoever he (or she or they) might be, composed for the moment of performance or for memory or for a lettered script? Again, this is a crucial determination, but in the scholarship also an elusive one.

For our reading or study of the drama, of Homer, and—as I will urge—of Plato as well, there is the problem concerning what might be called the *protocols* of reading what the writers of these texts wrote.[3] Modeling the "situation" of narrative discourse on a sentence's dependence on "associated non-linguistic factors," the French critic Roland Barthes writes:

> . . . one can say that every narrative is dependent on a "narrative situation," the set of protocols according to which the narrative is "consumed." In so-called "archaic" societies, the narrative situation is heavily coded. . . .[4]

---

2. Here one might also include the matter of "Platonic myth" and its problematic relationship to *logos* in the dialogues. For an overview, see another influential discussion of Ludwig Edelstein's, "The Function of Myth in Plato's Philosophy," *Journal of the History of Ideas* 10 (1949): 463–81.

3. A *prōtokollon* is, first, a table of contents pasted to the outside or the beginning of the bookroll. Hence, the *prōtokollon* literally covers the book, mediating the intercourse between the inscription and its various uses as minute or record, as contract, as charter, as code of conduct. Later, a protocol is a draft agreement to a negotiation, a transcription of the propositions agreed to. Later still, *protocol* covers the formulas and etiquette employed in diplomatic charters and affairs of state. So by protocols of reading, one can conceive the customs, conventions, rules, procedures, or strategies by which one decodes, applies, transmits, or translates the inscription. For a general discussion of the contemporary question of protocols in interpretation, see Robert Scholes, *Protocols of Reading* (New Haven, Conn.: Yale University Press, 1989), especially pp. 50–88.

4. Roland Barthes, "Introduction to the Structural Analysis of Narratives," in *Image/Music/Text,* trans. Stephen Heath (New York: Hill and Wang, 1977), p. 116. Barthes draws the phrase "associated non-linguistic factors" from M. A. K. Halliday.

A religious liturgy or myth, for example, is "heavily coded," extensively dependent on the "non-linguistic factors" of its sacred situation. How heavily coded, scholars have often asked, is the situation of the ancient drama performed during the civic festivals of Dionysus and answering to specific expectations and attitudes of its audience, perhaps its all-male audience? Plato's interest in such questions is suggested by Socrates' claims in the *Republic* concerning *mimetic*, or direct, and *diegetic*, or indirect, discourse in the epic (*Republic* III, 392D–394B). The dangers that Socrates sees in mimetic discourse reflect his suspicion that such discourse is not "heavily coded" but should be. Agamemnon's discursive situation should be unique, not endlessly imitable by generations of rhapsodes or schoolboys.

By contrast to the heavy coding of "archaic" ritual speech, Barthes describes how

> . . . our society takes the greatest pains to conjure away the coding of the narrative situation: there is no counting the number of narrational devices which seek to naturalize the subsequent narrative by feigning to make it the outcome of some natural circumstance and thus, as it were, "disinaugurating" it: epistolary novels, supposedly rediscovered manuscripts, author who met the narrator, films which begin the story before the credits. The reluctance to declare its codes characterizes bourgeois society and the mass culture issuing from it: both demand signs which do not look like signs. (Barthes, p. 116)

These discourses bring along their own situations, which readily graft on to the natural attitudes of the common sense shared by consumers or decoders. Thus for the legislators of the ideal state, Homer proves disconcertingly viable in the open, unencoded market situation for discourses, not needing a formal "inauguration," or setting of limits between profane and charismatic. I also cite Barthes at length, however, because his specification of "narrational devices" exactly matches a prominent feature of the self-encoding of Plato's dialogues—the celebrated literary framing, the happenstance narrative occasions (e.g., in the *Symposium* or the *Theaetetus*), the cunning use of directly and indirectly narrated conversation. Plato, in these ways, has minimized these texts' dependence on "associated non-linguistic factors" (time, place, context, inaugural or institutional framing, audience, speaker, etc.). For much of the history of the West, it has been possible to bring texts of Plato right into a later moment, a later common sense, a later natural attitude, without making this *translatio* very conspicuous at all. Thanks in part to these "narrational devices," Plato's is the most natural, the most accessible of philosophical texts.

Ancient literature is already dissembling, however, even before historical obliterations enter the picture to scramble "non-linguistic factors." Whether by accident or by some deeper affinity, *dēmos*-minded ancient Athens shares with "mass culture" this demand for accessible discourse: "both demand signs which do not look like signs," signs that may be consumed or decoded without necessary reference to a learned exegesis, but signs which, for that very reason, seem at times to call for a "hermeneutic of suspicion" to pierce their rhetorical disingenuousness. Even if we knew the inaugurating protocols of Homeric epic or Athenian tragedy, in other words, we would still encounter interpretive problems of the sort that Barthes alludes to. This is because much of Greek literature, even overlooking the gaps left by historical change, is already devious and elliptical about its protocols, often dissembling one thing as another, circulating a fiction as a fact, passing off written text as impromptu speech, camouflaging an artful sign as something natural.

One has only to think of the literary culture that Ion inhabits, the deep duplicities of which Socrates happily points out in developing his facetious claim that Ion possesses an art of being possessed. Or one might recall how Critias in the *Charmides* grafts his self-interested interpretations of objective knowledge on to Delphic or Socratic wisdom. Or there is the rhetoric of false pretenses invoked in the *Phaedrus*. In this dialogue an ambiguous erotic speech of Lysias in its various impersonations and transformations is symptomatic of a rhetorical culture in which writers like Lysias enable an amateur to speak in public with the polish of a professional. Which is the appropriate set of protocols for public speech under such conditions? Do we gauge a defendant as an amateur improvising a candid defense? Or as a mouthpiece possibly no more than repeating the promptings of some expert *logographos*? Ion, Critias, and Lysias would seem to accept an externally imposed "heavy coding"—that is, the nonlinguistic factors with which institutions hedge a speaker—but in fact Plato suggests that these performers use discursive resources to outmaneuver that heavy coding, to insert their own signs as the common or natural facts, and so to make a weaker case the stronger. Such discursive attempts to conjure up or rearrange extratextual authority go back at least to Homer, Hesiod, and their invocation of the Muses, about which Hesiod, for one, is less than straightforward (*Theogony*, lines 22–35).

In trying to legislate the relevant Plato protocols, one might begin by modeling reading, as Barthes tends to, on decoding. By this assumption, one must try to hold to the same code in decoding that a writer referred to in encoding a message. Knowing the protocols we can mentally approximate the semiotic circumstances of the text at its inception. Whether we choose to be bound to these protocols in our own transmission of the text is, of course, another question. But the point is that, in theory, it is crucial to know a gendering of the dramatic audience so as to be able to gauge the sociolinguistic dimension of the dramatic discourse, for the simple reason that men usually talk differently to women than they talk about them. And it is crucial to know to what extent our protocols of the written text—for example, concerning its structure, its coherence, its argument in a broad sense—apply to Homer's composition, or whether we need to construct, as some Homerists have sought to, a radically different discursive mentality with very different protocols involving oral improvisation, formulaic structure, acute audience consciousness, and the like. The Spartan recipient of a secret message wraps the ribbon of skewed text around a *skutalē*, the shaped baton exactly like that used by the sender. The skewed text thereupon resumes its legibility. Similarly, a reader of Plato might wrap the ribbon of text skewed by the dialogical manner around a *skutalē* carefully shaped to the relevant protocols, to the assumptions, intentions, linguistic and literary codes, and traditions invoked by Plato.

On this communicative model, every text would seem to imply some agreement or understanding between two or more parties that underwrites a text's legibility—for example, some shared language and experience of a sender and receiver of an epistle, or some consensus among parties bonded by a written contract. Hence, the decoding of texts that originate prior to or outside of current understandings ought to elicit that effort of interpretation that Clifford Geertz, adapting literary explication to the analysis of "social text" generally, has termed "thick description": "sorting out the structures of signification . . . and determining their social ground and import,"[5] sorting out significant

---

5. Clifford Geertz, "Thick Description: Toward an Interpretive Theory of Culture," in *The Interpretation of Cultures* (New York: Basic Books, 1973), p. 9.

features in light of the relevant protocols, that is, of the "associated nonlinguistic factors." For Geertz this is not necessarily an easy correspondence between "structures of signification" and "social ground." Signification, like dreamwork, often processes risky content into more comfortable shapes; some signification is effective for what it does *not* explicitly say. And the social ground may be fractured, layered, stressed. But Geertz recognizes the deviousness of such mediations; he asserts only an interaction between the two levels that a hermeneutic process then tries to tease out of the evidence. Furthermore, the reconstructed dynamic between text and ground is both an end of and the means for interpretation according to a dialectic of ends and means that tries to move out of the hermeneutic circle.

Such necessary flexibility of hermeneutic theory and practice has, however, made clear protocols hard to come by in the study of challenging texts like Plato. Why these protocols are so elusive is part of the problem with Platonic texts, even part of the problem explicitly posed *in* Plato. For one thing, Plato virtually inaugurates the "philosophical dialogue" as a literary form, and so his dialogues embody their protocols as much as they borrow them from a tradition we might use in their decoding— as the interpretation of Homer, for example, has used Serbian oral tradition.[6] Because of their deliberate innovation, the Platonic dialogues constantly but implicitly press general questions concerning how they should be read. But this issue of protocols is also made explicit, most infamously in the *Phaedrus*'s discussions of how one ought to write (*Phaedrus* 274Bff.). There the preferred solution to this problem— avoiding writing altogether—is obviously problematized, if not invalidated, by the fact that even Socrates, like Plato, obviously read and composed text with some relish.

We are additionally perplexed in the case of Plato, of course, by the powerful example of Aristotle, who imposes on Plato the protocols of his philosophical discourse. What this means we know by comparing the typically slender Aristotelian précis of Plato's philosophy to the richly textured passage or dialogue it summarizes—for example, the allusion to the *Gorgias* in the overture to the *Metaphysics,* or the famous but brief and

---

6. In the work of Milman Parry and Albert B. Lord. See, for example, Lord, *The Singer of Tales* (Cambridge, Mass.: Harvard University Press, 1960). For a recent survey of Homeric protocols, see Seth Schein, *The Mortal Hero: An Introduction to Homer's "Iliad"* (Berkeley and Los Angeles: University of California Press, 1984), especially pp. 1–88.

astonishingly uncomplicated synopsis of Plato later in Book I, chapter 6. This, we might remember, is evidently the same Aristotle who in the *Poetics,* for the sake of philosophical economy, dismisses the actual dramatic production as a surplus or supplementary business:

> The Spectacle, though an attraction, is the least artistic of all the parts, and has least to do with the art of poetry. The tragic effect is quite possible without a public performance and actors; and besides, the getting-up of the Spectacle is more a matter for the costumier than the poet. (Ch. 6:II, 1450b)[7]

This view of the drama fits Aristotle's disregard of the spectacle of Platonic dialogue and its emphasis on "public performance and actors." It seems true for Plato, incidentally, that spectacle does indeed interfere with philosophy; such spectacle, like the artless Ion, is in a sense inartistic, "more a matter for the costumier" than the artist. But such spectacle is not so irrelevant to the poetics of Plato, who positions much of his writing in the strife between art and its embodied performance, between theory and its human practitioners, between philosophy and philosophers. It is possible, I suggest, to make such a Plato a critic as well as a precursor of Aristotle's philosophic refinery.

Nor can we forget that this matter of the protocols for reading Plato offers one example of the larger concern with institutions of text transmission that has long fascinated classical studies, necessarily fascinated classical studies, which in view of what has been lost seems fortunate to have any texts at all. Perhaps it is hard to think that any of these texts might have been in some sense addressed to us moderns, who have had to work so strenuously to intercept, to piece out, or to reconstruct the contents of the drama, for example. Often we regard ourselves as outsiders trying to reimagine an alien mentality or discursivity—for example, Milman Parry trying to specify the oral basis of Homeric poetry or Eric Havelock proposing a fascinating but narrow view of Plato's use and critique of this musical tradition.[8] More recent studies of Havelock and others have aimed at elucidating the date, extent, and forms of Greek literacy so as to gauge its impact on a culture both

---

7. Trans. Ingram Bywater in *The Basic Works of Aristotle,* ed. Richard McKeon (New York: Random House, 1941), p. 1462.
8. Eric Havelock, *Preface to Plato* (Cambridge, Mass.: Harvard University Press, 1963).

favoring and troubled by the medium of oral discourse—the speaking body or person in assembly, theater, agora, courtroom, or schoolroom.[9] Other studies argue anew the old disposition of sophistry in order to challenge Plato and embark on a kind of post-Platonic rehabilitation of rhetoric.[10]

As a matter of orientation, let me collect in very general terms some of the interesting or urgent attempts to decide upon reading protocols appropriate to the case of Plato. These might be roughly divided into four groups: (1) protocols of the professional disciplines, especially philosophy; (2) philological protocols; (3) historicist protocols; and (4) humanistic and hermeneutic protocols. My own makeshift approach to the *prōtokollon* of the Plato text borrows from and critiques all of these in the name of what might be termed "literary protocols." No doubt this betrays my own professional bias, but by *literary* I also mean to foreground the Plato of book culture, for whom a literary problematic includes issues we have since decided to compartmentalize as philosophical, historical, anthropological, or philological, as well as literary. Writing is for Plato of a far less determinate status than it has been for us, and I ask my reader to reserve judgment, if at all possible, on where Plato's writing should fall in disciplinary schemes of ends and means.

(1) Aristotle and many philosophers after him—in our time notably Anglo-American philosophers—have decoded Plato's texts according to specifically philosophical interests, finding there both method and thematic content of interest to a developing professional domain such as philosophy.[11] Thus Aristotle construes Plato's texts as logical arguments

---

9. For example, Eric Havelock, *The Greek Concept of Justice: From Its Shadow in Homer to Its Substance in Plato* (Cambridge, Mass.: Harvard University Press, 1978), *The Literate Revolution in Greece and Its Cultural Consequences* (Princeton, N.J.: Princeton University Press, 1982), and *The Muse Learns to Write: Reflections on Orality and Literacy from Antiquity to the Present* (New Haven, Conn.: Yale University Press, 1986); also *Communication Arts in the Ancient World*, ed. Eric Havelock and Jackson Hershbell (New York: Hastings House, 1978); more generally, Walter Ong, *Orality and Literacy: The Technologizing of the Word* (London: Methuen, 1982); and now William V. Harris, *Ancient Literacy* (Cambridge, Mass.: Harvard University Press, 1989).

10. A few of many examples of current revaluation: Jacqueline de Romilly, *Magic and Rhetoric in Ancient Greece* (Cambridge, Mass.: Harvard University Press, 1975); Samuel IJsseling, *Rhetoric and Philosophy in Conflict*, trans. Paul Dunphy (The Hague: Nijhoff, 1976); Jasper Neel, *Plato, Derrida, and Writing* (Carbondale: Southern Illinois University Press, 1988); Renato Barilli, *Rhetoric*, trans. Giuliana Menozzi (Minneapolis: University of Minnesota Press, 1989); and C. Jan Swearingen, *Rhetoric and Irony: Western Literacy and Western Lies* (New York: Oxford University Press, 1991).

11. For a critique of the present state of this trend, see Kenneth R. Seeskin, "Formalization in Platonic Scholarship," *Metaphilosophy* 9 (1978): 242–51; and Harry Berger, Jr., "Levels of Discourse in Plato's Dialogues," in *Literature and the Question of Philosophy*, ed. Anthony J. Cascardi (Baltimore, Md.: Johns Hopkins University Press, 1987), pp. 77–100.

that include methodological strictures for testing or arriving at valid propositions. Or he hears lectures reporting philosophical dogma, for example concerning a theory of abstract but real essences. A version of this professionalism evidently developed by a consolidating philosophical tradition becomes very visible in Diogenes Laertius's account of Plato, which offers various more elaborate schemes for dividing and categorizing—and indeed constituting for philosophy as an effect of these schemes—"Plato's thought." In general, the Platonic text in this tradition is construed as expository or informative and, where possible, also as an example of method, specifically as an example of argumentation. This sort of specialization and its protocols are also evident in other domains that derive themes and methods from Plato and use similar protocols of reading on Plato. Besides the discipline of philosophy, we can number politics, rhetoric, history, and literary criticism as also construing Plato as an expository writer of doctrines or concepts relevant to these domains.

(2) But what if Plato is not an expository writer adopting the dialogue as a disposable ornamental device and so conforming to one's expectations regarding informational or argumentative prose?[12] Another set of protocols would construe Plato's texts on the basis of the "spoken conversations" those fictions re-present, as documentary, as preserving the life of famous men, or as subordinating Plato's own argument or truth to the dramatic *kairos* or *logos* of philosophy publishing itself in these famous discussions among celebrated personages. This documentary value of the dialogues makes a particular contribution to antiquarian and historical studies and to the matter of linguistic and literary history within the great tradition of classical scholarship that extends from antiquity through the Renaissance to the present. The philological construction of the protocols would embed the Platonic text in the conventions, beliefs, and rules that govern face-to-face interaction in the fifth-century agora or that guide written composition in the fourth-century school. In this realm considerations of ordinary language, literary style, community belief and prejudice, forensic rhetoric, and common sense would help in "sorting out the structures of signification" and so determining meaning.

(3) Armed with a philological reconstruction of these ancient protocols of ordinary language conversation, one might be able to critique protocols

---

12. A lucid survey of some of the interpretive possibilities is Philip Merlan, "Form and Content in Plato's Philosophy," *Journal of the History of Ideas* 8 (1947): 406–30.

that assume the philosophical or informational transparency of the Plato text or protocols that anachronistically construe the text beyond the boundaries of the intentionality of the discourse (i.e., the boundaries set by an author's reconstructed intention or by the plausible intentionality of fifth- or fourth-century Attic Greek or Hellenic thought, etc.). At one extreme increasingly influential in scholarship, this specification of the protocols—of the guidelines by which Plato should be read—would hold him to the ideology of Athens in the fifth or fourth century, and his writing would be radically historicized according to the horizons of his historical chronology, insofar as we can critically reconstruct and imaginatively reconstitute them in our study.[13]

So severe a historicist reconstruction makes the text an object of its archaeological procedures and so tends to deny a writer like Plato strategic leverage over his own project, as well as the ability to make a critical claim on the future or to turn skeptically against the ideologies that empower the project. Plato's status as a purposive agent, a subject, or an author becomes in large part an effect, not the cause, of our own historical situation and ideology. In similar fashion, ancient drama (the *Antigone,* say, or more obviously the *Oresteia*) becomes a complexly elaborated excuse or mystification of a cultural status quo. And Plato's text, too, would be in large part a product of his class, his gendering, his wealth, and his familial and political associations. Within so radicalized a historicist approach, it is as if from our retrospective we spy on the past through a double mirror. Caught unaware within the ideological determinations necessary to make his discourse legible, the idealizing writer projects a fiction or a future that is really only a mirror image of a constraining historical present, while we gaze back through a glass at historical difference more clearly, better able to piece together the occulted forces—the historicist protocols—that caused and conditioned past texts and past thoughts.

(4) Critiques of historicism eagerly point out how it flatters our own disenchanted enlightenment and our own historiographic technique, even while it underestimates the indeterminacy of historical pasts, of historical

---

13. Michel Foucault has been the key figure in the articulation of this post-Marxian historicist problematic in *Les Mots et les choses* (Paris: Gallimard, 1966), translated by Alan Sheridan as *The Order of Things: An Archaeology of the Human Sciences* (New York: Random House, 1970); Foucault takes his critique of modern humanistic thought back to antiquity in *L'Usage des plaisirs* (Paris: Gallimard, 1984), the second volume of his "Histoire de la sexualité," translated by Robert Hurley as *The Use of Pleasure* (New York: Random House, 1985).

persons, and of our subjection to *their* projects. In arguing the power of continuities against a historiography that accents differences and ruptures, such criticism makes more attractive some of the protocols constitutive of the humanistic and hermeneutic Plato. These views—one more traditional, one more modern—hold Socrates and Plato to be in some sense ambivalent citizens of their historical moment whose philosophy transcends that moment in making its appeal to us (that is, to whomever that appeal encounters at any moment in the afterlife of the inscription). It requires no great stretch of the imagination to hear the Socrates in Plato's *Apology* or in the *Phaedo* making such an appeal to some future vindication, and so these humanistic and hermeneutical views reorient the usual double mirror of historicist "archaeology" of the dead. Socrates and Plato's sense of history, that is, overlaps our sense of history; their present tense merges with our present tense; we share certain communicative protocols that enable them to address us in words we can understand. According to these hermeneutic protocols, two intentions merge or communicate in a common horizon or project that we might as well, after Socrates, name *philosophy*.[14]

This version of the text suggests apparently transhistorical protocols that enable readers in the fifteenth, nineteenth, or twentieth centuries to participate in a Plato otherwise dead and lost in historical otherness. This merging of intentions also recognizes and depends on a historical common ground—for example, the tenuous lines of continuity that connect ancient Greece and the modern world. Greek history and human nature are not our history and human nature, and yet ours in some part derive from theirs in ways that the humanist tries to understand better in the reckoning of *tradition,* which has meaning in the West only against the backdrop of incessant change in the "social ground and import" that sustain such inherited "structures of signification" as canonical texts. This canon itself comes under incessant pressure to change, so that *tradition* as a humanistic concept is sometimes seen as a custom most honored in the breach.[15] The tendency to undermine the humanistic

---

14. This position is theorized by Hans-Georg Gadamer in *Truth and Method*, trans. Garrett Barden and John Cumming (New York: Seabury Press, 1975) and developed for literary history by Hans Robert Jauss, *Toward an Aesthetic of Reception*, trans. Timothy Bahti (Minneapolis: University of Minnesota Press, 1982).

15. This is one argument of Erich Auerbach's *Mimesis*, trans. Willard Trask (Garden City, N.Y.: Doubleday Anchor, 1957), which tells the literary history of representation as the repeated intrusion of a "middle style" into a scheme polarized by classical norms of "high" and "low" styles. See, too,

canon is made more pronounced by the implication of humanistic protocols in all forms of pedagogy, where "structures of signification" and "social ground and import"—namely, texts and their recitations or interpretations in the schools—engage in endless dialectical contest.

The way I will try to read Plato, in part by raising the problem of his writing and the problems we face in deciding how to read it, will suggest how Plato displaces such contests into the medium of his dialogues and into the question of protocols for mediating structures of signification and some social ground or import. This is to suggest that every reading— every appearance of a text in a classroom, say—renews a crucial Platonic problematic about the motivation of the text and thereupon risks a disabling *aporia*. In these dialogues and in their questioning of signification, Plato's problems persist as our problems, and there our problems find a history in his history. Perhaps this is still to conjure, like Simmias, Cebes, and the generations since them, with *eidōla,* or shades, in the hope of deferring or reinventing the end. We imagine the living dead, the canonized saints, to constitute our tradition; various hermeneutics may then amount only to so many ways of conjuring with these powers. Or perhaps to read the writer of the *Phaedo* is to respect the different ways that Socrates, Phaedo, and Plato render the histories of this missing person, and in so doing move us with the desire of something precious we lack. What, then, constitute literary protocols? Let me pursue this question in general terms before trying to exemplify an answer with studies of particular dialogues.

II

The epigraphs to this book invoke Theodorus and the Stranger from Elea on the philosophical problem of the "problem" partly so that I might turn the paradoxical manner of the Heracleitans back against these critics and so gloss the "problems" of my subtitle. Immediately addressing Socrates, among others, Theodorus (*Theaetetus* 180C) and the Eleatic Stranger (*Statesman* 279C–D) in those epigraphs each makes a "problem"

Auerbach, *Literary Language and Its Public in Late Latin Antiquity and in the Middle Ages*, trans. Ralph Manheim (New York: Random House, 1965). A general picture of the classical tradition is developed by R. R. Bolgar, *The Classical Heritage and Its Beneficiaries* (Cambridge: Cambridge University Press, 1963).

out to be a kind of solution. Each in his way responds to a lesson that Socrates, lacking more explicit teachings, so well imparts: the virtue or power of the problem as a figure, as a form of thought, as a strategy of defense, and as a provocation. Indeed, Socrates embodies this problematical virtue or power and so imparts to Plato's writing of Socrates, too, the virtue of the problem. And henceforth with Plato's writing we face a problem.

In this way I would indicate a fine and celebrated difficulty in Platonic philosophy—the problematical status of everything in Plato that intervenes between our thought and Plato's thought. This is the difficulty incurred by Plato's covering problems with more problems, the fine difficulty, exemplified by my epigraphs and their contexts, of displacements, defenses, and substitutes—both hindrances and helps—that come between human being and human thought, that come more particularly between Socrates and his thought. Plato in turn lets this problematical Socrates, this hindrance and help, come between him and his thought with the remarkable result that Plato's writing has since come between us and our thought. And this writing, I suggest, imparts the unshakable, uncanny impression of something perpetually missing from its representation of Socrates and Plato. If it is by missing Socrates or by missing Plato that we hope to find philosophy, then this plot is already figured into the medium that became Plato's recourse, his makeshift method, his second, or alternative, sailing (*Phaedo* 99D).

Consider, for a moment, one small instance of the problem we face with Plato, perhaps no more than a trick of history turned on a minor Platonic document, which is possibly not the work of his hand at all. A letter that was to be destroyed, Plato's second epistle, gets through to tell on its author. By getting through, it illustrates its author's stated concern ("it is impossible that written things should not be divulged"), and it defeats his intention ("farewell and obey: read this letter now again and again and burn it"). Now that it has inadvertently come into our possession, how are *we* to read this letter and, in particular, to apprehend its mysterious claim that "there is no writing of Plato's, nor will there be; those that are now so called belong to a Socrates become beautiful and new"?[16]

One way to read this letter is to let its paradoxes and self-contradictions

---

16. I use the Loeb text of the epistles in *Plato VII*, ed. R. G. Bury (Cambridge, Mass.: Harvard University Press, 1961). Except where noted, translations of Plato are mine.

argue against its authenticity as a "writing of Plato's." This way in effect immolates the letter and so realizes its author's stated intentions. Another way is to authenticate the letter, perhaps by reasoning in acceptable scholarly fashion that its daring shows the confidence of the master rather than the caution of the imitator or forger. Authenticating the letter as Plato's defeats the author's intentions but confirms his suspicions of a power of writing that exceeds philosophical reach.

In fact, the letter and its tradition do not allow either possibility: It is impossible to ignore the letter, even if you doubt it; but it is also impossible to take it seriously and, so to speak, literally. Even if he did not in fact write the second epistle, Plato has exploited with great subtlety the relatively new technology of writing and the sociology of literacy to help construct the conditions of the letter's forgery and of its problematical reception: how it necessarily "provides learners apparent, not true wisdom; for they will learn without instruction and so seem to be knowledgeable when for the most part ignorant" (*Phaedrus* 275A–B)[17]—a consequence, incidentally, quite like that which Socrates attributes to his discussions and their direct and indirect impact on others (*Apology* 23C–D, 33C).

As well as anyone, Plato seems to know about, and to chart for others, the tangles he enters when he puts stylus to papyrus. He knows that the stylus leaks and that papyrus circulates, yet Plato writes. And so he throws in his lot with the problems of textuality and the imponderables of time, subjecting his thought about being to the problematical being of letters in history. Plato voluntarily writes under these conditions. Because he knowingly enters this game, one just has to interpret the second letter provisionally and somewhat dialectically according to an open combinatorial of possibilities. Thus the letter either might genuinely be Plato's or it might be a forger's. If it is Plato's, it might transcribe his straightforward, literal expression of intention, or it might engage in play, double-talk, or literary expression. If it is a forger's letter, it might be a straightforward deception bent on the usual sordid gains, or it might constitute a faithful forgery in a Platonizing spirit, a replica trying authentically to reproduce Plato's views. Of course these divisions could be pursued further.

Such possibilities might drive one to exorbitant helps against their

---

17. I use the Loeb text of the *Phaedrus* in *Plato I*, ed. H. N. Fowler (Cambridge, Mass.: Harvard University Press, 1977).

paradoxes, even putting one in mind of Jacques Derrida's celebration of "the mail that always might not get through" as the condition of a general textuality—a textuality that depends on the risk of delay, dissemination, *différance*.[18] The letter, as a substitution, indicates the absence, distancing, or death of its author. The second letter writer's futile effort to dissemble this absence or substitution by wishing to burn the epistolary bridge between sender and receiver has only made this absence more apparent. For Derrida, the very notion of a letter communicating an intention depends on the possibility that it might not have communicated, on the possibility of rupture, counterfeit, misprision, or detour, possibilities that the second epistle's travels so readily seem to illustrate.

This textualist view of the Platonic epistle shows how, as has been widely claimed, Derrida's "post"—his sense of the writing of grammatology—frames or outflanks Plato. There is the writing or letter that intends to reach its destination to be consumed in communication; its external sign wants to disappear into the significance of its internal sense. But this letter always might be waylaid, always might never reach its consummation and *parousia* in the understanding of an addressee. For if the Platonic message—"consume this letter"—had reached such a destination, it would not have reached us. On the other hand, however, is the possibility that Plato's literary project is open to these consequences, that this project can accept or handle such fortuitous effects. Perhaps the second epistle is a kind of joke *of* Plato, not a joke *on* Plato. In this view, as has not been at all widely urged, Plato's subtle letters can be thought to frame or outflank Derrida's critique with a Platonic textuality, a Platonic problematic of writing faced with Socrates. By this post is routed a letter that, in a sense, is never written ("There is no writing of Plato's"), that does not exist as a letter because it does not want to get through ("The greatest safeguard is not to write but to learn by heart"), but that inadvertently arrives.

And so I would post the following program of divided loyalties and

18. Derrida examines the philosophical conditions of mail in his study of Jacques Lacan, "Le facteur de la vérité," in *La carte postale de Socrate à Freud et au-delà*, pp. 441–524, esp. pp. 470ff. In the "Envois" of the same book, Derrida meditates on the status of the Platonic epistles, esp. pp. 91ff. I come around in chapter 7 to studying Derrida and "dissemination" apropos of "Plato's Pharmacy" in *Dissemination*, trans. Barbara Johnson (Chicago: University of Chicago Press, 1981), pp. 63–171. For *différance*, refer to "Différance" in *Margins of Philosophy*, trans. Alan Bass (Chicago: University of Chicago Press, 1982), 3–27.

recognitions. Nowadays there is deconstruction's challenge to a humanistic tradition of letters—the letter that always might be lost and so, in a sense, is always already lost, abandoned, orphaned in its hapless vulnerability. But there is also in this case the particular Platonism that I would like to describe—the phenomenon of the nonletter, the Socrates, that thanks to unheralded textual strategies of Plato always might turn up in the mail ("it's impossible that written things should not be divulged"). In its probings of the conditions of communication, deconstruction has estranged the very possibility of all such person-to-person cultural mail in the Western tradition of *bonae litterae*; but the Platonism of the second letter also anticipates such estrangement in producing its own uncanny effect.

> But listen now to the wonder that has happened. Many people have heard these things, people able to learn and to remember and to judge by every test, veterans of no less than 30 years' learning, who now say that what first seemed most incredible to them now appears most clear and believable, what first seemed believable is now the opposite. (314B–C)

One should not be misled by the implied finality among the philosophically curious of these reported conversions and inversions, which resemble the turnabouts and deadends among which a Socrates leads Meno, Hippias, Critias, Euthyphro, and other intellectual veterans. There is insufficient warrant in such a report for much confidence that this "wonder" is somehow a certain truth that has finally arrived through the impassable thickets of *aporiai*. This wonderful *result* (*thaumaston . . . gegonen*) may only come perpetually around to what the *Theaetetus* celebrates as philosophy's *beginning* in wonder (*Theaetetus* 155D), its beginning in the uncanny effect of Socratic *logos* (*Symposium* 215A–216C), thus in perplexed assurance, in a deconstructed common sense. And in its own circle of certainty and perplexity, the wonder of this letter also provokes a similar marvel, I think, at the mysterious ways "these things" circulate.

The studies comprised in this book wish by hearing, learning, and judging by every test to confront from the standpoint of reading these enigmas of the Platonic text or letter. The sort of reading I refer to is a practice that, like Socrates, has found writing to be defective as a simple repository of communication and communal truth. Indeed, it is in large part through writing that the cultural and historical relativity of communal truth becomes apparent; through the recording of history, history is discovered. This insight has fostered a historical conflict—a conflict abetted, I believe, by Plato's writing—between reading practice and the tyranny of common sense. This practice of reading has become even more vexed, and more crucial, in the wake of literary, linguistic, and philosophical challenges to commonsense views of communication, challenges that point out, for instance, the many ways that readers also write the texts they peruse. The Plato of the second letter, like the Plato of the seventh letter or of the *Phaedrus,* is wise to such vexatious reading but also wise to the writer's countermeasures that can make reading a problematical activity quite conformable to the perpetual Socratic quest for the deeper sense of the commonplace.

To be sure, a Platonic tradition of the sort I first encountered in a college philosophy classroom had to a considerable degree routinized the charisma of the Platonic text, so that the Plato I first learned was a classic classified or methodized into certain doctrines, the learning of which saved me, perhaps mercifully, from the need to read the text this way. And my experience was an ordinary or commonplace one. It illustrates how interpretation as a cultural practice aims at routinizing or regularizing the traffic within highly charged, intersecting, sometimes contradictory institutional codes and conventions. As Nietzsche and others have asserted, purportedly disinterested interpretation dissimulates its own shaping of its object and thereby actually reinforces the codes or conventions it pretends not to be biased by. But this institutional inhibition of reading abetted by strict canons of interpretation—and the eventual failure of particular inhibitions—can also illustrate the decentering value of experiments in reading aimed at untapped powers of central texts. Critically minded readers throughout history have sought out unheralded or suppressed works in an effort to localize or outflank a dominant tradition, but I believe that it is also possible, as interpreters from the early humanists to Heidegger and Derrida have demonstrated, to read particular authors and texts against their traditional hegemony.

It is against such hegemonizing routines and habits that I would assert something like a charisma of Platonic text, an apparent charm or power that may compel a reader to question, even unwillingly, conventional interpretation or understanding. The point here is not to overthrow a tyranny of common sense—no doubt a task impossible by definition—so much as to articulate the pluralisms within the apparent totality of common sense, to discern its dialectical forms, to describe its internal differences, or to analyze its potential for change. I cite a textual charisma even though, in view of the institutions and technologies of literacy,[19] *textual charisma* must seem an oxymoronic designation. A text, after all, seems precisely to lack the vibrant presence of the charismatic personality. But as Socrates and Phaedrus witness, the text can have a power of personality, fetish, and *pharmakon,* or drug, all at once, no doubt because the text in some ways seems alive, seems to have a voice.[20] Such respect of the charismatic power of the text might hope to resemble that piercing Alcibiadean analysis of Socrates in the *Symposium,* an analysis that reveals the Socratic system, the modus operandi, but also pays begrudging respects to its mystery, its transcendence, its exceeding the analysis (*Symposium* 215–22). In this way a literary formalism preoccupied with textual effects shades into a lover's infatuation according to a mechanism that Plato well understands.

Moreover, I mean this analogy to cut both ways, as both a help and a hindrance: Textual charisma functions here, like *erōs* in Plato, as much as a problem as a solution. Specifically, the attractive, convention-breaking sense of textual charisma is offset by a sociologist's awareness that the sacred or charismatic status of the Plato text gets constituted by some sort of community we share. Charisma is a factor in an economy or dynamic set of interrelationships; it indicates reconfigurations of cultural power rather than revealed truth. To some extent, in other words, the charisma of canonical texts depends on our part in their power, on our willingness to suspend disbelief, to hear voices, and to enshrine the speaking book—on our attributing to such texts a magic.[21] The idolatry of Lysias's manuscript in the *Phaedrus* acknowledges such credulity in caricaturing it (228), and so the description of writing's impotence later in the dialogue (275D–E) must be discounted against this sense of writing's potential power.

---

19. For general studies of the interplay among culture, consciousness, and the technology of writing, see the previously mentioned works of Havelock, Ong, and Harris.

20. Giovanni Ferrari perceptively describes this effect in *Listening to the Cicadas: A Study of Plato's "Phaedrus"* (Cambridge: Cambridge University Press, 1987), pp. 208–12.

21. Two sociological traditions interact here—one more interested in the shaping of the person or individual, the other more interested in the shaping of communal and social beliefs, both in fact mindful of the interaction of these. See, for example, Max Weber, "The Sociology of Charismatic Authority," in *From Max Weber: Essays in Sociology,* trans. and ed. H. H. Gerth and C. Wright Mills (New York: Oxford University Press, 1958), pp. 245–52, and Emile Durkheim, *The Elementary Forms of the Religious Life,* trans. Joseph Swain (New York: Free Press, 1965), pp. 385–92, 405–13.

Plato's celebrated divinity, like Socrates', depends then on the virtuous circles of us admiring readers or auditors. But attentive to the sociology of the dialogues—to the contention among personages, factions, and schools that thwarts the pursuit of truth in the company of friends—the critic mindful of controversies might further insist how these circles of ours are constantly besieged from within by the text we enshrine, by Socrates and by Plato: We admiring auditors and readers everywhere receive, though we may not recognize, the message from Plato and Socrates that divinity, charisma, and admiration demand a deconstruction within the dialogues' general critique of rhetoric, oral tradition, and political and technical personality cults. Here a structure and a call for its dismantling coexist within the arduous, faulty impersonalism of the dialogues: The aversion to ad hominem rhetoric that Socrates professes more than he is able to practice; or Plato's careful anonymity, the self-effacement of the second epistle, that nevertheless produces "Plato" as an "author" par excellence.[22] As a response to this faulty impersonalism and as a first step out of the Greek norm of the personality cult, we need a dismantling of the hendiadys Socrates-and-Plato so as to delimit both Socrates' charismatic voice and the mesmeric effect of Platonic textuality in part derived from that voice.

Plato's authority stems from different communities—readers' communities dispersed through history—from that privileged group of contemporaries who help fashion Socrates' special status. This difference entails a number of discrepant features in Plato's works, especially between Socrates and Plato, that help to give a dialogical analysis its opening. For example, this provocative discrepancy: How can Plato sympathetically portray a Socrates who condemns writing? This difference of interpretive communities makes it possible for an analysis to pit against one another two authorities, two systems of domination—one personal, or Socratic, one textual, or Platonic. Paradoxically, in leveling them at one another, one also enables them to pay their fuller respects to one another, as I hope to indicate.

22. I do not mean to ignore the legacy of Plato as the "initiator of discursive practices" labeled Platonism (in the sense of Michel Foucault, "What Is an Author?" in *Language, Counter-Memory, Practice*, trans. Donald F. Bouchard and Sherry Simon [Ithaca, N.Y.: Cornell University Press, 1980], pp. 113–38, esp. pp. 131–37). My interest in the literary openness of Plato's texts, however, necessitates a different emphasis, for example, on differences between general "discursive practices" labeled Platonic philosophy and the poetics embodied in Plato's texts. This openness always makes it possible for an interpreter or a tradition to take or mistake a part for a whole; this openness is a condition, not a cause, of such mistakes, with which Socrates and Plato both seem quite familiar.

In doing so, my reading generally rides the wake of such revisionary studies of Plato as Paul Friedländer's, Hans-Georg Gadamer's, or Leo Strauss's,[23] which attempt to revalue Plato as less a philosopher in the usual sense and more as something else. And in the work these scholars have inspired, that alternative, whatever it is, tries to reckon with the lack of transparency in Plato's writing or the prominence of its literary features. Of course, Greek readers and classicists have long been to some extent aware of Plato's literary features, as well as of the textual grotesquerie visible among the classic lines of the father of philosophy, a fascinating texture that invites a view of Plato as in the first instance a writer. Not really knowing what to make of these textual and literary effects, however, classicists have kept Plato's peculiarities something of a secret. By contrast, Marsilio Ficino in the Renaissance was able to bring the symbolic and allegorical ingenuity of a hermetic Neoplatonism to bear, for instance, on the odd fact that the *Phaedrus* is set beneath a "Plato-tree" (the *platanos,* or plane tree). Construing the *Phaedrus*'s setting as an image of the Academy, Ficino's hermeneutic enabled him to recognize and process this textual datum, which has not yet been, but might usefully be, introduced into a modern, more literary and New Critically oriented study of the imagery of the *Phaedrus,* its tree lore in particular.[24]

The example illustrates how Plato is a function both of what he wrote and of what we are willing or able to see in his texts, and it points the need for adventurous studies aimed both at Plato's texts and, reflexively, at the activity of interpretation. In virtually forgetting Ficino's exorbitant insight, we have also lost some Plato worth retrieving or reconstituting. This is the Plato that gestates Adonis-like within the tree, the Plato that signs in during his *Apology* as the youthful modeler of speeches disdained

---

23. Paul Friedländer, *Plato,* trans. Hans Meyerhoff, 3 vols. (Princeton, N.J.: Princeton University Press, 1964); Hans-Georg Gadamer, *Platos dialektische Ethik und andere Studien zur platonischen Philosophie* (Hamburg: Meiner, 1968), some of these studies translated and collected with more recent work in Gadamer's *Dialogue and Dialectic: Eight Hermeneutical Studies on Plato,* trans. P. Christopher Smith (New Haven, Conn.: Yale University Press, 1980); the classic Straussian essay is "On Plato's *Republic*" in *The City and Man* (Chicago: University of Chicago Press, 1964).

24. Such a study is Kenneth Dorter's, "Imagery and Philosophy in Plato's *Phaedrus,*" *Journal of the History of Philosophy* 9 (1971): 279–88. A narrower explication of the botany is F. Daumas's "Sous le signe du gattilier en fleurs," *Revue des Etudes Grecques* 74 (1961): 61–68. Ficino's allegorization of the scene in his commentary on the *Phaedrus* came to my notice by way of Ronna Burger, *Plato's "Phaedrus": A Defense of a Philosophic Art of Writing* (University: University of Alabama Press, 1980), pp. 129 n. 27, 130 n. 34.

by Socrates (*meirakion platton logous*—17C), the Plato who, in these puns and in other textual, writerly ways, indicates his surrender—a surrender that Socrates cannot or will not envision—of the possibility of the last, full, climactic word or *logos* to a logic of textuality and with it to a structural irony or play of writing that exceeds one's mastery. Nowadays, one can process or construe this surrender only in so-called literary terms, thereby acknowledging the irrelevance or excess of such forms, effects, and manners to any project—political, philosophical, historical, transactional—that presupposes the rule of ordinary language, speech, and face-to-face communication. This rule hastens Plato's texts to ulterior motives, and it assigns Plato's literature to those philosophers, philologists, rhetoricians, or historians who sooner or later peel back and discard the sophistication of Plato's writing in order to discuss the "thought of Plato" they find within, and despite, the writing.

This is to suggest, as others have, that the form or *manner* of Plato's texts modifies and sometimes subverts their ostensible content or *matter*, thereby increasing the likelihood of the mail's diversion, diffusion, or delay. But this difference of manner and matter further collaborates with a difference in media—a difference between a Platonic text and a Socratic speech, or *logos*. As various readers and commentators have attested, the distinctive literary manner of the Platonic dialogue consists, on the one hand, in the dialogical dramas, in their careful plotting, in Plato's frequent portrayal of "rounded" characters, in sometimes dazzling rhetoric and in finely styled speeches and conversations, in the problematics of tone, motivation, and temporality that stem from dramatized, existential situations, in the sophisticated use of imagery, in the appropriation of myth, in a careful setting of protagonists and dialogues in an epic and dramatic, as well as a poetico-philosophic, tradition. The qualities of such literariness invite the kind of interpretation developed as the literary New Criticism in America, one of the strengths of which has been its ability to recognize and elucidate the complexity of a text and to relate such complexity to literary purposes presumed to be relatively coherent, intelligible, and worthwhile.

But this inventory of Plato's literary polish and inventiveness tends to blur or postpone another important distinction: that between the discursive effects that are shown to originate in Socratic speech, or *logos*, and the textual effects inherent in Platonic writing. Many of the effects just mentioned—the style, the tone, the imagery, the appropriation of myth and tradition, even the plot—in the first instance originate with or attach to Socratic *logos*. Alongside these features of Socrates' richly inventive rhetoric, one might isolate, describe, and analyze distinctive features of Platonic literariness—for example, the larger plots and patterns within single texts or between and among different Platonic texts, plots and patterns that betoken intentionality and meaning beyond the range of the Socratic protagonist. Most notably, this literariness includes the coherent fictional biography of Socrates retrospectively worked out as the Platonic canon. In certain respects, Plato knows more about Socrates than Socrates knows about himself; the retrospective biography inscribes in every dialogue (in the *Charmides* or the *Gorgias*, for instance) the inevitability of the *Apology* or the *Phaedo* in a way inaccessible to the Socrates portrayed in the dialogues.

Given the peculiar structure, polysemy, and openness of writing, it is also possible—perhaps necessary—to press even further into Platonic literariness: into the very *texture* of the writing, where literariness falls through or beyond what one can communicate in face-to-face conversation. This texture is evidenced by the prevalence of apparently gratuitous puns, implicit wordplays, tacit echoes, allusions, parallels, repetitions, figures of speech, keywords, name games, and stylistic and grammatical quirks. Whether such effects qualify as *literary* in the favorable sense has long been disputed. They are, however, aspects of a strange design that merits study, and I will simply term them *textual* features, leaving somewhat aside questions of literary taste or intention. These features remain relatively inaudible or unanalyzable within the moment and register of speech. Where such features originate with Socratic *logos*—and they sometimes are so presented—they may be felt as pre-text: textual features needing a culture of writing to make them visible, legible, interpretable, meaningful. Because it so rarely receives its due in the dialogues' face-to-face discourse, this Socratic pre-text is presented as inviting, even demanding, a literary reckoning; Plato portrays such pre-text as tacitly authorizing his writing and our reading. The design or artfulness whereby Plato gives voice to this unmeant because unheard meaning of Socrates, to this other, textlike voice of Socratic *logos*, invites the perspective of French "new criticism" and its focus on structure and structural effects, more generally and more recently on its innovative regard for the general field of textuality and its study of how texts get produced and how they function, apart from conventional literary categories and distinctions (like those of *author* or *work*).

By overlooking subtle and not-so-subtle differences between spoken and written discourses and structures of speech and writing, one has a harder time speculating about the structure of that complicity of Plato and Socrates that so powerfully produces the Platonic text as traditional authority par excellence. To explicate this distinction of media, one might take stock of the ordinary interpretive powers and privileges of the reading situation—the potential to reread, to compare, to take literally, to externalize and manipulate the heretofore internalized voices that merge confusedly or musically with one's own thoughts. By these means the inaudible or unanalyzable effects of Socratic rhetoric can be arrested for questioning.[25] By these means Plato's writing manifests Socrates' authorship of numerous quasi-literary effects within what seems ordinary conversation.

French "new criticism" sometimes functions as an interpretive tool in current literary studies, for example, offering the techniques of structuralist analysis of narrative, of communication, or of sign systems to the studious reader. But in the case of Plato this French "new criticism" can also function trenchantly in an analogical fashion as a kind of heuristic. In its preoccupation with textuality much of this French "new criticism" is *poststructuralist*, critiquing the logocentric assumptions of the structuralism that drew inspiration from structural linguistics. Having broached the nonconscious productivity of sign, structure, and system in the making of meaning, structuralists found their consequent understandings of this productivity contested from all directions. In a poststructuralist writer like Derrida, who has criticized structuralist views of writing's subordination to speech, a Platonic situation is re-created as writing makes its painstaking case against speech's strong appeal.[26] Because Derrida's situation is comparable to Plato's situation in a way that I believe illuminates Derrida, Plato, and the tradition that joins and separates them, I am especially interested at points in the following discussions to put Plato and Derrida in communication of a sort. Plato's texts, the strong hypothesis of such a comparison might claim, are not

---

25. For a general entry into these issues that emphasizes Plato's traditionally understood place in the literate revolution, see Jean-Michel Charrue, "Lecture et écriture dans la civilisation hellénique: Interprétation philosophique de la lecture et de l'écriture dans l'antiquité," *Revue de Synthèse* 97 (1976): 219–49. A more speculative survey of these issues, with useful references, is Charles Segal, "Greek Tragedy: Writing, Truth, and the Representation of the Self," in *Interpreting Greek Tragedy: Myth, Poetry, Text* (Ithaca, N.Y.: Cornell University Press, 1986), pp. 75–109.

26. The best example of this structuralist-poststructuralist interplay is Derrida's readings of Saussure, Lévi-Strauss, and Rousseau in *Of Grammatology*, trans. G. C. Spivak (Baltimore, Md.: Johns Hopkins University Press, 1976).

only influential in the traditional way; all these years, they have also been *disseminatory* in a postmodern (but also, crucially, a *pre-*modern) sense, one that it now seems important to study and to articulate in a way sensitive and responsible to American traditions of scholarship, interpretation, and writing.

But such interpretive experiment also asserts the less adventurous hypothesis that the perspective of French "new criticism" can help elicit and explicate the unconventional logic of this textualist, writerly Plato, just as the spread of American New Criticism has helped a generation of students, including me, explicate a literary Plato who beautifully portrays a dramatic, existential Socrates. These two critical approaches, however, conceal a web of other interpretive debts and kinships that become increasingly important as one acknowledges the matters implicated in the manners of Plato's texts. Coupling Socrates' critique of Plato's literary culture with Plato's critique of Socrates' rhetorical culture, these texts reflexively address their own composition, not only in literary, technical, or psychological senses, but also in the widest possible cultural senses. It is hard to imagine a more ambitious, wide-ranging scholarly question than to ask what produces, enables, or impels Platonic textuality. Hardly any fact or idea of Greek experience is irrelevant to this question; and because readers and transmitters are a condition of this textuality, the whole enterprise of Western civilization is continually implicated in the answer. Just as Plato partly produces Socrates, so we partly produce Plato. In broaching these ambitious questions, a revisionary approach can learn from hermeneutics, from sociological and anthropological criticism, from psychoanalysis, and from contemporary rhetorical theory and criticism, as well as from structuralism and deconstruction. Of course, the effect of all this is, as often as not, the piercing humility of one's ignorance before so formidable a project.

But suppose this piercing humility is not yet fatal to curiosity, and take as an example of the convergence of approaches a problem that is philosophical and sociopolitical, as well as literary: the *critique of transcendence* in Plato. On this point, too, there is important, illuminating contact with modern critiques of philosophical transcendentalism (for example, Derrida's critique of a "metaphysics of presence") that have fueled "new critical" thought in America as well as in France. In the interpretation of archaic and classical culture, such a critique concerns itself with the human and material means for creating and preserving a sense of transcendent or divine ends, ends that in turn validate their means—the traditional institutions, codes, practices, and structures of authority.[27] By means of the detour or transposition of transcendence, cultural forms do not so much validate themselves as they get validated.

This useful English approximation of the Greek middle voice—this phrase "get validated"—suggests how humans habituated to a traditional (i.e., premodern) cultural attitude can neither actively create nor passively suffer this transcendence or divine sanction without jeopardizing its authority or the viability of their culture. Humans cannot be self-avowed creators, but they also cannot suppress their imagination or *erōs*, their desire to be godlike. Human beings can create the creators of the creation in which they are creatures, but only so long as they think of themselves as creatures and not as creators. One might flesh out this axiom with reflections on those human constructs—those kinship systems, religions, symbol systems, constitutions, customs—that would fail if widely perceived to stem from ordinary human rather than superhuman, divine, or transcendent origin. To cope with the threats to stability and continuity posed by technical and material change, traditional culture must evolve strategies, techniques, and habits for the *nonconscious* creation and revision of transcendence and of transcendentally grounded institutions: Humans must routinely reinvent the divine so that the divine can routinely reproduce human life.

In articulating this problematic of transcendence in Plato's text, one contemplates not only the disorientation introduced into Greek culture by philosophical nominalism and epistemological relativism but also structural changes within Athenian thought and culture in the times of Socrates and Plato (for example, the Periclean legacy studied by Thucydides), changes that jeopardize familial, educational, political, and religious institutions. The disenchantment of Athenian society, indeed of the Hellenic world, during and after the Peloponnesian War spurs Plato, on the one hand, to a critical description of this phenomenon—embodied in such disenchanted figures as Protagoras, Critias, Thrasymachus, Euthyphro, and Meno, as well as Socrates—and, on the other hand, to a representation of a reenchantment focused on the ambivalent, charismatic figure of Socrates. In the most familiar version of this problem, disen-

---

27. This discussion of transcendence is indebted to Harry Berger, Jr., "Naive Consciousness and Culture Change: An Essay in Historical Structuralism," *Bulletin of the Midwest Modern Language Association* (Spring 1973): 1–44; rpt. in Berger, *Second World and Green World: Studies in Renaissance Fiction-Making* (Berkeley and Los Angeles: University of California Press, 1988), and "Outline of a General Theory of Culture Change," *Clio* 2 (1972): 49–63.

chanted politicians and intellectuals, by means of a rhetorical presence or mystique, look to appropriate the newfangled and popular demagogic mode most successfully developed and exploited by Pericles. In retaliation or remedy to this rhetorical reconstruction of political life, a Socrates cannot help but incarnate another version of the same demogogic mode; while he can defeat a hubristic demagogue at his own game in face-to-face combat, he loses the larger struggle against demagoguery as an intellectual and political style. By his own powerful example, Socrates makes a stronger implicit case for personal style than the explicit case he makes against it, and so, as Plato shows, he regularly defeats his own purposes.

Of course, the problem of personal style had become a familiar feature of the cultural tradition of Greek thought and action within which ambitious individuals, schooled in part by Homer, sought to glorify and memorialize their names. This tradition, through such diverse human bearers as Alcibiades and Callicles, Anytus and Meletus, construes Socrates' idiosyncrasies as symptoms of megalomania, and it thereby constrains him and conforms him to its own narrow view of human motivation. In this way Socrates, as we would say nowadays, proves too logocentric, too much a product of the public, oral, personalist culture he would critique. In a series of personal encounters, he tries to retranscendentalize or reenchant key traditional terms anchoring key traditional attitudes that have suffered demythologizing, but his efforts to humble or make pious newfangled opportunists like Ion, Euthyphro, or Thrasymachus prove too tightly entangled in the mischievous Socratic persona. And as if to underscore Socrates' lack of an Archimedean point of leverage, Plato shows how this persona is in turn too readily entangled in familiar social scenarios of debate, rhetoric, pederasty, and ordinary conversation to distance itself from what others are able or willing to hear so as to accomplish its own estranging, critical, renovating purposes. While Socrates in the *Crito* tries to direct Crito's attention to the transcendent laws, for example, Crito can see only his friend Socrates, and the fault here, if this is a fault, is not Crito's alone.

The fascination that the *Euthyphro* or the *Ion* holds for me can be partly attributed to these texts' concise, lucid concern with tensions between traditional transcendence and contemporary disenchantment and with the discursive media that condition problems of belief. This disenchantment issues not in genuine skepticism or science so much as in a kind of mania—a sense of self-consciousness, freedom, and opportunity—that has its downside in estrangement, anxiety, and doubt. Never before, perhaps never since classical Athens, has ordinary interpersonal discourse tried to serve so ambitious a mediating function in the creation and revision of traditions and institutions thought to originate beyond ordinary human being. And rarely has discourse more emphatically shown how problematical a means it is by which human being would clothe and hide its naked frailties.

While the embeddedness of issues in personalities and situations has usually told against the philosophical value of such dialogues as the *Euthyphro* and the *Ion,* this very situatedness helps adumbrate important problems of rhetoric, language, human being, and philosophy that seem resolved in the more abstract, intellectual, or detached discussions of a *Republic* or a *Statesman.* In applying the philosophical criterion to the Platonic dialogues, that is, there is a danger of begging the question: One decides to see Plato's philosophy only in ostensibly more philosophically textured dialogues, proleptically, if at all, in dialogues that seem to question the possibility of philosophic progress as we like to envision it. It seems plausible to me, however, that the so-called early, Socratic dialogues constitute a more inclusive case of Platonic philosophy than the so-called late dialogues. The late "philosophical" dialogues are a subset of possibilities structured by the early ones—a point reinforced in the dual chronology whereby the *Apology* is early according to composition-dating scholars but late according to the Platonic biographical fiction.

There is, in this view, a principle of verification available or at work throughout even these apparently more dogmatic dialogues. According to this principle, the more systematic texts of so-called late Plato frame themselves with the possibility of Socratic scrutiny and refutation developed in the texts of so-called early Plato. In the *Sophist* and the *Statesman* the Socrates who stands by while an Eleatic stranger discourses of logical and human types silently models this conspicuously excluded possibility of refutation on which philosophy depends.[28] Perhaps the Socrates poised in readiness even anticipates another deliberative intelligence excluded from or suppressed in the face-to-face discourse, this other who is to

---

28. This more critical sense of the *Sophist* is well illustrated by Stanley Rosen's energetic analysis, *Plato's "Sophist": The Drama of Original and Image* (New Haven, Conn.: Yale University Press, 1983), or by the translation and commentary of Seth Benardete, *The Being of the Beautiful* (Chicago: University of Chicago Press, 1984).

become an inadvertent letter's recipient. To this quizzical or critical reader is known the possibility and the wonder of error, irony, parody, *aporia*. To this reader it may seem that the sidelining of the idiosyncratic Socrates in the late trilogy is a sleight of hand, an expedient or factitious means for asserting without really testing the preeminence of an impersonal, universal type—the sophist, the statesman, the philosopher—over the person.

It may be, in any event, that we know how to process one set of dialogues comfortably in light of our philosophical concordat but that another set of dialogues does not so conform to our hopes or expectations for positive knowledge or progress. And so, like the Stranger from Elea, we in effect invite these troublesome dialogues to fade peacefully to the margins of our demonstrations. These so-called early dialogues register a more obtuse resistance to philosophical programs than do so-called later dialogues, but it would be perilous, in my view, to bracket out that resistance when Plato may in fact be thematizing it. If we supply their standby Socratic perspective and critique, it may be that the revisionary Eleatic philosophy of the *Sophist* or the *Statesman* turns away from the intransigence of Athenian daily life in an escapist rather than in an authentically philosophical mode, the stranger's shepherd-king in the *Statesman* paralleling the more carefully hedged, wish-fulfilling pastoral hyperboles of the *Phaedrus*. Thus it may be that the idealism, the utopianism, of what we take to be Plato's mature philosophy is actually inoculating itself against pride of knowledge by allotting to itself only one phase of a movement that has not forgotten or rejected another of its phases, a phase critical of idealistic and utopian—indeed, misanthropic—impulses in the philosophic life. Nor is this really a radical suggestion, inasmuch as Plato's readers have always subjected the systematic conceptions proffered in some dialogues to questions and doubts worthy of the Socrates sometimes featured in those same dialogues.

Is this to read Plato as he intended? No answer here can avoid paradoxes that result both from the multiple senses of the term *intention* and from the resilient structures of Platonic writing and its fictions. For example, would Plato intend for us to judge his work by the standards of the intentions of a man named Plato, or would he intend us to judge by some other standards—for example, the criteria of *philosophia* (which we may not, of course, yet have in our possession any more than did Plato)? Plato, after all, is nearly anonymous, and what little of Plato there is seems to exist only so that he might lose himself in his thaumaturgy, in this wonderful institution of the philosophical question.

For now, then, let the uncertainties concerning the second epistle epitomize the ambivalences of this larger case. These letters, these texts of Plato, are hindrances and helps, simultaneously to be read and burned, lost and found. Developmental views of Plato's philosophy assume that Socrates is Plato's mouthpiece; but the opposite is also and simultaneously possible, indeed inevitable. Though Plato's dialogues are well-crafted fictions, they are fictions saturated with Athenian and Hellenic culture and history, as well as with personal history. Especially for Plato, this culture and this history are so embodied by the life, language, and style of Socrates that it is possible to make out as "clear and believable" the incredible wonder that these texts come not from a Plato, but from a dazzling Socrates, "beautiful and new."

Two / Missing Socrates

Plato's *Apology of Socrates* marks a climax and a beginning. It shows Socrates in the *dikasterion*, or assembly of jurors, attempting the climactic defense of his life, his citizenship, his vocation, and his integrity. The defense is a failure, however, a very precious failure. Its failure provokes the long tradition in which others try to pierce or resolve the enigma of Socrates that Plato's *Apology* displays with such force. This tradition tries to save Socratic power, to make him a better defense, to reinterpret him as apologizing better than he knew. The *Apology*, the *Crito*, and the *Phaedo* in different ways, through different phases of the enigmatic tale, reveal how these necessary, inevitable attempts to save Socrates paradoxically jeopardize the possibility of philosophy after Socrates.

In his commentary on Plato's *Apology*, Paul Friedländer makes an appealing and important analogy that haunts me for its easy characterization of a very difficult thing. Remarking on the relationship between the goad of Athens and his later textualization, Friedländer writes, "Plato's *Apology* is meant to be such a gadfly to the reader" as Socrates claims himself to have been to Athens.¹ The strange thing about this remark, and about Friedländer's very fine analysis generally, is that in some respects it does the opposite of what it says and of what it wants to do. Friedländer's claim for a gadfly *Apology* concerns provocation; therefore, like Socrates, it should, and in a way does, provoke. But even more it reassures and soothes; it tells us what we want to hear, what we enjoy hearing. While purporting to indicate the trauma of reading the *Apology*, the remark in fact reassures us about a continuity of the *logos*—"Thank goodness, Socrates lives on"—and so the remark paradoxically defeats its own purpose. It illustrates those Socratic half-truths about writing in the *Phaedrus* that make out inscription as a way of forgetting, not remembering.

In underestimating a problematic, Friedländer only follows his original, for in provocatively likening himself to a gadfly, Socrates belittles himself, his defense, and all of Athens, making light of what he professes to take most seriously. It is hard enough to compassionate a sleeping horse, let alone a horsefly. The downward comparison lessens Socrates' moving perplexities in his apology and thereby keeps his anguish at a more manageable distance, as if the fable were the crucial thing, which a reading can now be content to commemorate as a discourse saved. The self-deprecatory gadfly invites us to relish a Socratic apologue rather than to renew or work through Socratic *logos* in all its difficulty, all its temporality, and all its rich texture.

I

The paradoxical desire, embodied in Friedländer's commentary and in every other that I have seen, to be simultaneously stung and assuaged is a true legacy of the *Apology*. It answers to the bittersweet narrative of Phaedo and to Socrates' marvel at the conjoining of pleasure and pain when his fetters are finally removed (*Phaedo* 60A–C), this marvel that

---

1. *Plato*, 2:167. I know that Friedländer, who is so wonderfully undogmatic, makes an unlikely target here. But my point is addressed less to this fine commentator than to the schemes of commentary, narrative, and closure that at times work against even Paul Friedländer's better judgment and so, no doubt, against my own as well. The strenuous last paragraph of his study of the *Apology*, for instance, almost inevitably both denies and asserts a dogmatic truth of Socrates' death (pp. 171–72).

foreshadows the ambivalences of the ensuing discussion and death. If death has a sting, it is not in the loss of Socrates, we are told in the *Phaedo*'s second apology (*Phaedo* 63Bff.), so much as in the impending loss of the *logos* should one prove unwilling or unable to resuscitate it (*Phaedo* 89B–C). At this prospect, Socrates allows himself a moment's musing over the possibility that he will leave his sting behind when Simmias or Cebes awakes to find his arguments for the soul's immortality unconvincing (91C). Thus, renewing the *logos* in the Platonic retrospective also means renewing the difficulty or pain so easily deemphasized in elegiac recitations, like Phaedo's, concerning Saint Socrates, first martyr to philosophy.

Recent trends in interpretation of the *Apology,* in part inspired by Friedländer's superb Plato studies, have tried to restore to Socrates' defense its bitterness and its fuller, truer difficulty in order to correct widespread tendencies to apologize for Socrates' apology by construing it in a way that justifies his rancor, sarcasm, flippancy, and role playing. Recent interpretations, most notably those of Eva Brann and Thomas West,[2] have sought to reconstitute the dramatic *agōn* and to specify some of the many ways that Socrates brought the death penalty on himself and, in doing so, proved the indictment plausible and at least technically true. As practical rhetoric, the *Apology* can serve as the epitome of all bad examples of "how *not* to argue your case in court."[3] But the pragmatics of the discourse, Socrates' attentiveness to how his defense looks on this judicial scene in the light of common sense, should not eclipse the mystery of some extraordinary sense from which this apologia condescends to common sense, estranging the ordinary assumptions of pragmatic discourse. For what extraordinary reasons, one might ask, does Socrates intentionally flout ordinary language?

---

2. Eva Brann, "The Offense of Socrates," *Interpretation* 7 (1978): 1–21; Thomas G. West, *Plato's "Apology of Socrates": An Interpretation with a New Translation* (Ithaca, N.Y.: Cornell University Press, 1979).

3. The list of Socrates' purposeful forensic blunders, many indicated by Brann, West, and others, is impressive and dismaying. These blunders include, for example: Socrates' imprudent multiplication of his accusers to include a silent majority, against whom he repeatedly levels personal attacks; his flippant, irreverent calling of the god at Delphi as sole witness against the charge of impiety; his boast of trying to refute the oracle he claims piously to follow; his arrogant, self-serving construing of the oracle (it said that there were "none wiser," not that Socrates was "wisest"); his abusive interrogation of Meletus, which portrays Socratic dialogue in the worst possible light and that by conspicuously sharp practices evades rather than answers the charges (e.g., the equivocation on "believe in gods" and "believe to be gods"—27B–E); his betraying of his demand for a dispassionate verdict by his pugnacious, rabble-rousing stance; his professing ignorance in know-it-all tones; and his repeated casting of doubt on his seriousness or good faith ("And perhaps I shall seem to some of you to joke"—20D). This list might be much extended.

Nor does a change of venue unforeseeable to Socrates, a fortuitous change that transfers the trial from ancient Athens to the court of history and philosophy, easily cancel out the rancor of Socrates' "deliberately maladroit speech."[4] In striving to acquit Socrates in this universal court in the name of higher truth and right, one repeatedly stumbles over the matter of ends and means, over the matter of how jurors become the dupes of philosophic policy: Socrates uses them to martyr himself so that he might aggrandize his philosophic self on some larger scene that he can only vaguely allude to in his parting curse (39B–E).[5] After Brann and West, one can also more readily tabulate Socrates' cheap shots—for example, his obstreperous contempt for the ignorance of the jurors (by the reckoning of his own principles, this means the *innocence* of the jurors); his unjustified disdain of the body, of the body politic, and of practical affairs in general; his conspicuous sophistries that apparently insult what intelligence his jurors possess; his transparent self-glorifications; and his sometimes pointless blasphemies of gods, *nomos,* and common sense. These are the unsettling works of a provocative Socrates. If I seem to exaggerate and to relish them, impute it to my wish to unfetter this text, to read Socrates out of his knots and double binds, to allow the sting and its complex pleasure some scope.

Xenophon probably first records the scandal of Socrates' performance in court, though Plato's Crito, as always the model of discretion, already reprovingly alludes to the *"agōn* itself of the trial as it came about" (*Crito* 45E).[6] By *agōn,* Crito doubtless refers both to the trial and to Socrates' peculiar battle there. And the vagueness of Crito's reference already suggests a public consternation, common knowledge at least among Socrates' associates, over the trial; Crito can allude to this consternation without needing to spell it out further. Xenophon, however, finds more to report when he perceives Socrates' performance at his trial to be motivated by "the fact that Socrates already considered death preferable to life."[7] Later, Xenophon adds, "Because Socrates magnified himself, he

---

4. West, p. 81.
5. See especially Brann's case for the jurors in "The Offense of Socrates."
6. I use the edition of John Burnet, *Plato's "Euthyphro," "Apology of Socrates," and "Crito."* Translations are mine.
7. I use the text of "The Apology of Socrates" in the Loeb *Xenophon IV* (Cambridge, Mass.: Harvard University Press, 1974), section 1, my translation. Subsequent citations of this text occur by section number in parentheses. It is a moot point, incidentally, whether Xenophon's or Plato's Socratic apology was written first.

brought envy upon himself in court and made the jurors more disposed to condemn him" (32). Supplementing other reports of the trial that emphasize this vaunting, magisterial way of speech but do not see its ulterior motives, Xenophon maintains that Socrates' grandiloquence reflected a kind of death wish, that his speech became a deliberate if admirable perversity enabling him to escape "the hardest part of life and [gain] the easiest of deaths" (32).

Xenophon seems not to notice an unsettling problem here: that Socrates' appearance of great and haughty courage in the face of death in Xenophon's view actually dissembles a cowardice. Socrates, that is, follows a path of least resistance toward a virtual escape and "the easiest form of death," a result that Plato's Socrates says was *ouk anelpiston*, "not unexpected," but also "not unhoped for" (36A).[8] This confusion of courage and cowardice, of life and death, is an important legacy of Socrates' defense, if it is no accident that the *Phaedo* takes up the ethics of suicide or that the *Crito* tries to make principled and courageous the easy death that Socrates appears to embrace in the *Apology*. Thus Plato actually confirms the thesis of Xenophon. But he also compounds it with its antithesis. He complicates Socrates' situation by depicting him in a kind of "double bind" or perplex that does not allow a resolution in Socratic terms: To live is to compromise and seems cowardly; but to die is also to compromise and seems cowardly, maybe more painfully so in light of Xenophon's attempt to assimilate Socrates' motivation to his own conventional wisdom—namely, to die easy is to die happy. In Plato, in short, the Socratic choice comes to either death in life or life in death, to two forms of despair or hopelessness. At age seventy, as Socrates is only too well aware, he has nowhere to go, no *poros* to his *penia*, no resource for his need. The remarkable resourcefulness and openness of his life and thought must be bounded by a death irremediably hostile to this openness.[9] His standpoint, as he might say, is *atopos*, "nowhere."

Unlike Xenophon, Plato makes this double bind his theme and also, as Friedländer implies, his opening. The Platonic text does not resolve Socrates' dilemma so much as it indefinitely attenuates it and supplies it a place, the mixed blessing of the controversial book. In his *Apology*,

---

8. See West, pp. 42, 64 (note 105).

9. Like the *pantoporos* in Sophocles' "ode on man," "Never without resource [*aporos*] he meets what is to come; against Death alone he will find no ally . . . ," *Antigone*, Jebb edition, lines 360–61, my translation.

Plato shows us Socrates cornered, his avenues of escape apparently closed off in one direction by prosecutors, court, and jury—the dark epitome of the *polis*—and in another direction closed off by a self-hate that infiltrates his defense as what in the *Phaedo* he will term misology and misanthropy—the dark epitome of the philosopher. It is an enormous structural irony, one not lost on Socrates, that in the theater of the court, the perplexed philosopher comes to resemble those avatars of Proteus that he corners in his aporetic conversations.[10] In this setting, Socrates finds himself to be a sort of rhapsodic Ion unable not to entertain his judges with the show they expect, with a rendition of Socrates as a protean, manifold man whose duplicities in large part reflect the different ways Athenians have insisted on perceiving him. His parting insults to the adverse jurors, in what Guthrie insists "we may be sure . . . is the authentic voice of Socrates,"[11] acknowledge this irony while struggling to avert it:

> Perhaps, gentlemen, you think me overcome for lack [*aporiai*] of such arguments as would have persuaded you, if I thought it necessary to do and say everything to escape the penalty. Hardly. But still I have been overcome for a lack [*aporiai*], though not of arguments, but of audacity and shamelessness and of the willingness [*tou . . . ethelein*] to say to you such things as you would most gladly hear. . . . (38D)

This is restless language: syntactically, in its coordination and qualification ("But still," etc.); figuratively, in the suggestion of combat in the verb *overcome (healōkenai)* or in the ambivalence of *audacity (tolmas)*, which continues the same combat metaphor. Like these sentences, Socrates restlessly reorganizes himself, moving between the petitioner and the belligerent, between reasoner and threatener. He cannot or will not really take a place at the trial, but neither can he refigure or transcend *its* rules or codes with *his* rules or codes, despite this passage's increasingly shrill protests of self-command.

Guthrie's feeling for the "authenticity" of this passage supports one's intuition of something important at stake here. Perhaps this sense of

---

10. See *Ion* 541D, *Euthyphro* 15D.
11. W. K. C. Guthrie, *A History of Greek Philosophy*, 4 vols. (Cambridge: Cambridge University Press, 1975), 4:74.

crux reflects the repetition of the keyword *aporia*, a term that sometimes threatens to envelop all the contests *of Platonism*, as well as all the contests *in Plato*. Here, Socrates acknowledges how the adverse jurors hope for a poetic justice in which the aporetic disputant par excellence is himself brought to bay in the *aporia*, or perplex, and here Socrates frets the term as if to ward off this poetic retribution and to reserve the dispensing of situational ironies for himself. Especially revealing is the second citation of *aporia*, which cannot refer to a simple lack of audacity, shamelessness, and willful speech on Socrates' part. Indeed, these qualities can be plentifully illustrated from the *Apology*, for example by the audacity of these very remarks of disclaimer. To appreciate the extent of Socrates' *aporia*, consider how gratifying the jury must find these insulting remarks, which jurors can readily construe as the outburst of a desperate man. The apparent pain such insults try to inflict must in fact provide a sense of pleasure to those jurors who now have Socrates where they want him. At this point in the drama of the trial, decision has been reached; Socrates has lost the illusion of his self-command and its advantage; his rabble-rousing attempt to resume the rhetoric of power rings impotently through the iteration of *aporia*. In denying he has been snared, in boasting that he would rather die by this defense than live by any other, Socrates only entangles himself more hopelessly and only makes more apparent all the ironies arrayed against him, who would be master ironist.

As Anytus has said, anticipating the predictable plot unfolding here, to get Socrates to court is the sufficient condition of this outcome (29C). And Plato's Meletus, too, though momentarily embattled by an interrogating Socrates, still proves smug in his truth in light of Socrates' self-incriminating courtroom behavior. Worse yet and more obvious: In part thanks to Socrates, the trial lapses into theater and mere drama, not adjudication of claims; the trial becomes the staging area of poetic justice, not justice, and so this legal action has a hard time rising above the theatrical affects of catharsis and of pleasurable pain. If Socrates pretends to find himself a victim in a ritual or symbolic action, moreover, Plato shows him to be quite complicit in theatrical self-presentations, to retaliate to Meletus's lies and misrepresentations in kind. Such complicity, to be sure, is characteristic of Socrates' ad hominem conversational rhetoric, and so, really, a life-long problem with his philosophical method has at last reached its showdown.

In the *Apology*, Socratic conversational drama undergoes grotesque deformations in its struggle within the Athenian political theater, and both the philosopher's style and the city's style are devastated by the outcome; both are revealed to be terribly flawed and self-defeating, blocked by their means from reaching their ends. Socrates' distinctive manner, Harry Berger, Jr., writes

> is locutionary—the mode of speech acts—face-to-face, charismatic. The Socratic *logos* is embodied and phonocentric, and because of that, it is self-subverting. What Socrates has to *say* cannot be said the way Socrates says it; cannot be said by saying. . . .[12]

Socrates brings his preoccupation with speech against a political culture that he thinks is too preoccupied with speeches. Socrates' self-incriminating impulses may thus also reflect his awareness that he is inescapably his own enemy, that he is part of a problem that it is the concern of his philosophy to solve. And on the other side, we know, as few of the jurors do, how self-subverting this trial is to the democracy, how little this action furthers those Athenian ideals that the majority is doubtless trying to preserve.

II

The fatalism and hopelessness of Socrates' defense and the dumb optimism of Meletus reflect a shared awareness of impersonal designs or forces operating at the trial—designs beyond any purpose of Anytus or Meletus or Socrates, forces that bring out the city's worst and the philosopher's worst. In theory, of course, both Socrates and his prosecutors should be humbled before the impersonal logic of justice, a logic that Socrates at several points recalls. But the trial bends in other winds; the court serves the power and prejudice of an *un*legislated city by confirming, not truth or justice, but the guilt of all who come there. In Socrates' persuasive view, even those technically acquitted of specific charges cannot, having made the requisite defense, depart in all innocence, uncompromised. No one, Socrates would insist, could leave such a scene in good faith. In

---

12. "Facing Sophists: Socrates' Charismatic Bondage in *Protagoras*," *Representations* 5 (1984): 66.

court the city shows its power to bring all parties humbly into its debt; it consecrates there the complicity it calls citizenship.

I infer this cynical thesis from Socrates' extreme and unaccommodating stance and from his sense that his very appearance in court already contradicts or defeats the integrity of that stance. In composing his defense—most memorably in his ringing conclusion (35B–D) but also in framing his speech at the outset (17A–18A)—Socrates shows himself particularly alert to this possibility of structural self-incrimination, his being damned by the constraints of his situation no matter how he acts, no matter how righteous his private standards. At the outset, Socrates cites the standard; he specifies the virtues of a judge, solely to determine the justice of the plea, and the virtue of the orator, to speak the truth (18A). So perfect a trial would thus involve all matter and no manner, all presentation, no representation. To the extent that such an ideal trial is an impossibility, the actual trial is an injustice.

In his conclusion, Socrates returns to and amplifies this point in considering the practice of emotional and supererogatory appeals and in remarking how the judge breaks his oath in favoring such histrionics:

> But apart from reputation, O gentlemen, it does not seem to me to be just either to plead to a juror or, begging, to be acquitted, but rather to teach and to persuade [*didaskein kai peithein*]. For not for this was the judge impaneled, for giving justice as a private favor, but for judging these things; and he has not sworn to give favors to whoever seems right to him, but to judge according to the laws. Therefore one ought not to accustom you to perjure yourselves nor should you so accustom yourselves; for neither of us would then be acting piously. Thus do not think it worthy, O Athenian men, that I must do such things before you that I do not consider to be fine or just or holy, especially when, by Zeus, impiety is just the thing prosecuted here by Meletus; for clearly were I to persuade [*peithoimi*] you and, by begging, to compel you to perjure, I would teach [*didaskoimi*] you not to believe in the existence of gods, and simply in making my defense I would be bringing the accusation against myself, on grounds I did not believe in gods. (35B–D)

It is not at all clear to me that Socrates escapes this condition of self-incrimination; his naming it seems only to acknowledge his awareness of its inevitability.

Furthermore, this conclusion, which begins by questioning only the practice of certain appeals, ends by questioning the value of persuasion in general. Note how Socrates returns to the phrase "to teach and to persuade," a phrase that at first holds out hope for forensic oratory; but his later mentions of *persuade* and *teach* accent the cynical aspect of jurors' expectations: Socrates links persuading and teaching to begging and to compelling perjury, and he opposes these to the "fine or just or holy." "Neither of us would then be acting piously" if Socrates were to persuade and we were to be persuaded apart from a scrupulous concern for truth and justice. Customary courtroom persuasion and teaching would urge one to break one's oaths to judge only by the laws and by the truth. Socrates abandons any accommodation with such rhetoric when a practical admonition disappears into the all-or-nothing suggestion that one speaking rhetorically in court is unable not to incriminate oneself out of one's own mouth. The assumption coming into view here is classic Socrates: The genuine obligation falls on the juror *to learn* or *to know,* not on the speaker *to teach* or *to persuade.*

Socrates' gathering sense of double bind—on the one hand, his felt responsibility "to teach and to persuade," on the other hand, his clear insight into the impossibility of justly teaching and persuading under the circumstances—induces in him a powerful diffidence that at one point verges on the defense by total silence that he prophesies in the *Gorgias* ("I won't have anything to say in court"—521E).[13] At the end of the *Apology*'s prologue, when he reviews the strength of long-standing prejudices and opinions, Socrates exhibits a remarkably weak and abstracted resolve to speak:

> So be it [*eien*]; one must make a defense [*apologēteon*], Athenian men, and one must try to take away from you, in so little a time, the prejudice which for so much time you have been acquiring. Then I wish that this might turn out so, if it is better for you and me, and more, I wish to make something of my defense; but I think this to be difficult, and the sort of thing it is has not at all escaped my notice. All the same, let this proceed in whatever way is dear to the god; one must obey the law and one must make a defense. (18E–19A)

---

13. Also compare Callicles' prophecy of Socrates' *aporia*-like state at 486A–B.

West points out how Socrates pessimistically questions the value or possibility of any defense at all, making one—he here goes on record as saying—only because compelled by law.[14] Socrates' vagueness, his seeming indifference or inattentiveness, do not promise an energetic or heartfelt defense. At the same time, one hears in these lines hints of tragic recognition, of dark insight and doom from which, like Sophocles' Tiresias, Socrates may wish to shelter the jury or even himself.[15]

Socrates cannot change how he will be perceived here; he could not finally come clean of his irony, simply declaring himself in positive terms, even if he wanted to, for such a confession could not be distinguished from his usual dissembling manner. Rather than downplay this irony in court, Socrates in fact flaunts it—for example, in the repeated mentions of his peculiar manner that conspicuously cast the shadow of irony and doubt across his claims. Rather than earnestly disavowing an audience's perceptions, Socrates can only deform the prescriptions, the prior and imposed scripts for this performance; he can only finally embody an enigma, create a scene, give a sign to perplex Crito, Xenophon, and the rest. More particularly, Socrates struggles to make conspicuous the court's implied demand that an accused *play* at his innocence; "one must make a defense." The impersonality of this verb *apologēteon* marks the self-denial, the third-personing, of the merely persuasive or winning self-presentation, according to which the performer inhabits or impersonates the mentality of spectators. Hence one must *play* at one's innocence, as an actor rehearsing a social script; one must pretend to be innocent, even if one really *is* innocent. In representing rather than presenting one's innocence, even the truly innocent, if such defendants there are, must hypocritically pretend to be innocent. For *being* here in court can hardly depend on its true seeming or self-evidence; quite the contrary.[16]

In the most uncompromising view, such theater forces being to play by the rules of seeming, forces virtue to play by the rules of a kind of vice, indeed corrupts virtue to vice insofar as that virtue would go public or accommodate itself to the codes of civic life. Such pretense, one imagines, is likely to arouse guilt in the tender minded or truly innocent,

---

14. See West, pp. 83–84.

15. Leo Strauss, for one, seems to broach this possibility: ". . . one of the many things [Socrates] does not know is whether it is not better for the Athenians to keep their prejudice intact," "On Plato's *Apology of Socrates* and *Crito*," in *Essays in Honor of Jacob Klein* (Annapolis, Md.: St. John's College Press, 1976), p. 156.

16. West discusses this paradox of the *Apology* at greater length, pp. 77–80 and passim.

who are unaccustomed to forcing their being into a mere seeming. To prove your innocence, that is, you must first cast it off. This is the Desdemona perplex, to borrow from Shakespeare a familiar case of idealism wrecked by social bad faith. In the Attic court, similarly, by the Socratic standards of truth and being, everyone becomes guilty as Desdemona comes to see her guilt—she who proves guilty of complicity in a fallen world and of faithful participation in institutions that deny one the means to conform to their demands. No wonder Socrates at first makes an issue of his presentation, stating a problem, contemplating silence, before proceeding to revel in the representational possibilities of a dazzling antirhetoric and antitheater. Though his standards are as high, Socrates, of course, makes no very convincing Desdemona. In fact, his acerbic retaliation against ordinary human evils might remind one more of the cynical, misanthropic, role-playing Iago, who also proves all things to all people for reasons that certainly include his contempt of their bad faith.

Socrates' explicit surrender to external imperatives ("one must make a defense") begins a backsliding of philosophy into theater that Plato must be inscribing with deeply mixed feelings, if only because this theatrical Socrates, for all his cantankerousness and grandstanding, is not unattractive. Offsetting a sense of his duplicities, maybe even animating those duplicities, is a sense of something genuinely and pathetically heroic, a sense of a Socrates who, like Achilles in a passage his defense alludes to, keenly feels "that gall of anger that swarms like smoke inside of a man's heart / and becomes a thing sweeter to him by far than the dripping of honey" (*Iliad* XVIII, 109–10).[17] But because this temporary Achilles is only one of Socrates' alter egos in the *Apology*, we should be wary of taking this impersonation too seriously. Indeed we should be wary of taking any one of these Socrateses too seriously, since the coherence of this performance as a performance is evidently the democratic vision of wholeness: wholeness as a patchwork, a jumble, a flea market of characters. His accusers have represented a Socrates so persuasively, Socrates claims at the *Apology*'s outset, that he has almost escaped his own notice. Socrates answers this "persuasive" representation of himself, this duplicitous role unjustly thrust upon him, by vigorously representing additional roles and impostures, giving his jurors what they want

17. Richmond Lattimore's translation, *The Iliad of Homer* (Chicago: University of Chicago Press, 1961), p. 378.

with a vengeance. He draws these additional roles from past misrepresentations, for his present accusers are not the first to take him out of himself or to pass his proper name as common currency. Aristophanes appropriated the name of Socrates, Chaerephon took it, Delphi took it, the thirty tyrants took it; in trying to come to grips with old public ascriptions and with Meletus's present misconceptions, Socrates finds that he and Anaxagoras, a Socratic nemesis, may have switched names.[18]

Ascription, I believe, is the right term here, thanks to its implication that one gets collectively written according to communal codes of human legibility. We are what others are able or willing to interpret us as. So Socrates articulates primordial accusations against him, placing these alongside the current *graphē,* or indictment. Unable cogently to deny or evade these ascriptions ("you won't heed me, on account of my being ironic"—38A), Socrates chooses to inhabit them, to deform them, to parody them. He recirculates various spoken and written versions of Socrates: the Socrates of the *graphē,* or indictment; the Socrates of Aristophanes' comedy; the Socrates who is Delphi's pretext and messenger; the Socrates who is Anaxagoras (i.e., "lording it over the agora," debunking the idols of the marketplace); Socrates the new Achilles; Socrates the gadfly; Socrates the exemplar of old Athenian virtue, of *philia* and *aretē,* "minding his own business"; and finally the Socrates who is a scapegoat or inverted civic champion. It is possible that Socrates, as he impersonates them, in some way tests the validity of these impersonations, but he rests with none, in the end takes none seriously, and why should he? Each of these self-presentations, I believe, acknowledges an ascription, an image or character of Socrates in the minds of the community, a community of which he is so imperfectly a part. Socrates can thus only indicate a difference from these ascriptions. If he promptly cues his judges regarding his manifold public self, reminding them of the incoherence of his personage, it is to repay a prior indebtedness to their preemptive, crazy-quilt readings of him.

In this way, before the democracy of the court, Socrates impersonates "democratic man" with a difference, as well as with a vengeance. This is the difference that Socratic philosophy makes and that the Platonic text must insist on—a very slender resource, this. The *Republic*'s caricature of

---

18. For different understandings of this Socratic plurality, see West, pp. 220–21, and John Sallis, *Being and Logos: The Way of the Platonic Dialogue* (Pittsburgh, Pa.: Duquesne University Press, 1975), pp. 25–27.

"democratic man" is not a perfect fit to this Socrates, but, as it progresses, perhaps the description comes close enough to the *Apology*'s many-minded Socrates to indicate the problem. Democratic man

> lives along day by day, gratifying the happenstance desire, at one time intoxicated with drink and entertained by the flute, later imbibing water and being wasted away; then again, working out in the gymnasium, later unemployed and heedless of everything; and then as if with philosophy passing time [*hōs en philosophiai diatribōn*]. Often he meddles in politics and, starting up, says and does whatever occurs to him; and if he envies any warriors, he is carried off towards that pursuit, of if any businessmen, then towards that one. And neither order nor necessity is set over his life, but calling this life sweet and free and blessed, he makes this use of it continually. . . . Both manifold and full of the most numerous manners [*pleistōn ethōn*], both fine and many-colored, just like that city, so I think is this man, the life of whom both many men and women would envy, because it has the most instances both of constitutions and temperaments [*politeiōn te kai tropōn*]. (561C–E)[19]

In the zany rhythm of this description, democratic man becomes the champion of "both-and," multiplying himself according to the opportunities of democracy. Closer study would show this description surprisingly parallel to Socrates' self-presentations in the *Apology*, especially to the way the democracy has multiplied him beyond himself, confounding the "both-and" of his irony with the "both-and" of the open city.[20]

Of particular interest is Socrates' resemblance to what ought to be his

---

19. I use the edition of John Burnet, *Platonis Opera*, 5 vols. (Oxford: Oxford University Press, 1972), Vol. 4.

20. One might mention the defense's envy of warriors and merchants and its preoccupation with honor and money, as well as Socrates' reputation for drinking parties, for gymnastics, for asceticism, for political meddling, for passing time as if with philosophy (as he does here in court), and for evincing a certain impulsiveness or musicality in his choice among such pastimes. In general, these traits map Socrates' need to inhabit what the Platonic tradition too casually assumes to be his clear antithesis. The successful ancient accusation that, we think, mistakes Socrates for a sophistic, self-indulgent busybody shows how slender and unreliable this supposedly antithetical difference really is. The bias toward a clear antithesis, on the other hand, may stem from an interpretive will to regularize a discourse made obscure by art, by profundity, by the interplay of inherent structures and constraints in oral and graphic media, or by situational and historical ironies.

antithesis. Defending himself, he becomes an inverted demagogue, but a demagogue nonetheless, showing himself all things to all comers. Like the politicians, he professes himself, he pretends to be, so many valuable characters, though of course the slender difference his tone makes everywhere marks this pretense as a pretense. In this his first oratorical foray into such an assembly, Socrates construes the court as a radical showing of democratic situation, a situation in which speakers re-present audiences, telling people what they want to hear, what they are able to hear, what they have always already heard within the horizon of their common sense. It is no surprise, then, that Socrates cannot not entertain this jury by purveying a plurality of selves they have ascribed to Socrates, selves that more accurately reflect Athenian than philosophic wishes and needs—for instance, the wish that Socrates enact the role of heroic savior and protector or the need that Socrates fulfill the role of scapegoat whereby an unofficial city can purge and reconstitute its bad faith.

III

The bizarre Socratic enactment of the social script I have been describing makes a prologue to another script—the text Plato wrote—and this must also be figured more carefully into the reckoning. Jacques Derrida has made an interesting accounting of mutual debts in this case, which I would like to draw on to suggest a reformulation of the general problem of Plato's part in Socrates' defense.

According to Derrida's tendentious précis of Platonism, proper symbolism, as used for example in the pursuit of truth in memory, should not be open or ambiguous; it should not dissemble another as the same. Only the Ideas themselves should have the authority to reproduce faithful replicas. Exactly the problem with opinion, mimesis, and writing is their deceptive variegation, their seeming to be what they are not.[21] And such variegation is at home equally in the freewheeling democracy of Athens and in the unregulated economy of the text. Here is Derrida drawing the status of writing as analogous to that of the "democratic man" we have lately met, the democratic man who wanders

21. See Derrida, "Plato's Pharmacy," in *Dissemination*, pp. 134–42, 146–50, passim.

like a desire or like a signifier freed from *logos,* this individual who is not even perverse in a regular way, who is ready to do anything, to lend himself to anyone, who gives himself equally to all pleasures, to all activities . . . this adventurer, like [writing] in the *Phaedrus,* simulates everything at random and is really nothing. Swept off by every stream, he belongs to the masses; he has no essence, no truth, no patronym, no constitution of his own. . . . Democracy is orgy, debauchery, flea market, fair, "a bazaar (*pantopōlion*) of constitutions where one can choose the one to make one's own" (557D).[22]

While Plato, for Derrida, strives to oppose this unmoored signifier wherever it might turn up, Plato has nevertheless made an unacknowledged alliance with such perversion by inevitably inscribing his philosophy with scriptural fables, metaphors, and figures of speech that contaminate noble philosophy with its bastard kin. Such contamination ranges from obvious surface phenomena of the literary text to the deep complicity of the "theory of forms" in a general writing or grammatology.

But as with democratic man earlier, so in the case of personified writing one should not be too eager to accept Derrida's reconstruction of a figure antithetical to Socrates, particularly as set against the *pantopōlion* of the *Symposium,* against the variety of Socratic faces and poses in the *Apology,* or against the society-page Socrates—symposiast, pederast, talebearer, freethinker, corrupter of youth—routinely alluded to in Plato's dialogues by Socrates himself. If Socrates and Plato in fact oppose the variable character of democratic man and of writing, as Derrida accepts that they do, their crusade is nevertheless handicapped by Socrates' resemblance to this signifier without *logos* of its own, a midwife, gossip, or medium, a signifier belonging to anybody, representing the understanding of whoever would think to possess it. If such representation is disallowed by Platonism on Derrida's counts, wherefore does Socrates escape reproach? Is he not open, ambiguous, and dissembling, a participant, as Nietzsche observed, "in all temperaments"?[23]

---

22. Derrida, p. 145.
23. *The Wanderer and His Shadow*, no. 86, in *The Portable Nietzsche*, trans. Walter Kaufmann (New York: Viking Press, 1961), p. 69. "The roads of the most divergent philosophic ways of life lead back to [Socrates]; at bottom they are the ways of life of the different temperaments, . . . from which one might well infer that the most characteristic feature of Socrates was that he shared in all temperaments. Above the founder of Christianity, Socrates is distinguished by the gay kind of seriousness and that *wisdom full*

Indeed, in claiming to see that to which Plato was blind, Derrida verges on saying that Socrates circulates through Athens like the orphan that personifies writing in the *Phaedrus* and in Derrida's essay.[24] He verges on suggesting that Socrates himself incarnates, as a paradoxical overlord of *différance,* the ambivalences and misgivings that a monological Plato-Socrates, according to Derrida, would deny to the symbolic and representational orders.[25] By collapsing the problem of representation back into Socrates, what is incompatible in the abstractions of philosophy can find an uncanny coherence in the person of Socrates; Socrates becomes a sorcerer, or *pharmakeus,* by verbal magic able to tissue over the deep contradictions within a Socratic-Platonic philosophical project, seeming to solve in his person, for instance, the problem of "participation." If we complete this interesting connection where Derrida's criticism stops short, we may have, I think, a better notion of the motive or strategy of Plato's writing.

Socrates condemns the ontology of writing, specifically its distance from conversation and the dialogical situation of embodied language, its helplessness before willful interpreters, its inability to present its author's unmediated intention. Socrates claims all this, and yet there is much that is disconcertingly writerly about the language style of this master of face-to-face discourse. In its strategies and effects, for example, Socrates' apology is about as close as you can get to the marginal being of writing without writing, which is to say that, in a sense, Socrates *wrote* his own *Apology.* I differ from Derrida, first, in believing that Plato takes pains to document, to manifest rather than to suppress, this liability of Socrates, and, second, in thinking that Socrates' critique of writing's ontology, writing's flawed way of being, is thereby engaged in a *writing's* critique of Socrates' ontology, his flawed way of being. Plato's writing represents Socrates as already the charismatic focus of "participation"—a precariously theatrical solution to a philosophical problem that wants a different, non-Socratic solution for the sake both of Socrates now and of philosophy later.

of pranks which constitute the best state of the soul of man." Incidentally, an attempt is made at *Republic* 5:475Cff. to distinguish the *philosophos* from the so-called *philodoxos,* but this distinction, as so often happens in these Socratic discussions of philosophy, does not very well comprehend the Socrates who supervises it.

24. *Phaedrus* 275D–E; Derrida, pp. 145–47.
25. Derrida, pp. 63–171, especially section 5 ("The Pharmakeus") and section 6 ("The Pharmakos"), pp. 117–34.

For Derrida to recount how Plato makes Socrates legible against Socrates' stated preference for voice, then, is less to undermine the Platonic project than it is to describe it. To talk about Plato's complicity with Socrates in a philosophical legacy, we need deep commitments both to drama and to text, both to the voice and gesture of Socrates and to the style and manner of Plato. One might link this doubling with "grammatology" in an attempt to discourage or defeat the anxious appropriation of the Socratic-Platonic relationship into a binary or dialectical system, whereby one might be tempted to assert, for example, that Plato transcends Socrates or that Plato subordinates himself to Socrates. Instead, perhaps there is in Plato an endless strife, almost pre-Socratic, so to speak, between *logos* and *graphē*, speech and text, between dramatic, existential encounter and belated production of the monument, the *sēma*, that locates and manifests the missing Socrates, the Socrates that Socrates himself perpetually misses as well. It will never be possible to determine whether Plato is Socrates' mouthpiece or Socrates is Plato's mouthpiece. It will never even be possible finally to regulate the exchanges between these two possibilities, or between them and the possibility that I am Plato's mouthpiece or the possibility that I have made Plato my mouthpiece. Such are the conditions of Platonism as well as of its tradition.

IV

Much discussion, particularly in Europe, has sought to evoke a potential of dialogue and dialectic for transcending self or subjectivity, in order to institute a *logos* in which participants do not "adapt themselves to one another but, rather . . . come under the influence of the truth of the object and are thus bound to one another in new community."[26] This respect of the truth of the *logos*, or concept, apart from persons—about the truth of the object justice, for instance, or the object temperance, or friendship, immortality, piety, holiness, or any other estimable conceptuality—would preserve the common of self and other, say, from some intrusive "third man" or some dissembled third person. Hope for such a dialogue may lie behind Socrates' request that we hear only truth;

---

26. Gadamer, *Truth and Method*, p. 341. Such figures as Lacan and Habermas also share in their own ways in these dialogical projects.

certainly such a hope for dialogue lies behind virtually every hermeneutical understanding of the Platonic text dependent on a fusing of horizons—that oddly spatial metaphor for the mutual permeation of historical relativities.[27] And yet this hope, voiced at the outset of the *Apology*, is immediately betrayed by the ungainly object at issue, the subject Socrates himself. The *logos* here, the discourse of the truth of the object, is not something Socrates or we can readily adapt ourselves to impersonally; the object, the *logos, is* Socrates. Following the memorable analogy of the *Theaetetus* (149–51), we would have to imagine Socrates trying to be his own midwife in labor at the birth of himself. An impossibility: In the pertinent words of old Yeats, "Man can embody truth, but he cannot know it."[28] Self-knowledge at this level of sophistication is deflected into an abyss of mirrors that curves out of sight of one's attempt to see the truth one embodies.

Part of the difficulty of this abyss involves the warping of *enunciating* into *enunciation,* whereby the subject who expresses a truth about him- or herself would, in uttering it, move from active to passive standpoints, from the speaker or subject to the spoken or direct object, from expression to ascription. But such a subject can only imperfectly or incompletely disappear into what passes for the truth of such an object.[29] We cannot rigorously say ourselves without undergoing a transformation, conversion, or alienation. This transformation from speaking subject to spoken (or written) subject or theme (of discourse) is both an abstraction and a reduction. As Socrates has found in reviewing the impressions he has made, what the truth about Socrates gains in mobility, currency, or iterability it loses in presence and genuineness. The Socrates who is everything in the public forum proves really to be nothing. Plato, who could have simplified Socrates' dilemma by presuming to give us only what Socrates said, his enunciation or truth, instead chooses to foreground the enunciating, to foreground Socrates speaking, and so he bequeaths us the impasse, what I have ambiguously termed the missing

---

27. This is true even of so considered a revisionary hermeneutic as Ricouer's; for example, in Paul Ricouer, *Interpretation Theory: Discourse and the Surplus of Meaning* (Fort Worth: Texas Christian University Press, 1976).

28. From a deathbed letter intended for Lady Pelham, quoted in Joseph Hone, *W. B. Yeats: 1865–1939* (London: Macmillan, 1967), p. 476.

29. See the summary discussion of the "question of enunciation" in Vincent Descombes, *Modern French Philosophy*, trans. L. Scott-Fox and J. M. Harding (Cambridge: Cambridge University Press, 1980), pp. 39–48.

Socrates. Plato chooses to let the problem of medium permeate the message.

Most messages, of course, readily dispense with this problematic speaking presence. Most messages allow reasonably faithful repetitions or transcriptions that mute feedback from the medium itself. They function effectively within common sense and common language. They accept the virtual assimilation of surface structure into deep structure, of manner into matter. But one might resist so taking for granted, so glossing over, the case of the apologetic Socrates, of the enunciating whereby Socrates speaks himself. For Socrates, in an extraordinary sense, is his reserve; he is terribly inexplicit in himself, and this renders his endless explications more paradoxical, more moving. As Alcibiades eloquently suggests in the *Symposium* during his envious celebration of Socratic charisma (215–22), this Socrates is who or what withdraws from explicit representations of his truth, thereby instantiating, almost, a kind of holiness, an uncovering of a hiddenness that even Socrates himself greets as a revelation, if we can believe him and his talk of a *daimonion* or of an ignorance that he finds so formidable and unsettling. All Socrates knows is that he does not know; this is his *self*-knowledge, knowledge, that is, of a self that eludes him. However Socrates puts it, however he appears, as Alcibiades laments, he comes to a Socrates who is hollowed out by otherness or elsewhere. He cannot candidly, transparently offer this self in deep apologetics without ceasing to be himself; he cannot therefore offer himself in deep apologetics. Yet Socrates apologizes. How is this possible? we ask. What does this mean?

The design that in the *Apology* eclipses the usual conceptual object favored in philosophical discussion (some virtue, term, or idea) with a human subject exactly reflects the central Socratic problematic: Philosophy is incarnated in Socrates, and it must be disembodied, textually disembodied, as we know. The parenthetical element in this phrasing, the *textuality*, is of course yet to be supplied, its absence marked by the paradox and absurdity of Socrates' defense. Thus Socrates asks his jury to forget Socrates while he discourses on the subject of Socrates, and this, I am urging, is a profound rather than an incidental paradox of the *Apology*, of the *Crito*, of the *Phaedo*. How can Socrates talk about himself without calling attention to himself? Probably this is the paradox for all of Plato, since what perplexes Socrates comes to produce Plato.

Another statement, then, of the double binding of Socrates: He must ask us to forget Socrates while he discourses of Socrates. There are, to be sure, slippages and ambiguities; the defense varies its registers of truth. At places, truth seems of the matter-of-fact sort: Are Socrates' questions and conversations subversive? the jury must ask itself. Does he profess the gods? Has he sponsored new divinities? Elsewhere the speech invokes a more existential version of truth: Is Socrates just? Is he true to himself? These two ways of truth conform to the two sides of the double bind: one too empty of Socrates, one too full. One tradition's tendency, for example, to respond in the more existential register of truth tends to undermine Socrates' own efforts to get outside himself or to remove himself as the issue. To vindicate Socrates, as do Phaedo and the others, is to downplay a *logos* or philosophy independent of Socrates.

Of course, to hold to matters of fact is to miss larger issues and to deny Socrates any charisma, which even his detractors acknowledge by thinking him the source of all Athens's woe. To scapegoat Socrates paradoxically is also to commemorate or deify Socrates while trying to put him out of sight and out of mind. Here one returns to the sense in which most appreciations of Socrates' defense and of Plato's *Apology* unwittingly or at least paradoxically subvert both defense and *Apology*, dispelling pain in a kind of pleasure, drawing in ever-new jurors who postpone philosophy when they, like Plato inaptly opening his purse at the trial (38B), are most meaning to be for it. And conversely, criticisms of Socrates, like the jury's, like Derrida's, invert themselves as homages of a sort, given the possibility that they more provocatively stage and restage the injustice and the misrepresentation of this Socrates who speaks with a vengeance and with a *différance*.[30]

It should be hard to draw closed this argument for so open and ongoing an *Apology*. Let me do it this way, by borrowing the fine words of one who knew what Socrates was trying to do, trying too hard or too conspicuously to do, as I think:

> . . . we men do not sufficiently reach out and turn toward what properly gives food for thought; the reason is that this most thought-provoking thing turns away from us, in fact has long since turned away from man.
> And what withdraws in such a manner, keeps and develops its own, incomparable nearness.

---

30. So West, for example: "In order to understand Socrates, it is necessary to contradict him; those who accept what Socrates says without question will never learn the truth. Perhaps the Athenians who condemned him to death understand him better than those who voted for him," p. 227.

> Once we are so related and drawn to what withdraws, we are drawing into what withdraws, into the enigmatic and therefore mutable nearness of its appeal. Whenever man is properly drawing that way, he is thinking—even though he may still be far away from what withdraws, even though the withdrawal may remain as veiled as ever. All through his life and right into his death, Socrates did nothing else than place himself in this draft, this current, and maintain himself in it. This is why he is the purest thinker of the West. This is why he wrote nothing. For anyone who begins to write out of thoughtfulness must inevitably be like those people who run to seek refuge from any draft too strong for them.[31]

In this marvelous renewal of Alcibiades' encomium, one can see the "purest thinker" already becoming the thought, provoking thought, turning away from us, withdrawing, keeping and developing his or its own incomparable nearness, raising a draft too strong for the rest of us who, like Theodorus, like the Stranger from Elea, like Socrates himself (*Phaedo* 99D–100A), must seek shelter from such purity, such dazzling wholeness, in the problem. And this problem, Heidegger volunteers, inevitably concerns why we must write.

But Heidegger, seeing thinker-becoming-thought, also sees his own thinking in jeopardy, and so he proceeds to correct himself, repositioning Socrates in a more accurately Platonic perspective as neither thinker nor thought but more as a mysterious, a problematic sign of transfer with which we merge—watch now the subject "man" sliding into "we"—even as we remain detached, trying at last to read ourselves, now illegible in this self-division or estrangement, in this democracy of "both-and," this city of language that seems to intervene between our thinking and its object:

> When man is drawing into what withdraws, he points into what withdraws. As we are drawing that way we are a sign, a pointer. But we are pointing then at something which has not, not yet, been transposed into the language of our speech. We are a sign that is not read. (Heidegger, p. 18)

---

31. Martin Heidegger, *What Is Called Thinking?*, trans. Fred D. Wieck and J. Glenn Gray (New York: Harper and Row, 1968), p. 17.

In this context, in this Socratic draft, the Platonist becomes a sign in reading the complex of the human, the Socratic, the first person. Becoming a sign in reading this sign—then this is Platonism.

Three / Plato's Architexture

*T*hanks partly to Socratic complaints about the protean rhetoric of poets and sophists, Plato has acquired a reputation among his reconstructors as a defender of common sense and ordinary language, as a savior, that is, of linguistic appearances. These he tries to save by fortifying them with careful definition, technical hierarchies, and systems of epistemic competence—the intellectual weapons we see arrayed against such pseudotechnicians as Ion and Euthyphro. Plato wants meanings to stay put, it is said; we are taught that he wants words to refer, however mediately, to realities, to universals. Maybe Plato shares with many Athenians a nostalgia for straight talk. But as the *Apology of Socrates* suggests, I think, key features of Platonic writing, features that seem to take their cue from inconsistencies of Socratic style and rhetoric, argue against such nostalgia and so complacent a view of Platonic linguistics.

This is partly because Plato, far from mystifying such reconstruction with noble lies,[1] so clearly foregrounds the work of cultural revaluation, so clearly attaches it to Socrates, and so clearly shows it more in the light of problem than of solution.

I

Plato is distressingly *writerly*[2] for a defender of common sense or of authentic interpersonal communication, that is to say, face-to-face communication. He frequently overthrows the common noun and strict sense in puns and wordplay—wordplay that is a constant challenge and a constant delight to readers of Plato's Greek, if not to philosophers who eschew those modes of language that are "parasitic" on the so-called normal use.[3] Socrates' fable of the rings in the *Ion*, for instance, seems partly but illogically motivated by the similarity of *daktulios*, "ring," and *dactyl*, the distinctive poetic foot that Homer enchained in his *epos* and that Ion releases in his recitation. Socrates' implication in this pun is not clear—that is part of the point—but perhaps the immaterial dactyl already criticizes or subverts the too material *daktulios* of the clanking ring myth. Note, furthermore, that though the pun might be a Socratic jeu d'esprit in a conversation with Ion, who may or may not appreciate such play, in a Platonic text that pun inevitably assumes a deeper, more complex destiny by inviting textual interpretation and by fostering the

---

1. *Republic* 414B–417B invokes the possibility of a "well-born lie"—an expedient myth that would explain and justify utopian social interests. A temptation to be resisted, I believe, is imagining such a lie to inform other aspects of Plato's fiction or his project generally.

2. One could recast Barthes's distinction (from *S/Z*, trans. Richard Miller [New York: Hill and Wang, 1974], pp. 3–16, and elsewhere) in the Platonic idiom this way: Apollodorus in the *Symposium* regards the adventures of Socrates as *readable*; he uncritically purveys a tale for verbatim consumption. Alcibiades, on the other hand, perceives a more *writable* Socrates in his parable of Marsyas and the Silenus statue (215A–E).

3. The terms are J. L. Austin's, *How to Do Things with Words* (Oxford: Oxford University Press, 1962), p. 22. My allusion follows the widespread targeting of "ordinary language" philosophy that has resulted from poststructuralist critiques of communication theory (e.g., Derrida, "Signature Event Context," in *Margins of Philosophy*, pp. 307–30). The "logocentric" bias of communication theory, as well as of a structuralism drawn from structuralist linguistics, has proven unsuited to the reading of literary texts *as texts* in general and to the close analysis of discourse (i.e., of so-called surface structure) in particular. This contention between structuralist and poststructuralist, which involves among other things an opposition between oral and graphic media, illuminates a similar contention in Plato, as Derrida has argued ("Plato's Pharmacy," in *Dissemination*).

impression, as my first Greek teacher put it, that everything in Plato occurs for a reason. Such wordplay, at the least, can provoke a reader's reason into the chase of Plato's reason; such wordplay elicits hermeneutics, interpretation. The argument of the dialogue attacks this problematic art, but the textual playfulness of the *Ion* seems to foster it.

A similar play between materiality and musicality or spirituality may account for Socrates' punning on *melos,* "song" or "lyric," and *meli,* "honey," in the same dialogue:

> For the poets tell us, I believe, that from honey-dropping [*melirrutōn*] fountains in certain gardens and glades of the Muses they bring us songs [*ta melē*], just like bees [*melittai*], even fluttering like these. (534A–B)[4]

If *daktulios* is too harsh a likeness to music (dactyls), *meli* is too easy or sweet a likeness to music (*melos*). But such an interpretive possibility is in any case only zanily implied, spoken or written beneath strict sense as a curious alternative to simple acceptance of this rhapsodic account of musical tradition. While such language play is not beyond Socrates, it probably is beyond an Ion who is in some ways less musical than Socrates. Such language effects, therefore, seem not to exist within the horizon of a discursive, *logos*-centered dialogue or spoken communication. Such language effects are in an important sense *textual.* If Socrates participates in such verbal play, it is not as part of a game with Ion; it is as part of a proleptic discourse, across time and media, with Plato, whose writing both emulates and fulfills Socrates' repressed textuality.[5]

Such puns as that on *melos* and *meli,* it seems to me, break down the easy communication of sense, the transparency of signifier to signified;

---

4. I use the text of Burnet, *Platonis Opera,* Vol. 3. Translations are mine.

5. I borrow the phrase "repressed textuality" from Harry Berger, Jr., who uses it to refer to the play or wobble of the signifier and to the interpretive privilege that produces unintended meanings from such wobble, as this play and this privilege are inhibited or repressed by cultural practice and belief. See Harry Berger, Jr., "Bodies and Texts," *Representations* 17 (1987): 144–66. In the *Phaedrus,* for example, Socrates argues the view that a *logos* should be constructed "like living being with a body" (264C), and from this standpoint he later criticizes the artificiality of writing. Artificial discourse, he argues—archly argues—does not win the respect, the freedom from inconsiderate interpretation, that natural discourse enjoys (*Phaedrus* 275). Socrates' disingenuous anchoring of discourse in living body and in nature would repress the textuality of that discourse, inhibiting the revisions and interpretive appropriations to which mere human art is more vulnerable. One might further note the paradox that Plato both follows Socrates' stricture in conforming his discourse to a living being (i.e., to Socrates) and radically departs from the directive in better conforming that living being to the textuality he represses.

they call attention to vagrant meanings and also to the "materiality" of the phonic or graphic medium. They also contribute to the problems facing idealist philosophy, not to their solution. If Socrates in one respect only parodies rhapsodic imprecision and poetic illogic, in another respect he willfully fosters a philosophy of inspiration that has persisted throughout our literary history. As he subverts Ion's mastery or authority in the face of a larger theatrical economy, Socrates also subverts his own authority in the face of an intriguing but elusive linguistic economy.

A second kind of linguistic debasing often practiced by Plato (and to a lesser extent by Socrates) concerns the proper name and a Platonic version of the *nomen-omen* motif. The proper name is not supposed to be transparent to common denotations. "Euthyphro" as a proper name does not denote "orthodox" or "right-minded," but instead merely refers to an acquaintance of Socrates. But Plato often awakens the sleeping figures or provenances of such names. Ion, Plato insistently reminds us, comes from Ionia, like the Homer he represents, and he embodies the Ionic contribution to Attic culture. In this respect, the impersonal denotation of "Ion" far exceeds the reference to a celebrated, self-promoting ego with whom Socrates is acquainted. In fact, the text in effect remotivates Ion's name—a name that as the participial form of *eimi*, "to go" or "to come," seems to invoke Ion's *transience*, the elusive mediacy or inauthenticity of rhapsode or actor. Opposed to this transient signifier, we have Socrates' aggressive name-dropping in the dialogue, which tends to confine the nondescript Ion of Ephesus to relative obscurity in the company of legendary artists and heroes whom the *Ion*'s catalogue motif reduces to enchanted circles of very fine and musical names. This is so even for the recent painter Polugnotos, son of Aglaophon (that is, "much-renown," son of "splendid-voice"—532E). At the climax of this name-dropping, Socrates compares Ion to Olympus, Thamyrus, Orpheus, and Phemius (533B). This crescendo of famous names crests with "Phemius, the Ithacan rhapsode," then in close parallel "Ion, the Ephesian rhapsode." And it is tempting to hear in this series an accent on the famousness of Phemius, Orpheus, and the others compared to Ion of Ephesus and so an accent on the power of impersonal speech (*phēmi*, "speak") to overleap mere sense—what solidity, after all, do all these legendary references have for Ion or for us?—in Socrates' rhapsodic manifesting of divine voice (*phēmē*). Such quibbling over names as a form of speculation about origins, at any rate, foreshadows the next stage of the discussion, where Socrates tries to account for the voice (divine or demotic?) that possesses Ion and depersonalizes or disappropriates him.

Another example of such unnaming, this time from Socrates, occurs in the *Euthyphro* with Socrates' mention of his nemesis Meletus, whom he sarcastically praises for his conscientious husbanding of the city's human resources:

> . . . for it's right first to take care [*epimelēthēnai*] of the young, so that they will be as good as possible, just as it's probably right for a good farmer first to take care [*epimelēthēnai*] of the young plants, and afterwards the others; and so Meletus [*Melētos*] is perhaps first purging us who ruin the young sprouts, as he says; then afterwards it's clear that, having taken care [*epimelētheis*] of the elders, he will become responsible for the most and greatest goods for the city . . . (2C–D).[6]

This purposeful wordplay shows Meletus enacting the injunction of his name with the care, in a positive sense, of a good husbandman, or with the care, in a negative sense, of a hurt child (Meletus, says Socrates, comes "to the city as to a mother"—*hōsper pros mētera pros tēn polin*, 2C). The puns reinforce Socrates' sardonic tone. But they also project a larger economy of language, of politics, of care as a pathology[7] in which Meletus and his identity function impersonally as a force or instrument, as an *agnōs*, or "unknown" (2B). In a way, Meletus becomes *care* in its fullest, ambivalent sense, a pains-taker bringing his care, his pain, to the city as to a mother. Again, even though Euthyphro may not hear this sense from Socrates, we can read it in our text.

Making a name transparent or common (as with Ion) or decomposing or disseminating a name (as with *Melētos* or with two further, more interesting cases we will inspect shortly) dispossesses the named of his or her own self and gives that self back to the community of culture and

---

6. I use the edition of John Burnet, *Plato's "Euthyphro," "Apology of Socrates," and "Crito"* (Oxford: Oxford University Press, 1979).
7. Pursuing "care" as a theme here would involve a long detour that would have to include on its itinerary, for example, Heidegger's interest in the concept in *Being and Time*, especially Part One, Section VI. *Meletē* also has the increasingly familiar sense of rhetorical "practice" or "exercise" audible in Socrates' mocking report of the novice Meletus's political debut.

language, often with disturbing implications for the proprieties.[8] Such name games may imply, for instance, that the subject is not a subject in simple legal, moral, or grammatical senses. Or perhaps Socrates or Plato wishes to shake or show, respectively, the false composure—the inauthenticity—of Euthyphro, Ion, and others by such unnaming, making them not so prepossessing as they would be, not self-determined or self-knowing. In the *Theaetetus,* however, even Socrates loses his name to the "elements" (203), suggesting that one's doubts about linguistic certainty might exceed this simple defaming of Socratic adversaries like Euthyphro and extend to all linguistic property.

Since action at the level of subtext, pun, and phoneme often wars against the intentions of participants in a dialogue, the textual features I am describing add an unnerving complexity to the puzzles that Plato has scattered before the hermeneut, who may find him- or herself wandering in Heidegger's shadow in quest of the unsaid, of the innermost dynamic of a text.[9] If the Platonic text I am describing is indeed our text, we may have to forgo the wish we have heard so finely advanced by Gadamer and others to make of interpretation a kind of Platonic dialogue or conversation in which partners do not "adapt themselves to one another but, rather, . . . both come under the influence of the truth of the object and are thus bound to one another in a new community."[10] To some extent, Gadamer's remark fits the *logos*-centered aspirations of Socrates, who sometimes claims to be concerned with the truth of the *logos,* not with the person who voices it.[11] But so hopeful a description emphatically does not square with the text-centered practice of Plato, where Socrates' breaches of this claim stand forth as naked as his refuted interlocutors. Even apart from crucial differences of media in the deployment of the "dialogue" analogy, Gadamer and others have not sufficiently allowed or

---

8. I adopt, though with some reservations, the terminology of property, proper name, and proper or literal sense from Derrida, *Of Grammatology*. Incidentally, Homer anticipates and seems to authorize this problematic of the proper name. I refer to the Cyclops episode, when Odysseus too truly puns on his name in denying it. See George E. Dimock, Jr., "The Name of Odysseus," in *Essays on the "Odyssey,"* ed. Charles H. Taylor, Jr. (Bloomington: Indiana University Press, 1963), pp. 54–72.

9. I think of Heidegger's well-known strictures in *Kant and the Problem of Metaphysics*, trans. J. S. Churchill (Bloomington: Indiana University Press, 1962), pp. 206–8.

10. Gadamer, *Truth and Method*, p. 341. As the body of Gadamer's work makes clear, this is fortunately less a call to imitate the dialogues portrayed in Plato than a call to repair or supplement such dialogue. Gadamer makes a much fuller case for the importance of dialogue to the development of Platonic thought in *Platos dialektische Ethik* (Hamburg: Meiner, 1968).

11. A few among many such references: *Charmides* 166C–D; *Protagoras* 348C–E; *Phaedo* 90C–91C.

accounted for the chronic failure of "dialogue" and "new community" everywhere in Plato's dramatic renderings of Socratic conversation.

Referring selectively but in some detail to Plato's *Euthyphro*, I would like to specify further the linguistic and rhetorical challenge the Platonic text, as text and as hermeneutical model, sets before philosophical interpretation. And I would like to suggest an infernal or diabolical sense in which Gadamer has correctly gauged the binding to one another in "new community" of Socratic dialogue. But because the medium of this bond is bad faith, not good faith, complicity, not complaisance, this new community of Athenians (perhaps of us interpreters as well) proves, alas, *dys*topian.

II

For a number of reasons, *Euthyphro* invites a doubled reading, not just because Euthyphro and Socrates oddly reverse or double one another and not just because the character of Euthyphro is neatly split in the critical commentaries, where some glossers see him as harmless, friendly, and supportive, if a little quaint, while others see him as disingenuous and sinister.[12] Plato's regular staging of Socratic doubles—whether of sophistic adversaries or of supposed Athenian or Eleatic allies—makes this *Euthyphro* plot representative and thereby generally illuminating of other dialogical situations. The specific doublings of *Euthyphro*, I think, reflect a doubled discourse, a duplicity held together in a few especially interesting places that invite an excavation of the subtext. I will try to indicate a few of these places and suggest what is reserved or implied there.

---

12. Euthyphro is traditionally regarded, in part because of his name ("right-minded"), as a representative of Greek orthodoxy, "an earnest and simple believer in the old traditional religion of the Hellenes" (P. T. Geach, "Plato's *Euthyphro:* An Analysis and Commentary," *The Monist* 50 [1966]: 370). But the view of Burnet (*Plato's "Euthyphro," "Apology of Socrates," and "Crito"*), seconded by Taylor (*Plato: The Man and His Work* [London, 1949], pp. 146–56) and by Robert G. Hoerber ("Plato's *Euthyphro*," *Phronesis* 3 [1958]: 95ff.), is that "everything points rather to the conclusion that Euthyphro was a sectary of some kind" (p. 85), whom Plato sympathetically portrays. Elsewhere, we encounter the impression of Euthyphro as "an extremely corrupt young man" (Daniel E. Anderson, "Socrates' Concept of Piety," *Journal of the History of Philosophy* 5 [1967]: 1), or as a worshiper of "the morbid creations of his unbridled selfishness" (Harry Neumann, "The Problem of Piety in Plato's *Euthyphro*," *Modern Schoolman* 43 [1966]: 269).

One face of *Euthyphro*'s duplicity concerns a theological discourse touching on the Olympian "holy family" and on the apparent failure of this family to meet philosophical standards of holiness and piety. His conduct of this critical discourse on this holy family throughout his life in Athens is the ostensible cause of Socrates' indictment, as he suggests to Euthyphro: "Now isn't it just this, Euthyphro, on account of which I flee the charge [*tēn graphēn pheugō*] . . . ?" (6A). But so unfounded are the charges of impiety, though superficially valid, that witnesses—Plato, say—are driven to seek far different causes for the prosecution. Whence emerge the fragments of a second, infernal discourse centered on an unholy family—the kinship or complicity of Zeus, Euthyphro, and Meletus as dutiful, indeed zealous sons "who come to the city as to a mother to accuse me" (2C) for reasons strange to philosophy, but in reality all too *familiar*.

Socrates and Euthyphro meet just outside the halls of town justice, where each has legal business—Socrates to answer the indictment of Meletus, Euthyphro to sue his own father on behalf of a rowdy who died through his father's perhaps criminal neglect. The two litigants marvel as they hear one another's cases, then briefly discuss the issues. Flattered by Socrates, Euthyphro expertly holds forth on the justice of his indictment, then on holiness in general until, pressured by Socrates' questions, he reveals how inconsistent, self-serving, and demotic his expert views really are. At the conclusion, Euthyphro's vainglorious expertise, the target of muted Socratic irony throughout the conversation, is openly held up to ridicule by Socrates.

In their charting of developments in Plato's thought, philosophically minded commentators have tended to regard the *Euthyphro* as a dialogue of refutation in Plato's "early" style, remarkable for its place in the chronicle of Socrates' trial and death, for its testimony in regard to religious practices and beliefs, but especially for its "early" display of the "Platonic Idea," its active-passive distinction, its species-genus or its part-whole distinction.[13] Socrates' attempts to elicit definition of piety or

---

13. This literature is surveyed in Guthrie, *A History of Greek Philosophy*, 4:102–3. For other informative summaries and bibliography in various perspectives, see R. E. Allen, *Plato's "Euthyphro" and the Earlier Theory of Forms* (London: Routledge and Kegan Paul, 1970); Henry G. Wolz, *Plato and Heidegger: In Search of Selfhood* (Lewisburg, Pa.: Bucknell University Press, 1981), pp. 49–52; Albert Anderson, "Socratic Reasoning in the *Euthyphro*," *Review of Metaphysics* 22 (1968–69): 461–81; Neumann, "The Problem of Piety," 265–72; W. Gerson Rabinowitz, "Platonic Piety: An Essay Toward the Solution of an Enigma," *Phronesis* 3 (1958): 108–20; and Jan H. Blits, "The Holy and the Human: An Interpretation of Plato's *Euthyphro*," *Apeiron* 14 (1980): 28ff.

holiness have come to be regarded as typical of those Platonic definitions that try to transcend the particular experience of a Euthyphro or a Socrates in pursuit of a universal definition, in this case of *to hosion,* "the holy" or "the hallowed."[14] These cogent discussions of the dialogue's first, abstract, philosophical discourse, however, leave unacknowledged a complementary discourse bafflingly fused with the first. This counterdiscourse is marked by the *Euthyphro*'s seemingly strange digressions and ill-regulated examples, for instance the confusing and apparently arbitrary series of terms that exemplifies the active-passive distinction at 10A–C. This series of verbals—formed from the verbs *carry, lead, see, love, become* (or *be born*), *undergo* (or *suffer* or *experience*), and *love* again—at first seems only to shed the light of arbitrary examples on the questions of theology that frame the argument. But reseen from the standpoint of a second discourse, and this is my point, this sequence of verbals exactly implies the actions and passions of child nurture and of child-parent interaction, the family scene of piety.[15] And these same relations in turn mirror or reverse key moments in the *therapeia,* or service, of the divine as the conversation at several points alludes to it.[16] Think again of *carry, lead, see, love, be born, experience, love* in their various modalities and voices, in both family and cult contexts. If this is theology, it is theology on a Freudian kind of detour;[17] and if this detour is not *Ungesagte,* or "unsaid," it is, nevertheless, like most detours, poorly and obliquely signed.

But let us take a slower run at these difficulties, beginning for a moment at the beginning in an attempt to focus more clearly the mindset of Euthyphro. Euthyphro's sensitive approach to Socrates at first arouses our sympathy because he seems so well acquainted and so sympathetic with Socrates. He knows Socrates well enough to know that the philosopher is out of place in the stoa of the court. He knows Socrates

---

14. See Richard Robinson, *Plato's Earlier Dialectic,* 2d ed. (Oxford: Oxford University Press, 1953), pp. 49ff.

15. The classic text on patriarchal religion in the ancient world is N. P. Fustel de Coulanges, *The Ancient City* (Garden City, N.Y.: Doubleday, n.d.), especially pp. 34–116. Familial piety in Euthyphro is briefly but lucidly sketched by James P. Hoopes, "Euthyphro's Case," *Classical Bulletin* 47, no. 1 (November 1970): 1–6.

16. This *therapeia* is explicitly an issue at 13A–D, but it is also at stake in the mention of the *peplos,* the robe of Athena carried to the Acropolis during the Panathenaea (6C).

17. E. R. Dodds speaks of "the barbarous tale of Kronos and Ouranos," where "the mythological projection of unconscious desires is surely transparent—as Plato perhaps felt when he declared that this story was fit to be communicated only to a very few in some exceptional *mysterion* and should at all costs be kept from the young [*Republic* 377E–378A]," *The Greeks and the Irrational* (Berkeley and Los Angeles: University of California Press, 1966), pp. 46–47.

well enough to hail him easily by name and even to chide him humorously in terms appropriate to Socrates' celebrated love of the new:

> What novelty, Socrates, has come about that leaving off your diversions [*diatribas*] there in the Lyceum, you now divert yourself [*diatribeis*] in the stoa of the king? For surely there doesn't happen to be a suit of yours before the king as there is of mine? (2A)

Euthyphro knows and speaks the language of Socrates and of the Lyceum, or so we might suppose from his use both of the "diatribe" and of a faintly aggressive irony. Euthyphro also knows Socrates well enough to realize that Socrates, without some falling off about which Euthyphro might be curious, cannot have brought an action against another: "What do you say? Someone, as it seems, has brought an indictment against you? For of that indeed I do not accuse you, of bringing one against another" (2A–B). Oddly, this remark, even if a witticism, implies that Euthyphro knows that bringing an accusation itself involves a kind of moral offense to which the high-minded Socrates would not likely stoop. Euthyphro volunteers, perhaps he is also confessing, that there may be a stigma attached to what he himself is doing. This note of self-accusation hints at difficulties to come.

After learning of Meletus's plan to save the city by prosecuting Socrates, Euthyphro remarks, "For he simply seems to me to begin by doing ill to the city at its core [*aph'estias*], trying to do you injustice" (3A). Here again Euthyphro's sympathy harbors a lightly paradoxical reference, implying valuation of something, the household hearth (*hestia*), that Euthyphro's indictment of his father, lord of his household, itself seems to jeopardize. Euthyphro's professed respect for Socrates once again shelters an implied disrespect for himself and what he is doing. Euthyphro's sympathy with Socrates develops hereafter through an understanding reference to Socrates' *daimonion* (*Manthanō,* Socrates, "I know all about it"—3B) and finally concludes with a strongly implied kinship between the philosopher and the soothsayer. Speaking of the opinions of the many, Euthyphro reports:

> For even at me, whenever I say something in the assembly concerning divine things, foretelling them of future things, they laugh as though I were maddened [*mainomenou*]. And yet in what I have foretold them I have said nothing not true, but they are

similarly jealous of all such as us. But one should not be mindful of these [*ouden autōn chrē phrontizein*], but muster resistance. (3B–C)

We must not be anxious about these critics, Euthyphro urges, but must stand up and fight. Though his own manner and actions belie this slogan, it has an uncanny relevance, like the braggart's stated wish that reverses an actual fact: Since we cannot muster resistance, we must be mindful or anxious concerning these critics. "Now about this, how they might regard me, I don't much desire to try out" (3C), Euthyphro soon admits.

Later (and it takes a while for the sheepish Euthyphro to confess his case to Father Socrates) when Socrates marvels at the temerity of Euthyphro's indictment and wonders about the justice of accusing one's own father of murdering an outsider, Euthyphro retorts with a quasi-Socratic sense of impersonal, even absolute right:

> It's laughable, Socrates, that you think there is a difference, whether the murderer is an outsider or household member, but this alone it is necessary to regard [*dein phulattein*], whether the killer killed justly or not, and if justly, let him off, but if not, go after him, even if [some urge the sense "only if"[18]] the killer is of your hearth and table. (4B–C)

Euthyphro's claim, though it seems archaically puritanical, actually calls to mind the radical argument of the *Gorgias*[19]—one should seek rather than avoid the judicial correction of one's self and one's kin—just as Euthyphro's phrasing and syntax again call to mind Socrates' own idiom. Hence the objection, coming from Socrates of all people, strikes Euthyphro as laughable.

These opening statements and exchanges mark an interesting reversal and begin one movement in the dialogue's dramatic irony: Socrates and Euthyphro have in effect changed places, the one proceeding like the sophistic philosopher, the other defending the pious concerns of tradition and common sense. This reversal soon culminates in Socrates' offer to

---

18. For example, Jan H. Blits (following Burnet, p. 23) in "The Holy and the Human," p. 22. A problem for this view, as Blits points out (pp. 24, 26, 38 n. 17), arises when Euthyphro later ignores so scrupulous a distinction.

19. For example, *Gorgias* 480B–D.

become Euthyphro's student as protection against Meletus's suit. Then, should Socrates continue to fall short of Meletus's standards of piety, Meletus could bring suit against Euthyphro, "my teacher before me, on the grounds of corrupting the elders, both me and his father, me by his teaching, and the latter by his correcting and chastising" (5A–B). Meletus, Socrates tells Euthyphro, should bring the indictment "against you instead of me" (5B). In trying to oblige Socrates with his sympathy and likemindedness, Euthyphro has exposed himself to what sounds like ridicule when Socrates just as theatrically takes on an unexpected, contrary role.

Euthyphro escapes this fanciful day in court, but only to come under the sterner cross-questioning of Socrates in this dialogue. And though the dialogue does in fact drop fine hints about a problematical reciprocation of piety and holiness, Socrates' bullying, prosecutorial manner ("Since you seem to me so lax, I myself will embolden you [*soi sumprothumēsomai*] . . ." [11E]) seems to reinforce in Euthyphro a fear or nervousness that precludes his seeing any love or desire that may be planted in Socratic piety and that may be presiding over a philosophical discussion begun in the name of (Zeus) Friendship (*pros Philiou*—6B; compare friendly terms of address at 3C, 10A, 10E, 14A, and 14D). As evidence of his piety, Socrates at 14E–15A extols the generosity of the gods, "For what they give is plain to all; for we have nothing good but what they give." But Euthyphro is shy and shamefast about a suggested commercial model of theology, even if it may shelter a true reciprocal dependence of piety and holiness, of the human hallowing thanks to which the divine is hallowed or holy, so such suggestions never get off the ground, never assume more sublime form. Instead, Socratic piety and its attempt to sustain, perhaps even to create, the holy is conspicuously absent from Euthyphro's outlook and from the discussion, which keeps desublimating or demystifying the holy to the terms of family, economy, and state and to relationships predicated on need and constraint rather than on love and goodwill. At 15A, again, the question of a religious economy in a large sense never gets past the question of barter—what stuff the gods need from us in exchange for all their gift goods.

We do, however, see Euthyphro relishing one of these divine gifts, if I may shift the reference a little abruptly. He welcomes, of all things, an argument from the gods, an argument that seems to say, "Don't expect gods and fathers to reward your reverence with gifts." Euthyphro uses this divine gift, this argument, to try to justify his prosecution of his own father:

> Then, Socrates, see how great a proof I speak to you of the right usage [*tou nomou*] that pertains here—a proof I've already spoken to others—that this correctly takes place, not letting off the impious one, no matter who he happens to be; for people themselves really happen to believe that Zeus [*Dia*] is the best and most just of the gods, and they concede that he chained [*dēsai*] his own father because he gulped down his children illegally [*ouk en dikēi*], and the latter, too, had cut out his father on similar grounds; but they harshly provoke me because I proceed against my injurious father, and thus they speak in contradiction with themselves concerning the gods and concerning me . . . (5E–6A).

Of course, Euthyphro's example is outrageous and his argument ridiculous: Gods and mortals are supposed to follow different standards; that is what makes them gods, us humans. Euthyphro's thinking the contrary pretty well shows the short range of his theological insight, unless his expert hermeneutic involves assumptions very different from these. It is just possible that Euthyphro, after the sophistic manner briefly sketched in the *Phaedrus* (229C–D), reads in this theogonic fable a law of nature, a law that binds gods and humans alike. We will explore this interesting possibility in a moment.

But first, notice two competing impulses in Euthyphro's self-justification. On the one hand, Euthyphro, the religious expert, does not seem to believe literally in the events of the myth; his little speech follows the plot and employs the diction of a refutation. The manner of that recitation clearly indicates that his standpoint is rhetorical rather than theological; hence, perhaps, his confidence in going to court. His sophistication, as well as an odd scrupulosity, is also reflected in his carefully avoiding the admission of his own belief in the myths; instead, like Ion with his audience, he focuses on the expressed beliefs of other people, beliefs that he can turn to his advantage rhetorically and, depending on what legal settlement he expects from his father, perhaps monetarily.[20] Euthyphro says, to be exact, *autoi gar hoi anthrōpoi tungchanousi nomizontes ton Dia tōn theōn ariston kai dikaiotaton*; that is, again, "for people themselves really happen to believe that Zeus is the best and most just of the gods." Euthyphro may, as I think, suggest by this phrasing some incredulity; but he certainly suggests by his syntax greater interest in the belief of others than in the truth of Zeus.

With one reservation—the second interpretive possibility I mentioned a moment ago, according to which Euthyphro assumes an unconventional hermeneutic. Though it seems odd that Euthyphro is so committed to so fantastic an argument, this impression is lessened somewhat if we see a law of nature working through the particulars of his recitation. According to so sophistical an interpretation, the gods become exemplary instances of physical, natural, or moral universals rather than charismatic counterexamples to the human condition who by their license help reconcile us to our bondage. Thus Euthyphro seems to focus, not on how *in*human gods are, but on how the mythical pattern, even in its particulars, parallels and illuminates his rivalry with his father. If Phaedrus would see in Boreas mostly wind, Euthyphro would see in Zeus mostly son. The theogonic war between fathers and sons that ends in bondage, emasculation, and obscurity is reproduced on a small scale when Euthyphro's father catches, binds, and buries the homicidal client (*pelatēs*—4C) of the son:

> . . . the one killed was a certain client [*pelatēs*] of mine, and as we were farming in Naxos, he worked for hire at our place; having gotten drunk and then enraged with someone of our household, he slit his throat; then my father, having bound together [*sundēsas*] his feet and hands and having thrown him down into some ditch, sent a man here inquiring of the exegete what ought to be done. But in the meantime he made little of the bound one [*dedemenou*], and was heedless [*ēmelei*] on the grounds that he was a murderer and it was no great matter if he died; and that's the very fate he suffered. For from hunger and

---

20. For a survey of the legal setting, see Douglas M. MacDowell, *The Law in Classical Athens* (Ithaca, N.Y.: Cornell University Press, 1978), especially pp. 59, 60, 192–202. MacDowell's exposition repeatedly illustrates the familiar and timeless use of legal institutions as prods or ruses for out-of-court settlements. The sycophantic Euthyphro may be trying to settle for cash or considerations above and beyond that cleansing of *miasma* as supposed by A. E. Taylor (p. 147), Hoerber (pp. 95–98), and others.

cold and the bonds [*desmōn*] he died before the messenger returned from the exegete. (4C–D)

This sordid little anecdote is notable for its pecking orders of freeman and slave, master and man, and father and son, as well as for the carelessness—and drunken carelessness—visited upon inferiors by superiors, on sufferers by aggressors, on the passive by the active.[21] But this is above all a scene of archaic family justice—Euthyphro's "client" (if this is what *pelatēs* refers to; perhaps the important point is that Euthyphro claims a proprietary relationship—*pelatēs tis ēn emos*, "my *pelatēs*"),[22] this client might have been Euthyphro, in a sense was a surrogate Euthyphro in representing some kind of proprietary bond—and the situation brings to mind the harsh terms of sonship intimated in Plato's *Lysis* and its more explicit discussion of *philia*. The note of despotism is most emphatically sounded in Euthyphro's story, as in the mythic paradigm, in the iteration of *deō* ("need," "bind")—in the binding and the bonds and in the *need* fused into the sense of *deō* and, in the climactic sentence, into the denial of *necessities* of food and shelter and freedom of movement. Euthyphro's legal action and his piety are born out of and borne against such need, and they are compacted with all this filial care and all this paternal inattentiveness.[23]

Euthyphro concludes his report of the Naxos incident in this way:

Now this is what both my father and my other relatives are annoyed about, because I in behalf of this murderer prosecute my

---

21. Some calculate Euthyphro's father to be seventy-five years old (Taylor, Hoerber), from which a certain feebleness is assumed (Hoerber, p. 97), a feebleness that makes more surprising Euthyphro's apparently impious prosecution. But according to Euthyphro's own carefully rehearsed account, the "old gentleman" (Taylor, p. 147) sounds neither "old" nor "gentle." Hoopes, too, sees a problem with the usual views here (p. 5).

22. This curious term has invited various glosses and translations, most of which are insensitive to the problem of the father's apparently having recklessly destroyed something of the son's. *LSJ*'s rendering of *pelatēs* as "client" seems a little misleading in view of later connotations in the history of that term; but "hired hand" or "free day laborer" does not do justice to the suggestion of free dependency of this worker on Euthyphro. See Hoopes, p. 5, and Burnet, p. 24, for speculation on Euthyphro's tie to the deceased.

23. "The theme of the vulnerable immortal is conspicuous in the myths of the Greeks. Perhaps it reflected a chafing of spirit under despotic lordships of local principalities, or an impatience with powers of a father, and secret daydreams of humiliating him and toppling him from place." Emily Vermeule, *Aspects of Death in Early Greek Poetry and Art* (Berkeley and Los Angeles: University of California Press, 1979), p. 125. For additional comment on the hierarchic sensibility in play here, see Walter Burkert, *Greek Religion*, trans. John Raffan (Cambridge, Mass.: Harvard University Press, 1985), pp. 189, 311, 321, 331.

father for murder; either he's no killer, they say, or even if he obviously killed, the deceased being a murderer, there is no need to be mindful [*ou dein phrontizein*] of such a one, for it's unholy for a son to prosecute his father for murder; poor knowers [*eidotes*], Socrates, of how the divine stands in relation to the holy and to the unholy! (4D–E)

The tone here evokes another hurt child, like Meletus, anxious to show up those who insist on belittling him, telling him what to do, those who seem to have overlooked his expertise in holy matters by sending "a man away to ask of the exegete what must be done." In the interval, the murderer dies and thereby supplies Euthyphro a chance to reverse his humiliation, to act rather than to suffer. More interesting still, the language of Euthyphro's report, its paraphrasing in indirect discourse, has Euthyphro's father and kinsmen urging him "not to mind" or "not to care." But perhaps that is not all: What they literally tell him is *ou dei phrontizein, Euthuphrōn,* and in this admonition one might hear some punning or playing on the man's name: *ou-dei-phron(tizein)*, no doubt provoking, goading, and teasing amid admonition, as one's familiars know best how to do. Here Euthyphro's name, which in theory might ironically denote "right-mindedness," when embedded in this much more tangled linguistic and social context, plays a crueler joke on him because it produces and it mocks his care. In one prohibition it summarizes the traditional wisdom that Euthyphro both believes in his viscera and doubts in his head: *Ou dei phrontizein,* one must not care, think, mind, heed.[24] Such a prohibition of course presupposes and preserves its contrary; and by its explicitness this particular prohibition, if taken in earnest, no doubt inhibits its own fulfillment. *Ou dei phrontizein, Euthuphrōn*! How do you render this in English? "Never mind, Ever-mind"? In this "specular name" lies a textual image of Euthyphro's *ēthos*.[25]

Nor does it seem an accident for this infernal name of our hero, this

---

24. For discussions of the relevant traditional wisdom: on the exegetes, James H. Oliver, *The Athenian Expounders of the Sacred Ancestral Law* (Baltimore, Md.: Johns Hopkins University Press, 1950); on *miasma*, Robert Parker, *Miasma: Pollution and Purification in Early Greek Religion* (Oxford: Clarendon Press, 1983).

25. Geoffrey Hartman reflects on such "specular naming" or dispersion of the proper name as a literary phenomenon in "Psychoanalysis: The French Connection," in *Psychoanalysis and the Question of the Text*, ed. Hartman (Baltimore, Md.: Johns Hopkins University Press, 1978), pp. 86–113. Some of the volatility of Euthyphro's name in this context might be glossed by the hopeful, euphemistic iteration of *euphrōn, euthuphrōn,* and other *eu-* words hoping to dispel the Furies in the final lines of Aeschylus's *Eumenides* (e.g., lines 1030–43).

injunction not to think, to turn around the syllable *dei*, a syllable uncannily active in this dialogue along a chain of resonant words, words of power: *deos* ("fear"), *deon* ("needful, " "proper"), *aidōs* ("shame"), *deinos* ("awesome"). And such words, like Euthyphro's argument, seem partly truly, partly falsely derived from *Zeus*, who is grammatologically rather than morally, theologically, or mythologically disseminated here.[26] This dissemination of syllables is no shower of gold. Rather, in such words lies the real force of piety and holiness for Euthyphro and perhaps for Athens, not in the philosopher's *eidos*, or idea, which has drawn so much notice in the commentaries on this dialogue. Though Euthyphro lacks knowledge and the courage to acquire it, he has fear (*deos*) in plenty and need (*deon*) and even a kind of shame (*aidōs*), at least before the more penetrating gaze of Father Socrates, where one keenly feels the more-than-conceptual difference between seeing and being seen (10A).[27] Here, it seems to me, is a peg on which to hang that peculiar manner with which Euthyphro first addresses Socrates, that flattery-cloaked-as-intimacy, that confessional tone of self-hate that inhabits this flattery. The source of such ambivalences is here in the tension between Euthyphro's *penia* and his *poros*, his neediness and his resourcefulness, his bonds to the family and his attempt at free self-assertion, in the tension between the confidence of his rhetoric and the dread of some nameless retaliation incurred by such freedom and confidence. Socrates plays the father, but Euthyphro also guiltily projects on Socrates his expectations of the punitive patriarch.

What I have called an infernal chain of signifiers—the hidden dynamic of the dialogue and of its second discourse—reveals itself fleetingly in a paradoxical citation of Stasinus at 12A–B shortly after Socrates has lamented his inability to fix and stabilize his words (11E):

Zēna de ton th'erksanta, kai hos tade
pant'ephuteusen

26. I adapt to my purposes the figure of "dissemination" from Derrida (*Dissemination*), though I confess a quite different estimate of this figure in Plato from that which Derrida describes in "Plato's Pharmacy." My view is closer to Hartman's, as developed, for example, in "Monsieur Texte: On Jacques Derrida, His *Glas*" and "Monsieur Texte II: Epiphony in Echoland," *Georgia Review* 29 (1975): 759–94, and 30 (1976): 169–97.

27. For Socratic play with this chain of signifiers, see *Cratylus* 418E–419B, and especially *Protagoras* 341A–B, where Socrates makes light of the terrible (*to deinon*).

> *ouk etheleis eipein: hina gar deos, entha kai aidōs.*[28]

Literally:

> Zeus [*Zēna*] the creator, even he who all things brought forth,
> you will not name: for where fear [*deos*], there shame (or respect) [*aidōs*].

This is the seminal passage for the dialogue's genus-species distinction in the first discourse of the philosophers (in fact for a logic-centered discourse within a *logos*-centered discourse);[29] but the citation's conspicuously irrelevant wordplay is also seminal for the second discourse, the discourse, may I say, of the deconstructors. What is irrelevant as conversation or argument achieves a deep sense as text. In fact, the quotation demonstrates some of the logic of that second, disseminating discourse when the forbidden name of Zeus, mentioned only to begin or originate the sentence, returns defaced and dispersed in the wordplay of *deos* and *aidōs*, two pious effects of the holy Zeus in the first place mentioned, but effects, unlike the bounty of all created things (cf. 15A), more likely to inspire fear than confidence, flight than pursuit, defensiveness than prosecution.[30]

---

28. This citation from Stasinus is disputed (see Burnet, pp. 53–54). I would urge, against Burnet, the retention of *etheleis eipein* over *ethelei neikein* as better matching quote with its context. Accepting Burnet's text, on the other hand, would involve modifications in my analysis: For instance, *ethelei neikein*, "he will not revile," more strongly accents blasphemy or profanation of Zeus, but at the expense of the hortatory immediacy of the second person.

29. In conversation, Harry Berger, Jr., has usefully distinguished three levels of interpretive interest in Plato reflected in the commentaries: what he terms, following the rhetoric of poststructuralist criticism, the *logocentric* level, where commentators take their cue from Socratic *logos* in varying degrees of philosophical, cultural, dramatic, or existential fullness or openness; within this *logocentric* area of interest, Berger also sees a *logicocentric* level, where commentators isolate and analyze the logic of Socratic argument and refutation; but Berger also sees a *textual* level in Plato, where commentators like Berger see *logos* and *logic* profoundly modified and mediated by the textual status of what we call "Plato." Where the *logocentric* interpretations of a hermeneutical commentator (Gadamer, for instance) emphasize a variety of Heideggerian *heeding*, the textualist interpretations of Berger—or indeed, of the present essay—tend to emphasize close *reading*. For a fuller discussion of these claims, see Berger, "Levels of Discourse in Plato's Dialogues."

30. The sleeping metaphors in Attic defense and prosecution, terms often repeated in the *Euthyphro*, denote flight and pursuit; this seems another instance of a kind of ambiguity or coexistence of the primitive and the sophisticated in the dialogue. In the critical reading of a text, these sleeping metaphors are much more apt to stir than in listening to a conversation.

The elliptical final phrase "where fear, there shame" reinforces this stern sense of prohibition with its gnomic packaging of traditional theology into a pious slogan or dictum. Of course, the official agenda of the dialogue ignores these vagrant linguistic effects as well as it can, as if the terms thrown out by the quotation were of no more import than the even and the odd (12D), to which Socrates disingenuously, not to say irreverently, compares fear and reverence. One problem with such traditional piety is precisely that you can so take it or leave it—*if* you have the mind to. But in fact the terms of Socrates' quotation subvert the official agenda of the dialogue, or, more precisely, they mark its subversion. In Gadamer's terms, the "truth of the object" binding this community is not what it should have been: the *holy,* the truth or epiphany of which would have bound a community into *piety.* But this binding takes place according to a mechanism that is undone by its question; the "new community" would be both condition and consequence of such dialogue, so Socrates and Euthyphro seem unable to attain it from where they begin. This objective has already—always already—disappeared with Zeus the generous creator into the dialogue's second, latent discourse and into its seemingly inert and arbitrary elements, its letters, phonemes, words, and offhand examples, where it leaves new unspoken fear and anxiety in its track. Though this discourse is most clearly legible in Plato's text, Euthyphro and Socrates, indistinctly and incoherently, to be sure, heed this subtextual discourse to the extent that they bind one another in mutual distrust and disrespect.

Thus in a way, and I have purposely termed this way *bad faith,* Euthyphro is wise to the old myths, that is, disenchanted with their truth, though sensitive to the anxieties projected into them by the human imagination, anxieties that in this case reflect the needful helplessness of the child before parental action, aggression, or omnipotence, anxieties that produce in him retaliatory urges to bind and dominate using the city and its courts as one's mother, in the place of Gaia and Rhea in the theogonic myths. Euthyphro, refashioned or framed by Plato's text as the injunction not-to-think, represents this *ēthos,* oddly both so careful and so heedless, so free yet so constrained, like the believer in bad faith in Sartre's analysis.[31] Or in the Socratic comparison, Euthyphro is a walking contradiction, like those famous aporetic statues of Daedalus, the ances-

---

31. This discussion occurs in Part One of *Being and Nothingness,* trans. Hazel Barnes (New York: Washington Square, 1966), pp. 56–86.

tral curse Socrates visits upon himself (11B–E). Or one might see Euthyphro suffering from the paranoid self-sufficiency, so to speak, the self-assertion compact with dread of nemesis that Socrates so marvelously reports of the sophists in the *Protagoras*. These are all figures of the impossibility of dialogue respecting "the truth of the object."

These are all also passive-aggressive figures for the suppression of the "middle voice" of mutual need, reciprocal relationship, and shared responsibility. In refuting Euthyphro's view of holiness as "what all the gods love," Socrates elaborately deploys an active-passive contrary to suggest that holiness transcends the love of the Olympians, that holiness is loved because it is holy, not holy because it is loved (10A). Beyond the purposes of this elegant but suspect refutation, however, the active-passive contrary also contributes some very interesting and legible peculiarities to the dialogue's discursive undercurrents. Here the excluded middle of Socratic logic that divides active from passive conspicuously excludes the Greek middle voice. Burnet comments how "the conception of a passive verb was exceptionally hard to grasp for a Greek, since the Greek verb [seldom] developed a special form for it. . . . The meaning had to be expressed by 'middle' forms or by 'intransitive' verbs . . ." (p. 128). It is also hard for the non-Greek to grasp the conspicuously excluded middle voice of Socrates' active-passive distinction. But we ought to make the effort, especially because the middle voice, in generally marking reflexive or self-interested action, captures a sense of complicity between agent and patient that Euthyphro's either-or moralistic and legalistic thinking, as well as Socrates' excluded-middle logic, wants to suppress. Thus there is carrying and leading, on the one hand, and being carried and being led, on the other, but somewhere too there must be a place for *getting carried* and *getting led*. This sense of the middle voice seems closer to the moral ambiguities, exchanges, and reciprocities that the *Euthyphro* concerns than do active or passive voices, and because these ambiguities were earlier broached in the discussion of Socrates' and Euthyphro's indictments and then bracketed, they can be felt here as present-excluded.

The exaggerated clarity of Socrates' active-passive hierarchy—more prescription than description—pulls along with it the train of verbal examples I have earlier mentioned: *carry, lead, see, love*. Though Socrates' argument renders the nominative subject of these verbals as nondescript (a mere *ti*, "something") the textual and contextual parallels have a way of filling in the nominative for the doubled reading. Plato's text and the conversational context in the lives of Socrates and Euthyphro suggest specific carriers, leaders, seers, and lovers—authors, actors, and recipients of these processes and predications. This infilling follows an aetiological impulse common to religion, as well as to law—an impulse prominent enough in this dialogue (who is to blame?—3A, 4B–C, 5B; who is to thank?—3A, 14E–15A).

In the shadows cast by carrying and being carried, by leading and being led, by seeing and being seen gather two parallel sets of unequal relationships—important cultural relationships inscribed beneath the simpler inequality of participial forms. One of these relationships, the main focus of Socrates' alleged impiety, concerns the hierarchy of humans and gods, in which gods are putatively active, humans putatively passive, so that there is creator (as in the Stasinus citation at 12A) and created. The second relationship, also central to piety, particularly in the ancient tradition, is that between parents and children, the main issue in Euthyphro's defense before Socrates of his prosecution of his father. Within the context of this second relationship, the verbals *carrying, leading,* and *seeing* constitute, not casually chosen examples, but terms precisely evoking parenting, nurturance, and guardianship, terms evoking the family scene that has obscurely brought about the long-suffering Euthyphro's action. Perhaps the series even respects the increasingly subtle forms of coercion and care that attend a developing child, who is earliest directed by carrying, then more gently by leading (something being led may be thought to depend on the same something's *following*), then more abstractly by shame or conscience.

The surplus of familiar meaning and reference in this series is a curse of philosophy in common language positioned in the commonplaces: such philosophy is damned by examples, damned without them. But Socrates' way with such examples is also a celebrated feature of his charm: the quality of dissembling or understatement whereby he always seems to mean more than he says. The excess touched in these examples throws a shadow across the conversation; the excess that I have sought to describe functions very much like Socratic irony in indicating a region of knowledge or awareness that the dialogue's explicit language is not reaching. But while critics, including his principal accuser, Meletus, argue Socrates' mastery of this dissembling (and their mastery of his mastery), the case is not so clear. Socrates may or may not intend stray references or connotations that here suggest the reciprocal dependence of active and passive, of divine and human. For whom would he intend such connotations, after all? The more certain point is that Socrates is himself both active and passive in such a case: active in *logos,* passive in text, where other meanings permeate face-to-face *logos,* in part with Socrates' tacit, "middling" acquiescence, thanks to his open, enigmatic, permeable discursive style.

By this route Socrates' exemplary concern for piety may rekindle a sense of the holy—or better, a sense of the problematic of the holy[32]—for Plato's readers. It is possible to glean from the *Euthyphro* the difficulty that arises for religion when the holiness of the divine depends on human holiness, on finite acts of human hallowing; when the hallowed as a condition is so crucial, but the agency and agents that empower such hallowing are so obscured.[33] Benveniste's conclusion—that *to hosion* is what is "permitted by divine law (to men)" (p. 465)—needs a further crucial, disenchanted elaboration here: *To hosion* is what humans permit to be permitted by divine law to humans, though of course the human creators of religious culture get occulted within that culture. In another way, if gods allow certain rites to humans, humans must still perform them in the tenuous light of this permission, thereby sanctioning not only the permission but the permitting gods.

32. Blits, for one, in "The Holy and the Human," makes a vigorous case for Socratic piety. I would stress the *problematic* rather than the *holy,* however, in the phrase I note. Socrates and Plato seem not to be fundamentally interested in resuscitating the traditionally holy per se. Traditional holiness is too much entangled in fear and shame to allow for the kind of discursive *philia* (though this term, too, is bound to Zeus, as at 6B) that Socrates seems to regard as important to human, political, and philosophical life. The term *problematic,* on the other hand, suggests both the problem occasioned by the decay of traditional holiness and the chance and mischance of revising traditional habits of thought through various critical strategies and philosophical practices. It should not be overlooked how the *Euthyphro*—indeed, Socrates in words at odds with his charismatic person—heralds a parting of ways in ancient religion, which on one side becomes more personal and on the other more philosophical. See Martin Nilsson, *Greek Piety,* trans. H. J. Rose (Oxford: Oxford University Press, 1951) and Andre-Jean Festugière, *Personal Religion among the Greeks* (Berkeley and Los Angeles: University of California Press, 1954).

33. *To hosion* is a very elusive term, and not just because our view of these things is obscured by Judeo-Christian influences (even without these influences, Socrates is perplexed). In its ambivalences, *to hosion* can refer to a quality of divinity transcending the human (like *to hieron,* "the sacred") or it can refer to the piety of the worshiper; it can refer to external observances (as at 14B) or to the internal purity, the wholeness, of the worshiper; *to hosion* can refer to sacred law or injunction, as distinct from positive or human law, which governs human action in other spheres of life, but *to hosion* can also denote *license*: what is permitted or required of humans, that is, what does not lie under taboo, proscription, or curse, what is *profane.* The problem for Socrates and for philosophy is how to distinguish such ambivalent, undifferentiated, primitivistic religious experience without too simply dispelling it. See Burkert, *Greek Religion,* pp. 55–118. On ambivalences in these contexts, see Jean-Pierre Vernant, "The Pure and the Impure," in *Myth and Society in Ancient Greece,* trans. Janet Lloyd (Atlantic Highlands, N.J.: Humanities Press, 1980), pp. 110–29. For illuminating attempts to comprehend the Greek language of the sacred, see Emile Benveniste, *Indo-European Language and Society,* trans. Elizabeth Palmer (Coral Gables, Fla.: University of Miami Press, 1973), pp. 445–69.

The sacred is what is so dedicated by human acts and only so long as such acts sustain it. Specifically, the condition of cosmos, something's being made or arranged, depends on acts of creating or ordering that in fifth-century Greece too visibly bear ordinary human signature. Euthyphro's later claim that piety is *therapeia* (12E) of the gods encounters just this difficulty when all the examples of therapeutic attention, in a startlingly apt inversion of human-divine hierarchy, have human craft overseeing domesticated animals. In attempting to correct this inversion, Euthyphro accepts Socrates' specification of such *therapeia* as service of masters—*hupēretikē* (13D). But *hupēretikē* (literally, "under-rowing") can allude to the *thētes*, the lowest and poorest class of citizens, who serve the fleets and epitomize the rambunctious rule of the *dēmos*, thereby marking another startlingly apt inversion of a hallowed hierarchy.

Opposite these implications of the Socratic standpoint is the way that Euthyphro's exemplary anxieties induce only his fitting revelation as a wolf or Meletus in sheep's clothing. Indeed, in face-to-face conversation Socrates is partly responsible for arousing these anxieties, turning would-be friend to foe, and forcing Euthyphro to seek other shelter. Impatient and alarmed at these improper inversions of cause and effect, Euthyphro in the recognition scene finally turns in exasperation upon Socrates with the popular and unexamined view of piety:

> Nevertheless I simply say that if someone knows how to say and to do the things gratifying to the gods, in praying and in sacrificing, these are the holy [*ta hosia*], and such things save [*sōzei*] private households and the common things of cities; and the opposite of gratifying things is impiety [*asebē*], which both overturns and destroys everything. (14B)

Here we have a personal care raised to civic proportions, pragmatically vacillating between *phronēsis* and remorse. And we have the helpless and helplessly opportunistic piety of the politicians who find their only saving power (*sō-cratēs*) in the penitential victims and scapegoats who can bear the weight of civic misfortune. The negatively inflected logic of this piety, so fearful of reprisals, does not involve returning genuine thanks for divine blessings, but staving off or paying the penalty for the misfortunes of an increasingly godless world across which the divine still casts its shadow. And this penalty we still pay. For the vicious circle of hubristic *phronēsis* and anxious remorse defers the holy truth of the object, loses it between the past and some future; and in its absence the infernal dialectic of calculating prudence and careful remorse binds its factions into a kind of community founded on the avoidance of truth, as well as on the repression of history.[34]

What then is "the object of which the text speaks"?[35] It is not really piety, nor is it the holy, that traditional category of transcendence itself. Respecting its otherness by their silence, Socrates and Plato may, perhaps, imply their piety by a conspicuous absenting of its object; but then this would be an object of which the text pointedly does *not* speak. Then again, in the wake of this prohibition, Euthyphro may be the text's object. However, this would not be a *spoken object,* but as I have tried to argue as well with the *Apology,* a *written subject,* dramatically presented as subject-in-dialogue, but also dispersed by Plato's writing into communities of language, kinship, politics, and belief that Euthyphro seems bent on suppressing. One might cogently argue that Socrates, too, would abstract himself from such communities were it not for the strenuous tethering of his will within makeshift conversation. In finally supplying that conversation its interlocutor, Plato secures its endless power and value. But Plato's text also tells on both Euthyphro and Socrates; as writing, it monumentalizes what they would evade or transcend, and it does so by way of textual strategies that need much further analysis and description.

---

34. Michael J. O'Brien provides a useful introduction to the newfangled *phronēsis* on this Thucydidean scene in *The Socratic Paradoxes and the Greek Mind* (Chapel Hill: University of North Carolina Press, 1967), pp. 22–55. It seems clear to me that the Platonic Socrates does not subscribe to the positivistic varieties of ethical intellectualism described by O'Brien. At the same time, in such conversations as that of the *Protagoras,* Socrates, bound by the structure of face-to-face communication, is unable to establish or to contribute more than his ironic distance from prudential versions of wisdom, and such ironic distance is not message or means enough for most philosophical ends. Irony, that is, is too easily uninterpreted or misinterpreted; thus irony too readily results in cases of mistaken identity where Protagoras and Socrates, like Euthyphro and Socrates, seem to shift or share positions. Berger, "Facing Sophists," lucidly discusses aspects of this Socratic liability.

35. Gadamer, p. 341.

Four / Person,
Tradition,
Text
in
Ion

For philosophy as we understand it, the *Ion* is the slightest of Plato's canonical dialogues. It does little more for the philosopher than epitomize the unreliability of poetry as a form of knowledge. All the same, the *Ion* makes a marvelous challenge to literary and rhetorical interpretation because the dialogue itself practices such interpretation at several levels. It both provokes and mirrors one's study, presenting and representing problems of interpretation as a form of knowledge. Its interest is less poetry per se than its focus on the mediations of tradition and especially on human media as they represent and misrepresent instituted truth.

In his musing over Plato's *Ion* and its legacy, W. K. C. Guthrie casually likens the dialogue to the "light, winged and sacred" poet depicted in it and remarks the scandal of a heavy-handed scholarship that "has done much, if not to crush, at least to take the bloom from its wings."[1] Guthrie is not serious about this comparison between poet and

1. Guthrie, *A History of Greek Philosophy*, 4:211.

discourse, but perhaps he should be, in part because the difference between a person and a *logos* is not at all clear in Plato, in part because the first "heavy hand" in a long tradition of scholarship belongs to Socrates himself, whose questioning of Ion is notably obtuse. In fact, a reader's puzzling over *Ion* reenacts Socrates' puzzling over Ion in a way that upsets the scholar's usual interpretive standpoint and privilege. We compose with Guthrie one of the *Ion*'s many rings, inescapably enveloped by the hermeneutic mediations and paradoxes addressed in the Socratic dialogue and addressed as the Platonic dialogue to unspecified future readers in an unpredictable tradition.[2]

Socrates greets an Ion fresh from a victory in a contest of rhapsodes, or performers of epic, at Epidaurus. Socrates interrogates Ion about the field of knowledge that informs his successful study and practice of Homeric poetry. When Ion is unable to present or defend his art systematically, Socrates teases him with a theory or speculation concerning divine inspiration—enthusiasm, "engoddedness"—that accounts for the behavior of poets, rhapsodes, and audiences. Understandably reluctant to accept this attribution of madness, which would make him the ancient equivalent of a natural jester or fool, Ion tries to defend his mastery of all the arts mentioned in Homer. After Socrates strips these away one by one (the charioteer, for example, not the rhapsode, is the true expert in chariot driving) Ion clings to the art of the general as the true sphere of his competence. Unable to shake Ion's self-esteem, Socrates ends the conversation with a crescendo of sarcasm.

In different ways, both Socrates and Plato refuse Ion and Homer their claims to autonomy, to wholeness, to the tyrannical art or power of the all-sufficient general that Ion, in the dialogue's recognition scene, aspires to. Plato's textualizing of Ion is an interesting and complex effect of his

---

2. Among those who have lately shared with me most helpfully in this tradition: Allan Bloom, "An Interpretation of Plato's *Ion*," *Interpretation* 1 (Summer 1970): 43–62; Kenneth Dorter, "The *Ion*: Plato's Characterization of Art," *Journal of Aesthetics and Art Criticism* 32 (1973–74): 65–78; Jacob Klein, "Plato's Ion," *Claremont Journal of Public Affairs* 2 (1973): 23–37; John D. Moore, "Limitation and Design in Plato's *Ion*," *Pacific Coast Philology* 8 (1973): 45–51; Jerrald Ranta, "The Drama of Plato's *Ion*," *Journal of Aesthetics and Art Criticism* 26 (1967–68): 217–29; and Joel F. Wilcox, "Cross-Metamorphosis in Plato's *Ion*," in *Literature as Philosophy, Philosophy as Literature*, ed. Donald G. Marshall (Iowa City: University of Iowa Press, 1987), pp. 155–74. Useful bibliographical information, as well as more cautious and traditional approaches to these issues—approaches less sensitive to the pluralism of the text—can be found in *Plato: On Beauty, Wisdom, and the Arts*, ed. Julius Moravcsik and Philip Temko (Totowa, N.J.: Rowman and Littlefield, 1982), and in Morris Henry Partee, *Plato's Poetics: The Authority of Beauty* (Salt Lake City: University of Utah Press, 1981).

writing. But Socrates, too, "textualizes" Ion in his own improvising way, abstracting him out of his vainglorious individuality and subjecting him to larger wholes or processes—for example, the scheme of *technai* (538Cff.)—that construct or determine Ion unaware. In a sense, Socrates makes Ion out to be booklike; or at best Ion is both a writer and a reader, perpetually moving between having and being had.[3] At the same time, Plato shows how this is happening to Socrates as well.

I

Socrates sees Ion in two contrasting lights, which he makes visible in his impromptu, rhapsodic account of musical inspiration. Like Euthyphro, Ion feels the giddiness of freedom and power, though he is also, when pressed, acutely conscious of his vulnerability. Socrates' elaborate flattery at the greeting (530B–C) elicits and establishes firmly before us this brave Ion, reveling in a sense of his own prepossessing ego. But Socrates' professed envy, in its repetitions of what an Ion must do, also emphasizes the rhapsode's bondage. Ion's appearance of insouciance, privilege, and power, Socrates will argue, conceals a number of mechanisms to which the freewheeling rhapsode or poet is actually enslaved. Socrates terms the master here a "godly power," but he characterizes it in a noisily ungodly way:

> . . . it is a godly power which moves you, like that in the stone which Euripides called the magnet but which the many call the Heraclean stone. For this same stone not only draws the iron rings themselves, but also puts into the rings a power so that they in turn are empowered to do the same thing as the stone, to draw other rings, so that sometimes a chain of rings, a very big one, is suspended; but for all of them, the power hangs on that one stone. And in this way, the Muse herself makes enthusiasts,

---

3. The phrase "having and being had" reflects my sense of Socratic wordplay at 536B on *katechetai* and *echetai* and middle/passive forms of *eksartaō*. This wordplay seems to ridicule or desublimate "possession" and, by wavering between middle and passive voices, to call attention to the reciprocal dependencies of divine and human actually operating in *enthusiasm*.

and a chain is suspended when, through these enthusiasts, others become enthused. (533D–E)

There is a deliberate, sustained tension here between skepticism and enchantment. The terms of the discourse debunk the "godly power" by reducing it to a kind of mechanics, but the matter is at the same time rendered in a pretty, rhapsodic manner that implicitly acknowledges the potential sublimity of speech. As the syntax and similes loop along, they suggest chains that weirdly befit their content. Socrates marks this equivocation between his debunking and his rhapsodic declaiming with two names for the magnet: a popular, mythological name (Heraclean stone) and a sophisticated, disenchanted name linked to Euripides (the magnesian stone).[4]

Speaking this way, Socrates is obviously playing with Ion. But we should also recall, as we have noticed before, how in a more baleful sense, since Ion is his only apparent auditor, Socrates is also playing *to* him, unable to make his criticism of rhapsody not also look like a kind of flattery. To engage his auditor, Socrates first enchants him. Thus the wordplay in the discourse of enthusiasm and at other points in the dialogue varies with the two media we study. Though one may read Socratic equivocation of "enthusiasm" with equanimity in a Platonic text, Socrates in person is surely not a master of all his speech's duplicities, even when his parodistic language indicates some awareness of them. In explicating Ion's servitude to code, convention, and tradition, in short, Socrates also silently exemplifies his own.

For only a few lines in his account does Socrates allow a space for more positively connoted images of musical tradition that correspond to Ion's professed sense of privilege. Poets, like Bacchants, draw off celestial fluids, themselves reporting

> that from springs flowing with honey, and out of the Muses' gardens and glens, they pluck their lyrics and carry them to us just like honeybees, even fluttering like bees; and they tell the truth. For a light matter is the poet, both winged and holy, and unable to make poems until he becomes engodded and senseless and the mind is no longer in him. (534A–B)

4. Bloom, pp. 51–52.

Despite some sweetness and light, however, Socrates' negative mentions of senselessness and "possession" (534A) make this Muses' garden a very precarious green or golden world; in philosophical daylight, even the poets' own wish-fulfilling description of their activity becomes ambiguous, more lunacy than luxury.

Socratic rhapsody against rhapsody should also put one on guard against a certain philosophical perversity here, since this magnet and iron chain model the conversation. Just as he locks poets, rhapsodes, and their musical garden into his myth of iron rings, a repressive Socrates can be seen to be chaining Ion into a methodical interrogation of *technē*, into what one reader aptly terms "the iron-clad necessity of the argument based on the arts."[5] Socrates drives the rhapsode through paces, narrowly channels his answers to force an outcome, in effect plays Pentheus to Ion's Asian stranger.[6] The "ancient quarrel between philosophy and poetry"[7] breaks out anew. But the mock-epic proportions of this encounter, distributing the ridiculous to all contenders, may also make one wonder to whose aid Plato is coming.

The analogy between musical power and magnetism is both weaker and stronger than it at first seems. On the one hand, the image, with its rocks and iron rings, seems firm-founded and iron-clad. But unlike a chain, this string of rings does not interlock. The rings depend on the mysterious and tenuous power of the magnet for their connection. Without the magnet's charismatic power, the chain atomizes and collapses. Any break in the chain breaks the chain at every connection below. There is therefore an apparently deliberate and intriguing weakness built into this model of necessity with which Socrates constrains Ion and his kind.

To see the unexpected strength of the image, on the other hand, translate the analogy into its most conspicuous referent along the bridge that Socrates has provided: I mean by way of the *dactyl*, a subject of some punning here. "Ring" in Socrates' account of inspiration translates

---

5. Bloom, p. 48.
6. As in Euripides' roughly similar depiction of encounters between an Asian free spirit and a Greek heavyweight, for example, at *Bacchae*, lines 215–63, 451–518.
7. *Republic* X, 607B. Friedländer, *Plato*, 2:136, rephrases the quarrel this way: "The primary intention of this dialogue is not to depict satirically the clash between Socrates and a vain artist. Instead, Plato has grasped the Herakleitean tension in his own nature as a thinker and has given it form as a poet." I would supplement this by pointing out the tension between the philosopher as talker and the philosopher as writer.

daktulios, a term with only an iota's difference from *daktulos,* the dactylic meter of Homer, the regular link in his powerful epic chains. The iron chain of Socrates' myth displaces or disguises the linguistic chains of Homeric epic, but the ring song, which is in this way less crazy than it seems, also draws a subtle strength from this musical connection of itself to its referent.

Here, then, is one way Socrates plays for greater stakes than implied by the simple parody of Ion in which the refutation is dressed. For if they resemble magnetic chains, charismatic linguistic chains, the comparison implies, are not firm or interlocked, but depend on a "godly power" of uncertain provenance, perhaps not so much a stone as one's way of naming it. These linguistic chains, as the sequel illustrates, are open to numerous distortions of emphasis, revisions, rearrangements, and thefts. The Homer that Ion and Socrates recite in the *Ion* is rendered conspicuously discontinuous, unchained, and problematic with respect to tradition, thanks to the very selective citation that Ion, Socrates, and Plato all practice. Even though learned by heart, internalized, armed for face-to-face performance, this Homer functions like the writing castigated in the *Phaedrus,* open to diverse understandings and appropriations, "rolled round and round among the heedful and the nonchalant alike" (275E).

Consider again the model of tradition that Socrates' fantasy of magnetic rings implies, for *tradition* here is a crux, not only to modern interpreters, but also, I believe, to the two founders of the tradition that I am trying to interpret. Socrates' spectacular *spatial* analogy of tradition—of chains suspended down to here from above—in effect suppresses a sense of time and change, which pose the harder problems for tradition, *nomos,* and transcendence. If presents, persons, and presence fully embodied tradition, we would not, I think, share the sense of rupture that troubles Socrates about Ion. But time, change, and difference infect Ion's presence, hollowing it out with the absence of past and future, recasting space as spacing. Noticeably escaping the closure of hierarchical thought are other relationships (Ion-present-as-Homer-absent, Plato-present-as-Socrates-absent, text-present-as-Plato-absent) that the dialogue as a work of time and tradition might be thought to invoke and depend on.

The ring song, by contrast, puts the poet in the same presence as his rhapsodic performer and melts that present time into a nostalgic atemporality of myth and legend. In a characteristic manner, Socrates' ring rhapsody mimics its adversary, marking its exceptions, its differences from Ionic music, in tone more than in structure, in tonal differences that risk misunderstanding. The poetic structure common to Socrates' and Ion's performances acknowledges a kind of pastoral or golden-age core, the musical garden, within the cultural machine. And so the Socratic account conserves the archaic ecstatic conjuncture, the primacy of sacred space, the power of magnetism and harmony, even while it strives to caricature and, presumably, to criticize them; Socrates embodies this power even as he tries to disembody it from Ion. The account's deep structure is skeptical, scientific, Euripidean, but its surface structure is still magnetically bound to a mythic, storylike, Heraclean fate.

The atemporality of the ring song answers in a quite relevant way to the pervasive present tense of theatrical performance, which brings all of time and space under the spell of its enthusiasms.

> Hold on, Ion, tell me the following, and don't hide away what I ask you. When you are reciting verses well and very much astonishing the spectators—you are singing of Odysseus, when he leaps to the threshold, becomes visible to the suitors, and pours out arrows at his feet; or you're singing of Achilles driving upon Hector or something pitiable regarding Andromache or Hecube or Priam—are you then in your senses, or do you become beside yourself and does your soul, getting engodded, think itself to be in Ithaca or Troy or wherever the epic has them? (535B–C)

The anachronistic sequencing of these selected episodes underscores the point; a true sequence (e.g., Troy before Ithaca) submits itself to the dramatic space in which Ion performs the equivalent of Homer's greatest hits.

It is not a higher muse, Ion admits, that dictates these selections. In contrast to the higher-to-lower vector of magnetic power, this admission shows more accurately which way the wind of inspiration is blowing. Though rapt, engodded, transported by some higher power through space and time,

> . . . from the dais, I look down at the spectators lamenting, every time, and casting dreadful glances, astonished with the narration. And it's most necessary that I set my mind on them; so if I bring them down to weeping, I myself shall laugh having taken the money; but if they laugh, I myself shall weep having lost the money. (535E)

When "it's most necessary," Ion volunteers this other vision of necessity according to which he is inspired first by the "godly power" of money; so Ion prostitutes his muse. This playing of the audience for money, however, seems an inevitable result of a sense of musical tradition predicated on performative and competitive space. Easy access to songs and easy access to popular enthusiasms obviate the need to think the past and tradition in their truer difficulty. Homer has become like his nepenthe.[8]

II

Now, however, what would happen if a critical reader, emulating Socratic meddling, took some time to undo this typical Socratic conversion of philosophy into fable and cosmos, if one temporarily tried to make time rather than space govern the image—or, better, concept—of musical tradition? Already this problem: The abstractness of temporality defies ready mimesis, or representation. How is thought in images ever to grasp a musical tradition as a discipline of time or a chronicle of difference and change? The magnetism, the charisma, is more nearly *back then*, not *up there*; we have it now as obscurely passed from some past, only from above by an illusion of transposition that identifies the authority of time with the authority of the divine. Socrates' lampooning account of music exploits this illusion even as it implies strong skepticism on his part of human attempts seriously to represent the authority or action of the divine; such attempts invariably seem to involve bad faith, a will to power dissembled as piety or as a will to truth. But if Socrates elicits from Ion the admission that his muse is really (or, more cautiously, also) *down here* as an audience motivating and shaping the performance, it is also true that the magnetism, the charisma, felt to exist *back then* also originates *now, among us,* as we read this text, imagine Ion and Socrates, and reconstitute the links from this present to that past.

This fact gives us some leverage on the more difficult reckoning of tradition, its uses, and its abuses within the dialogue. With Socrates and Ion tradition proves difficult to isolate, so many are its adhesions to

---

8. *Odyssey* IV, 219–21. Cf. Bloom: "In investigating Ion, Socrates studies a kind of popular substitute for philosophy," p. 48.

persons. What can be spoken is like a telegram: a few words from far away, not so much a knowledge as one's way of naming a power, thus a work of magic, not of art. Such tradition might only announce itself in the difficult representation of present-as-excluded, "Present yet absent," as in the Heraclitean proverb according to Heidegger.[9] Ion excludes or eclipses Homer in interpreting him; yet Homer permeates Ion's self-understanding and thus remains a force Socrates must try to reckon with.

The conversation's telegraphed tradition features names organized in catalogues that suppress difference from an original or that frame mimetic difference with genealogical regularity. For example, heroes are pretty much alike; nominal differences weakly belie essential similarity, and so such names are creatures of their particular context or reception. A catalogue motif in the *Ion* will help to carry this point in a series of name lists, whose distribution and coherence Ion and Socrates will attempt to justify. Socrates assumes—disingenuously, no doubt—the operation of conceptual unities within the tradition. Early in his examination, Socrates interrogates Ion's command of a whole field of poetry, on the grounds that "poetics is a whole" (532C) and that to be a technician anywhere in this field one must have the whole art. At 532D, in a characteristic maneuver, Socrates confuses a point in seeming to clarify it; apparently trying to be helpful, he questionably likens poetics to other arts: "Won't there be the same manner of inquiry into all the arts, whenever one takes any other art as a whole?"

To clarify his clarification, Socrates takes Ion on a brief tour of musical tradition, mentioning in quasi-epic fashion catalogues of famous technicians. Conceptual thinking may be hard for Ion, this strategy implies, but as an ambitious professional and descendant of Mnemosyne he certainly knows his Hellenic *Who's Who*. So Socrates will come at his abstract headings by enumerating famous heads. Socrates has already at this point touched on the poetic tradition ("Homer and the other poets, among whom are Hesiod and Archilochus"—532A) and now proceeds to survey the tradition of painters (Polugnotos, son of Aglaophon, the single citation here), the tradition of statue makers (Daedalus, Epeius, Theodorus), and the tradition of flute playing, lute playing, singing, and rhapsody (Olympus, Thamyrus, Orpheus, Phemius, and Ion). These latter catalogues begin with the most recent and historical personage,

---

9. Martin Heidegger, *An Introduction to Metaphysics*, trans. Ralph Manheim (New Haven, Conn.: Yale University Press, 1959), p. 130.

Polugnotos, and thereafter increase in numbers of persons or names, in legendary status (with the possible exception of Ion),[10] and in enigma. For while these lists presume to honor such intelligible wholes as painting, sculpture, and musical performance, they serve to confound other important categories: the living and the dead, the actual and the fictional, art work and war machinery (the Trojan Horse of Epeius), statuary and metal working (Herodotus informs us that Theodorus made bowls and rings).[11] Bloom points out, too, how Ion would be particularly sensitive to Socrates' indifferent mingling of statuses in the last category, where rhapsody is lumped together with mere flute and lyre playing (p. 49).

The profusion of names and references in Socrates' musical catalogues also parallels and entangles a number of other listing passages in the dialogue—for one, the earlier attempt to separate Homer from his matter by spelling out his work's place in an art of poetry (531C–D). Among such catalogues, there is also an implicit comparison with Ion's own enumeration of his competitors and coworkers—Metrodorus of Lampsacus, Stesimbrotus of Thasos, Glaucon, and by implication all the Homeridae (530C–D). And later, when exploring Homeric passages with Ion, Socrates singles out texts that accumulate further references to such cultic and craft fathers as Asclepius and Melampus—more names that help plot the line or curve or swerve of tradition. Nor in listing all of the *Ion*'s lists can we forget the contemporary personages named at 541C–D, even though everyone else has apparently forgotten them.[12] And we should add the list of Homeric passages at 535B–C, each passage focused on a person named (rather than on event or plot, concept, quality, or virtue). In these cases, the survey of tradition follows the inventory or anthology of genealogically linked proper names.

These circles or rings of names in their irregularities and internal differences are, however, anything but simple, uniform rings. Casually offered as plain illustrations of classes or types, these catalogues invite what in fact they have elicited from scholarship: careful review of particularities, along with curiosity respecting person, time, place, and stature. This scholarly second-guessing cuts against the sense of regular-

---

10. Mentioning him in such company, Plato may be raising a question that has puzzled later commentators: Is the *Ion* a total fiction? Is Ion historical fact or new legend? Whether intended or not, this uncertainty complements the dialogue's inspection of the problematical status of tradition.
11. *Histories* I, 51; III, 41.
12. Bloom, p. 61, but compare Moore's claims, pp. 46, 50.

ity that Socrates claims for this tradition, but our scholarship in this case also illustrates the different ways the present for its own purposes reconstitutes the past, a point relevant to Socrates' critique of Ion's weak scholarship. Broached under the category of the same, or of art transparent to itself (all poets, all sculptors, all music makers, all foreign-born generals), Socrates' lists are actually shot through with differences important to a critical sense of history and tradition. For us, however, they may depict an unhappy choice between philosophic thought laboring at its architectonic abstractions and the Ionic body of a variegated tradition proudly if stupidly resisting such rationalization of its proper names. Whether mindful of heads or headings, both Socratic and Ionic versions of authority cull only favorite points, telescope sequences, and focus a god's-eye view that elides human actuality.

Socrates' subsequent story of possession, in manifesting artistic authority, continues this strategy, substituting categories and statuses for names, a terminology or typology for a genealogy. To all the tradition-bound names and persons that the conversation elsewhere alludes to, we might contrast the virtual anonymity of his story of music, in which Socrates mentions by name only Tynnichus the Chalcidian. Tynnichus is a practical anomaly but a philosophical exemplar, the artist outside all art and convention who anchors Socrates' case for musical possession but also for a depersonalized sense of artistic function as dependent on a divine, not an artificial or genealogical, power. This enables Socrates to claim that music constitutes a special case in the arts. With respect to its celebrity, its difficulty of assured success, its "metatechnical" status as an art of arts, perhaps this is true. But in other important respects music presents a typical case, as the *Meno* makes clearer, of the chancy transmission of art, culture, and knowledge in a tradition of emulation like that adumbrated by the *Ion*'s lists and catalogues. In such a tradition, some practices have been thought through, but many more are governed by an interplay of social prestige, personal authority, imitation, and emulation. By downplaying these routine agons of tradition, Socrates stages an interpretation of the *technai* strongly biased in the direction of hopeful philosophic hierarchies of being and function. But in simultaneously foregrounding the contest between Ion and Socrates, the Platonic text shows the pervasiveness of traditional artistic and personal motives even here and so militates against the argument. The ring myth and its commentary, in effect, duel with Ion's weapons, and so they can only project an unlikely, mildly gratifying idyll of the philosopher-king as Socrates' countersong to the golden world evoked by Ion's muse.

Like his ring-myth, Socrates' hierarchic deployment of *technai*—what Friedländer calls a "grotesquely exaggerated emphasis upon technical knowledge" (2:130)—is deformed by this occasion and by its musical, mythical template. The idyll of self-consistent, rational *technai,* like the enthusiasm myth, is therefore more of a metaphor we must interpret than a dogma for us to purvey. This is indicated, I think, by the way the concept of art in such a scheme slides into the unanalyzed place of the divine. According to the Socratic account, the art, rather than the god, would possess and specialize the person; the art, like music, would receive its transcendent direction and channeling from the god it supplements:

> Hasn't the god given some project to each of the arts which each is able to understand? For the things we know from navigation, I suppose, we won't also know from medicine. (537C)

Each manifestation of art participates in some transcendent warrant that stabilizes its functioning and claims proprietary rights over individual projects and practitioners. This transcendentalizing of art, however, is all the more paradoxical in that art and the divine, technology and transcendence, seem patently discontinuous if not contrary, as Ion can witness. Yes, I must be divinely directed, he says in effect, but of course I am not.

In attempting to shift tradition from the artist to the art, from its past to its concept, Socrates thus also squares up against the cultural prestige of traditional Greek "rings" and "ringleaders": those guilds, cults, and associations that the dialogue alludes to in its mention, for example, of Homeridae, Melampodidae, and Asclepiads, also of Orpheus and Daedalus. The guild or cult traditions, living traditions descending from legendary names, are an important means whereby Greek culture has domesticated or instituted the charisma of the forefathers and winnowed experience from chance, art of a kind from experience.[13] The prominence

---

13. Compare the famous introduction to Aristotle's *Metaphysics:*
   Now from memory experience is produced in men; for the several memories of the same thing produce finally the capacity for a single experience. And experience seems pretty much like science and art, but really science and art come to men *through* experience; for "experience made art," as Polus says, but inexperience luck. Now art arises when from many notions gained by experience one universal judgement about a class of objects is produced. (980B–981A, trans. W. D. Ross in *The Basic Works of Aristotle,* ed. Richard McKeon [New York: Random House, 1941], p. 689)

of the name in these traditions reflects the prestige of the person (within narrow limits, of course) and so intimates the possibility in many of these arts of one's making a name for oneself. Behind this possibility exists a whole culture of imitation and emulation (rather than of conceptual instruction), a culture for which, because the medium of art is the person, the art can as well become a medium of the person.[14]

The art exists embodied in a range of personal attributes and skills, and so artist and person do not mutually exclude one another's functioning in the manner envisioned by Socrates' technological idyll. A person might be at the same time a good general and a good rhapsode, unity here being conferred by person and not by art. In fact, the sense of artistic excellence operating in such a tradition draws on the paradigm of heroic fame and so suggests a special kinship between martial and other agonistically toned arts. The exceptional Socratic example of Tynnichus, by contrast, shows an excellence emphatically not of one's person; Tynnichus's mystique, unlike that of other famous artists, is transpersonal, referring to some higher power that makes the person its medium and thus restores art's priority over persons.

The appeal of Socrates' idyll here—and its argumentative force can make it very appealing in a refutation—lessens when we find how the wholeness of art or theory involves the fragmentation of the person. When Ion claims to know "What is fitting . . . for a man to say and what sort of thing is fitting for a woman, what sort for both slave and freeman, what sort for both subject and ruler" (540B), Socrates disperses these persons into more specific actions that entail particular arts—a slave woman spinning, a cowherding slave assuaging angry cattle (540C). Socrates' implication here is again tricky, to be sure—those quickly but finely sketched "slaves" come into focus both as persons and as artists,

---

The whole of this introduction bears on the *Ion*—as the quotation of Polus from Plato, invoking a memory and an individual, may suggest—and in a way parallels it. For Aristotle, like Socrates, is running through *experience*, which has "knowledge of individuals" (981A), to reach *art* and its knowledge of universals.

14. Jeffrey Hurwit characterizes "the age of the individual" in the seventh century B.C. and after as suddenly "full of names." This he partly attributes to the alphabet that makes it possible for potter, sculptor, painter, builder, or other maker to sign the work, but also to "the impulse to sign—the desire to proclaim oneself and one's works—and something about Archaic Greek society (alone among the contemporary cultures of the ancient world) had to make that impulse acceptable. That something might as well be called the recognition of the individual." *The Art and Culture of Early Greece, 1100–480 B.C.* (Ithaca, N.Y.: Cornell University Press, 1985), pp. 140, 141.

both in political and in technical perspective—but the argument is claiming the perpetual self-surrender of people to *technē*, a formulation of depersonalizing that wavers between description and prescription under the pressure of Socrates' reiteration of "slave."

Given these ambivalences about the rule of either persons or concepts, in the *Ion* as in the *Republic* it is a very problematical task to gauge Socrates' appeals to the architechnical view of culture, a view that organizes all knowledge and value into a technological hierarchy. Such technocratic thinking, as he reports in the *Apology*, is one of his principal strategies for running rings around such proud technicians as Ion, but the value of this *topos* to argumentative contentiousness is itself perhaps reason for some suspicion of it. It is less clear (in the light of the *Charmides*, say, where the technocratic ideal is contested [171D–174D]) whether Socrates intends technocracy to have a more abstractable, positive function as a political view to be taken seriously. Such Socratic speculations imagine the depersonalizing or impersonalizing of "personality cults," even though the depersonalizing implicit in the scheme of *technai* fragments the whole person that Socratic self-examination elsewhere explicitly professes to constitute. So we encounter what is a frequent, unresolved crux in Socratic dialogue: a shifting of perspectives that enables particular refutations but also inhibits a firm grasp of Socrates' larger philosophical project; a wavering of ends and means between human being, anthropology, conceived as the end of philosophy and human being conceived as part or function of some larger whole—politics, physics, metaphysics, or even history.

The *Ion* exemplifies, moreover, how in Plato this shifting of philosophy between human and transhuman *telos* is embedded in contexts that deflect its progress or resolution. The need to depersonalize knowledge or aim at transpersonal objectives reflects the unsettling fact that Socrates is himself the center of a personality cult who reluctantly competes in a traditional way with the magnetism of such other ringleaders as Homer, Pythagoras, Parmenides, Heraclitus, Protagoras, or Gorgias. The case is made more urgent by the apparent social evolution of Socrates and his contemporaries: The equality- and freedom-loving fifth-century person, a new creature in Greek history, can, like Ion, more readily select his own models and emulate heroic personages filtering out of a different age or anthropology. If a person does not feel implicitly constrained by a status, then the only limits on one's career are knowledge, luck, opportunity, and the ability to imagine or fashion a better self.[15] The archaic person knew his place; the contemporary would know everything else. Thus what Socrates laments in the artisans of the *Apology* is the appropriation and aggrandizement of their artistic competence by their vainglorious persons.

> Finally I went to the craftsmen; for I was conscious that I knew nothing, so to speak, but these I knew that I would find knowing many fine things. In this I was not deceived, but they knew what I did not know and in this they were wiser than I. But, Athenian gentlemen, to me the good artisans seemed to have the same fault as the poets; on account of practicing his art finely, each believed himself wisest in the other greatest matters, too, and this false note of theirs obscured the former wisdom. (*Apology*, 22C–D)

Consciousness of *technē* and *epistēmē*, when set against the archaic ethical backdrop preserved in epic, legend, ritual, and folktale, becomes a corrosive to the soul, inducing a kind of *hubris*. Ion shows this ambition in his pretensions to the general's art: Knowledge of Homer fits him out for every other activity, especially that of a general, the conventional status of rhapsode notwithstanding. Such practitioners, perhaps as a function of inhabiting a position of humility or service, typically reveal a desire for a position of mastery beyond or outside the art, whether as general, as master of all trades based on skill with one, or as philosopher. And this is because, as we say, morality lags behind technology; the technically competent person is still dominated by nonartistic beliefs and cultural habits that make him or her much less intelligible, even while they reinforce the person-as-artist's delusions of wholeness or autonomy outside city, tradition, or institution.

---

15. This sense of a mobile self is familiar from Sophocles' Oedipus, for example, from his unlucky boast:

> I count myself the son of Chance,
> the great goddess, giver of all good things—
> I'll never see myself disgraced. She is my mother!
> And the moons have marked me out, my blood-brothers,
> one moon on the wane, the next moon great with power.
>   (*Oedipus Tyrannus*, lines 1080–83,
>   trans. Robert Fagles, in *The Three Theban Plays*
>   [New York: Penguin, 1984], p. 224)

III

Taking or playing part in conversation, perhaps a conversation about wholes, may be Socrates' means of chastening *his* will to power, which may be fueled by his sense of a personal wholeness. And such conversation certainly strives to chasten the world's narcissistic—and therein delusorily whole—Ions. But this activity remains one-sided so long as Socrates must mirror Ion, must seem to Ion merely another Ion working a different field. Socrates' seriocomic emulation of Ion is exemplified not only in the ring song but in the *Ion*'s conspicuously deformed discussions of Homer as well. Here we can distinctly hear the effects of the mechanical argument of the rings in turning a tin ear to the Muses. While Ion exploits, adapts, and anthologizes Homer by culling epic high points, Socrates in his interrogation antiphonally culls the low points.

Having just elicited from Ion proof of Homer's enormous spellbinding powers, Socrates proceeds to analyze selected Homeric passages through their technical applicability to nonpoetic knowledges (537ff.). Thus the wounding of Machaon, which directly spurs Patroclus's disguise as Achilles and begins a momentous turn in the *Iliad,* becomes a clinical text (538B–C). And the messenger of final peace to Thetis in the *Iliad*'s powerful anticlimax is made a fishing text (538C–D). Such oppressively literal readings seem to ignore poetic and musical texture altogether. The marvelous surrealistic prophecy of Theoclymenus to the suitors—crazier still—becomes an outrageous confounding of fiction and soothsaying expertise (538D–539D). In these cases, a deadpan Socrates mimics the sort of confusion of art and life for which, and with which, he had earlier ridiculed Ion:

> Why, what should we say of a person who, when adorned with party-colored clothes and golden wreaths at sacrifices and holidays, laments though having lost nothing, or is in great fear although standing among twenty thousand friendly people, with no one stripping him or injuring him at all? Should we say this person is in his senses? (535D)

Socrates' sarcasm here, as later, rests on his disingenuous refusal to acknowledge fiction, theater, or the suspension of disbelief,[16] though the very question, knowing well the conditions of theatrical performance, is predicated on such detachment from the literal.

Behind such raillery one finds other meanings at play, restraining this attempt to cut Homer up into *epistēmai* of fishing or pharmacy. Socrates'

---

16. See Dorter's description of comparably absurd situations, p. 72.

survey, for instance, veers from relatively simple practices like fishing or charioteering toward more problematical arts like healing or prophecy, both (though complementing one another as body and soul) competing with rhapsody, rhetoric, and philosophy.[17] Even the simpler charioteering example alludes to the rivalry of father and son in its glance at abstractable skills, lore, and *nomos*. And the case of prophecy inattentively confounds the genuine, possessed prophecy of Theoclymenus with the more routine and technical reading of bird signs. This last example, joining inspired prophecy and technical soothsaying, virtually reprises the original enthusiasm-versus-art debate, bringing us around full circle.

As Bloom perceptively argues, interesting moral problems are also overlooked in each of the texts and contexts that Socrates cites to support his claim that Homer belongs to every art but his own. Socrates of all people, one imagines, can hardly be forgetful of the problems concerning the right or just use of *technai,* and yet such problems, too, must be suppressed if we are to have our single, selfsame arts here.[18] This unspoken contest of art and right, often made explicit elsewhere (in the *Gorgias* or in the *Charmides,* for example) parallels controversies about Homeric teaching: whether, as Havelock argues,[19] Homer's teaching resembled that of an encyclopedic primer of arts that one literally memorized and mimed; or whether, in its cultural effect, it primarily addressed those "other greatest matters" (*Apology* 22D) we know as ethics and politics that one must more searchingly interpret and represent. In reviewing this question, Guthrie notes the tendency of a claim for the predominance of the former kind of teaching to drift into evidence for the latter (4:208–9). This point can be reinforced if we reflect how little Havelock takes account of the power of interpretation practiced by Ion and Socrates, further instanced by Plato, and then exemplified in Havelock's own argument—the power of interpretation to remotivate old discourses in new settings, to generate new meanings in old texts, or to appropriate old texts to new uses that can alter ethical and political assumptions embedded in the old.[20] The tendency, even in commentaries,

---

17. For the problematic of prophecy, see Bloom, pp. 56–59. For the far stranger problematic of medicine in Plato, see Derrida, "Plato's Pharmacy," in *Dissemination,* pp. 61–171.
18. Bloom, p. 55.
19. Havelock, *Preface to Plato.*
20. See Paul Ricouer, *Interpretation Theory: Discourse and the Surplus of Meaning.* The drift of prior discourse into new context is more elaborately treated in Derrida, "Signature Event Context," in *Margins of Philosophy,* pp. 309–30. For a commentary on these issues, see Jonathan Culler, *On Deconstruction: Theory and Criticism after Structuralism* (Ithaca, N.Y.: Cornell University Press, 1982), pp. 110–56.

for technical concerns to drift toward ethical and political concerns matches the very drift we have been following in *Ion*: how rote learning—traditional or technical learning—is readily implicated, unawares, in some more global interest, argument, or ideology. So Socrates turns up the admission that all the arts of Homer in fact belie the general, here doubtless a general of the Periclean type. This eruption of value-laden terms and names, slave as well as general, into a conversation about the internal coherence of arts bears out one's sense of the pastoral or idyllic partiality of the earlier discussion concerning whole *technai* magnetically united.

By reciting supposedly technical passages from Homer, Socrates competes with Ion (himself eager to recite but held at bay), but he also again flatters Ion with such imitation and reveals his own rhapsodic impulses. How can so avid a Homerist, many have wondered, prove so unsympathetic? Like Socrates' ring song, Socrates' Homeric anthology entertains with a comical or parodistic music of its own. But like the myth, the interrogation, in grossly oversimplifying its object, in forcing dactyls into the compass of *daktylioi*, proves inept at capturing the sense or significance of music. As the saying is, Socrates clutches three times at the shade of Homer, and each time comes up empty-handed. But if Socrates does not possess Homer, neither does the Ion who is made—and made to feel—increasingly marginal by Socrates' performance.

With Ion and his Homeric highlights, one thinks one is hearing and seeing the Essential Homer. With Socrates, on the other hand, looking for *his* Essential Homer, the Homer of *technai*, one feels Homer's power by its conspicuous absence or suppression, by Socrates' ridiculous hunting for Homer where he does not live. Paradoxically, what I have termed Socrates' tin ear rouses one's Homeric loyalties, makes one want to point up and defend the beauties that Socrates here pretends not to see or to feel. This complex critical stance oddly makes Socrates, not Ion, the truer Homeric contender; it is Socrates, not Ion who would rather be general, who takes Homer more seriously as a force in Greek culture.

Such inversion can also suggest how the uneven web of tradition allows no easy positive values or propositions that would lend themselves to hierarchic resolution. Ion, like Homer, proves a tangle of threads stretching out in many directions, and Socrates is unable to get clear of the fabric to put Homer in his place, Ion in his place, and his own philosophic self in its place. After all, how can one have an art of language—if philosophy indeed shares this burden with poetry[21]—without or beyond language, the nature of which is part of the problem here? Socrates' interrogation collapses or returns in circles upon itself because of Ion's textuality, because of poetry's textuality, which renders the *epos* anonymous, improper, possessive rather than possessed, endlessly mediating: *Die Sprache spricht.* For all his insurmountable concern with the physical body of his oral performance, Ion proves disembodied upon critical inspection; he is simply elsewhere, protean. His slipperiness evades the Socrates who explicitly formulates the case of rhapsody as an exception proving the rule of an overarching technical cosmos. But this explicit formulation is not nearly so dialectical as is his implicit practice of parody, overstatement, conspicuous allusion, or satirical role-playing—an implicit practice that the Platonic text makes available to a reader's explication.

To review the *Ion*'s thesis in more traditional terms: A hierarchy of arts cannot replace a hierarchy of enthusiasms, that paradoxical *logos* of coherence and dispersion with which Socrates has characterized the musical tradition as if he stood outside this tradition. From Socrates' apparently disenchanted standpoint of one no longer held within such a tradition, past cultural orders possess, as if by the magic of inspiration, a striking nonconscious coherence and power attested to by Ion's success. From his retrospective standpoint, Socrates pursues a sophistical sort of argument, asking in effect how it might be possible to emulate such innocence, such coherence, but artfully?[22] How might it be possible to impute a method to this madness and so give thought some purchase on artistic practice and tradition? How? Only with irony, the answer appears to be, for one still within the tradition or under the spell of the

---

21. Regarding apparent role shifting between rhapsode and philosopher mediated by the dialogue's language, see Wilcox, pp. 162–70. The concern for language problems is apparent at *Phaedo* 96–100 with the threat of "misology"—that is, despair induced by the chronic breakdowns of language and communication in philosophical discussion.

22. Characterizing the revisionary ambitions of Gorgias in the *Encomium of Helen*, Jacqueline de Romilly has this to say:
> Sacred magic rested on faith; Gorgias' magic rests on the notion that all truth is out of reach. Sacred magic was mysterious; Gorgias' magic is technical. He wants to emulate the power of the magician by a scientific analysis of language and its influence. He is the theoretician of the magic spell of words. (*Magic and Rhetoric in Ancient Greece* [Cambridge, Mass.: Harvard University Press, 1975], p. 16)

Wilcox suggests that, with Socrates' disenchanted explanations and his evident advocacy of a new *paideia*, "the cat . . . is out of the bag"; Socrates has embarked on a graft, similar to Gorgias's, of the technical onto the magical (pp. 167–68).

enchantment. A telling difficulty of supplementing artistic practice with philosophical rationale in the *Ion*'s equation, as seen in Socrates' impersonations of the rhapsode, is the risk such wisdom runs of becoming what it would replace. This is a fate to which the Platonic text regularly consigns its progressive sophists whose commitments to cultural innovation do not come hedged with Socratic ironic detachment: The revisionary *paideia* of a Gorgias, a Protagoras, or a Hippias thinly rationalizes a persisting enthusiasm without really touching or altering it; or worse, so wise a revision becomes possessed in trying to possess. Method's susceptibility to such madness reflects the fact that, given these discursive, conversational settings, there really is no "disenchanted standpoint" outside tradition or the sway of enthusiasm where thought might gain its ultimate leverage. As the encounters with dialectic in the *Phaedrus* testify, the belief that you can correct or methodize madness readily escalates into a greater if subtler madness. Such revision in the conversation with Ion thus confronts an obvious and stubborn impediment. Socrates speaks, but the only words to issue are those Ion can hear. The measure of Socratic reason disappears into the peculiar mania of rhapsodic and musical action, which both necessitates Socratic irony and renders it unintelligible to Ion.

So you cannot reduce Homer to an encyclopedia, nor can you (as the conversation of the *Republic* hopes) save only the manageable passages, those subject to your art, and then discard the rest. That would be destroying Homer but still trying to have it, evacuating the past, then trying to reconstitute it anew in all its prestige. The transparent manipulation of the sacred or charismatic drastically inflates the currency, consumes the reserves that it would draw upon, and, like the sophists, Ion here is rather too brightly candid about his bad faith to help conserve the charismatic source of institutional authority.

The person in the artist, the self that indulges artistic license, accounts for only one phase of a larger economy sure to exact its due, as Socrates struggles to make clear. Time and tradition do not subserve the space of thought and imagination. This is to presume, in the manner of Anaxagoras, whom Socrates regularly makes his straw man on this issue, the omnipotence of mind. From a reader's perspective, one cannot too much emphasize this point. For while a Platonic dialogue dramatizes *kairos* (the moment of opportunity), subordinates tradition and language to the face-to-face conversation of persons about "realities" and thereby fills the "space" of imagination, this theater is the effect of a work of memory and writing and thus is entangled in text, time, and a tradition, entangled in all the thickets of this dialogue, in the give-and-take not only between Socrates and Ion, but between Socrates and *Ion* and between the *Ion* and us. By contrast the prospect of Mind in its presence of Mind entails such miscalculations as that of downward flux: the flow of current in hierarchical constructions from better to worse, from the muse to the masses, from speaker to audience, from teacher to disciple, from the past to the present, from the top to the bottom, from the head to the feet. In fact, goes one lesson of the *Ion,* though hierarchical thought is inescapable, no hierarchy is so unilinear or so utopian, once it moves beyond the logocentric myths and hopeful advertisements of rhetoric.

IV

Homer is at the mercy of his audience, and so is his muse. What if an audience laughs when it should cry, or dozes off when it should alertly attend? If Ion depends on Homer, and of course to an extent he does, Homer also depends on Ion; if the arts depend on god, god too depends on the arts, particularly as the arts are enacted by people, by slaves as well as generals. The thematic insistence of technology and *hubris* in tragedy testifies to the power of these paradoxes on the sophisticating Athenian mind. These embodiments of the arts—the human mediation or human factor in divine or traditional authorities—are precisely what the turn to the Homeric text adds to the *Ion*'s abstract discussion of putatively abstract arts. The fact is that one cares enough about such wholes as Achilles and Andromache and Priam and Penelope to lament their sundering in the vain attempt to conceive some whole *technē*. But on his part, too, Ion fragments Homer. These facts give the abstract discussion of wholes a less than wholesome feeling of a sort worth pinning down.

To disperse or reorganize an embodied tradition seems necessarily to involve a *sparagmos,* or dismemberment, of some kind. In the present instance are dramatized two dazzling embodiments of such traditions, Ion and Socrates, each in a way the servant of his own personal presence. Consider for a moment with Socrates the striking example of Ion's adornment, his fashion, his manner—the special ways he *embodies* texts and thereby defeats more philosophic attempts to *abstract* from them.

Ion's characteristic boasting expresses just this dependence of tradition on embodiment:

> Well, it is really worth hearing, Socrates, how well I have been grooming Homer [*hōs eu kekosmēka ton Homēron*], so that I think I'm worthy to be crowned with a golden crown by the Homeridae. (530D)

Ion directly associates dressing up Homer with adorning himself. This equivocation breaks down distinctions between himself and Homer, his body and Homer's corpus, between theatrical sight and ancient *epos*.

In its magic revivals, we have seen how the conversation of Socrates and Ion in a number of ways blurs the line between proper name and common noun, between person and epos, between fact and word. Amidst such indistinctness, verbal antagonism also veers toward physical menace. Ion's *hubris* becomes obvious when, as general, he offers a kind of violence to Socrates; and, for his part, Socrates replies with an allusion to the violence done Proteus by Menelaus, on the one hand, and a reference to Ion's criminality, on the other. Ion and Socrates are both making explicit a violence latent in the earlier talk of possession involving Socrates' repeated reference to Corybants and Bacchants as similes for the kind of inspiration that he claims Ion experiences (534A, 536C). Possession of this sort would indeed do violence to Ion's will, even as the argument, in trying to drag Ion out of his element, by a kind of mimetic fallacy actually does do a certain violence to his will (536D). Such allusions to mystic transports, when joined with the mention of Orpheus (533B), might import rending and dismemberment—perhaps a concern shared with the Orpheus-like Ion by the Pentheus-like Socrates. A wordplay already glanced at may complement these allusions to mad maenads by linking rings, digits, metrical feet, and more, punning, at 534A–B, not only on "honey" and "song" (*meli-melos*), but on "song" and "limb" (both *melos*). Ion offers us only the appearance of agony, falsely lamenting in great fear (535C–D), when perhaps he should be made to experience true agony. After all, what risks did Thamyras or Orpheus or Phemius (534B) run? Or Marsyas, Socrates' alter ego in the *Symposium* (215C), who knew how to play when "stripped and injured" (535D)? Such thoughts, in Guthrie's terms, would take the bloom from anyone's wings.

On the one hand, the ambivalence of Ion's craft—moving among parts, shifting among self- and other-indulgence—brings him close to the Socratic analysis of rhetorical servitude: The orator caters to appetites, answering to external cues, not interior motives or signs.[23] Ion finally reveals this alter ego under its martial, Periclean aspect, the rhetorician reincarnated as the autocrat whose word is deed. He emerges as a general, the foundation for all his other identities—for man and woman, for slave and freeman, for subject and ruler (540B), a list notable for its attentiveness to reciprocal statuses and power relationships. The rhapsode proves a general, not a lieutenant; he fantasizes acting and acting upon, from a role he imagines to confer real power. At best Homer is not his inspiration, but his armor, or more exactly his armored personnel carrier—a powerful refuge and a full repertoire of mobile roles and types. Oddly, Ion apparently believes the general to be free from the tedium and tensions of audience and market and from the duplicity of performance. Both the wish and its form are strange coming from a man apparently so self-assured, so adept with an audience and the economics of his vocation.

The indirectness and daring of revision, interpretation, word, speech, and image manipulation produce in Ion a curious lust for domination and a marked distrust of the word, especially as a vehicle of meaning. The incantatory poet or enchanting god is not really strong enough; a disenchanted Ion (easing himself here, one imagines, with a typical nervous laugh) avidly wants this other, realer power that Socrates pretends to offer him. But in view of the ambivalences and in the setting of a democracy, the powers of general and rhapsode are unnervingly similar, and both functions are powerless in isolation, when unchained from muse, metier, and market, when locked up in an aporetic argument. The rhapsode standing at the present end of a human tradition typifies the lot and the art of many would-be technicians, like the politicians caught up in tremendously powerful cultural machines they find themselves unable to master, yet unable not to want to master.[24] As the world fills with mediating functions felt to be such, it fills people with dreams of autonomy and immediacy, with desires of utopia or with longings for the cultural nursery.

---

23. See, for example, Craig La Drière, "The Problem of Plato's *Ion*," *Journal of Aesthetics and Art Criticism* 10 (1951–52): 32. Also recall the traditional connection of poet and sophist (i.e., sage) in Pindar and others.

24. See W. R. Connor, *The New Politicians of Fifth-Century Athens* (Princeton, N.J.: Princeton University Press, 1971).

V

The *aporia* in this dialogue, however, also includes the frustrations of the discoursing philosopher, who impatiently invokes Proteus and finally binds Ion with an echo of his own medicine, the wishful magic of a spoken name: "You, Proteus, you!" But Proteus in particular is the demon of past and future that defies pinning down and defeats such attempts at magical or moralistic appropriation. So Socrates' mention of Proteus is both monitory and futile; what is worse, it seems to be the offshoot of more violent and angry impulses. And it does not hold Ion or even Ion's attention. The Platonic text, however, monumentalizes this admonition and its impulse; it uses the figure of Proteus to open up the possibility of reading and interpretation within the very intertextuality of tradition that Socrates cannot quite put his finger on.

In this textual perspective, Socrates' victory over Ionia looks woefully Menelauan. Trying to embark on a renewed life, Menelaus in the *Odyssey* becomes a striking image of the burden of the past; his memory binds him to the debacle of the war and to the spectral presence of lost comrades who fought to repair his honor and his home. Nor does Menelaus find anything but more loss and deprivation in his material wealth and in the company of Helen, who regards that war rather more positively as a moment of personal glory.[25] Such a Menelaus comes close to the *Apology*'s portrait of the stereotypical Athenian. And such a Menelaus appropriately represents the state in which the protean Ion leaves his audiences—with the form of a life, but not its substance—and this is also how he leaves Socrates.

This reenactment of Homer is distressing enough drama, constituting a sense of the past and of tradition that no more than mirrors one's hopes and anxieties. Through the rhapsode is visible only what we already see, what we already most desire and most fear, and so tradition becomes like a dream. No doubt these dispersions of tradition deserve to be lamented on moral and humanistic grounds. But they partly stem from that tradition's failure to keep people awake, to keep them from dozing off. This is the brute if comical fact against which all theory fails. By his own somewhat proud admission, protean Ion is absurd; sleepiness and alertness dictate his culture. Socrates can sting and awaken, but his charisma is limited; to Ion he is something of another sort of Ion. Besides, Socrates

---

25. See William S. Anderson, "Calypso and Elysium," in *Essays on the "Odyssey,"* pp. 73–86.

is himself something of a problem, since he must accept the present occasion on its terms, since he must be like Ion to question Ion, since he must play Menelaus to his Proteus in this "light-hearted little piece" of tragicomedy.[26] One does not wish to be cast as Menelaus—Socrates of all people, who presumes to be our goad, our Helen. It is too easy to be Menelaus, who embodies and evokes our most paltry concerns and our least noble impulses.

Still, the Homeric contexture is preferable to the pseudopious Socrates' imposing on Ion a choice between craziness and criminality, a choice Proteus eludes (later, if not now). Socrates, however, will not resign himself to the open and uncertain textual conclusion; he refuses, as in the *Phaedrus*, really even to acknowledge it, although he often entertains it, often approaches or embodies it in his attempts to disembody thought. Indeed, he himself is already textual, always already textual—in fiction, as fiction. But he does not keep this assignation or reach this altered traditional scene of dialectic until Ion, shifting shape to *Ion*, is finally enchained in a place.

---

26. See Ranta's claims for the *Ion* as a comic drama, claims that underscore my point: To see Ion as a character in a kind of play perforce also makes Socrates a character in the same play. From the standpoint of the represented conversation, this can only be a social theater, the effect of which is to reroute the dialogue's cultural and artistic criticism along conventional paths and to enclose or possess Socrates within a musical ring.

Five / Innocence and Experience in *Charmides*

Plato's equivocation between person and rubric, between body and text, between internal and external regulation of intention, bears closer inspection in the many places where Socrates is concerned with the nurture of the young in civic discipline. Freethinking discussions of education in Plato reflect the greatly altered conditions of political life in fifth-century Athens, when the onset of prudential rationality, social pluralism, democratization, and disenchantment threatens or breaks through more traditional and automatic restraints on individual behavior. These newer forces unsettle a person's traditional place in family, community, and Hellenic statuses and institutions, but as Socrates often complains, loudest in the *Apology*, his fellow citizens are slow to acknowledge the causes or deal with the consequences of such change.

Socrates at law, Euthyphro and Socrates in religious controversy, Ion and Socrates re-creating musical and artistic traditions—in each of these cases Plato shows as newly and urgently problematical the yielding of personality to a traditional demand of impersonality and self-discipline.

This problematic is occasioned by recognitions approaching self-consciousness (Ion's felt prestige, for example) and by a gathering, sophisticated awareness of how central to the functioning and transmission of traditional institutions is the medium of the physical, speaking human being. This awareness fosters the delusion that a sufficiently able and knowledgeable person—an Ion, a Euthyphro, a Critias, a Protagoras—might invert the symbiosis of individual servant and institutional master. In seeing how persons are fashioned as means to cultural ends, in other words, some persons think to learn how culture may prove a means to their personal ends. Such persons do not, of course, actually master institutions; but in sufficient numbers they silently change those institutions and the premises by which a social reality is constituted and reproduced. It is mindful of this unofficial constitution that Socrates at law mocks the jurors for encouraging a bastard jurisprudence at the expense of truth, justice, and the Athenian way.

Thanks to such unregulated merging of personal and cultural ambitions, crossing from Plato's more public settings to more intimate settings of the dialogues makes for a change more of standpoint than of substance. The sudden exchanges in the *Phaedrus* of *erōs* for rhetoric, of private seduction *(peithō)* for public persuasion (also *peithō*), then back again as if these were two faces of a coin, reflect institutional anomie, as well as that dialogue's pastoral collapse of great and little worlds.[1] In the *Phaedrus* and the *Charmides* one witnesses at the human-eye level in private conversation the concern for strategics, hierarchies, discipline, and the techniques of bad faith that also characterizes the history of Athenian institutions in the wider, god's-eye retrospective of the historian. If Athenian public life has become too personalized in the age of demagogues, the private sphere has conversely become too impersonal in its role-playing possibilities, its modeling of political intrigue, and its infatuation with pseudoscientific technique—all tendencies readily illustrated from the *Charmides* and the *Phaedrus*. There is no private life, as

---

1. Paul Plass, "The Unity of the *Phaedrus*," in *Plato: True and Sophistic Rhetoric*, ed. Keith Erickson (Amsterdam: Rodopi, 1979), pp. 193–221, esp. 214. Blair Campbell surveys these disruptions of common sense and commonplaces in "Thought and Political Action in the Athenian Tradition: The Emergence of the 'Alienated Intellectual,' " *History of Political Thought* 5 (1984): 17–59. For example,

> Intellectual norms, formed privately in response to aims having little to do with politics, have superseded those embodied in the *nomoi*. . . . [The intellectual] is to judge political affairs by such [technical] standards as "interest," "benefit," or "advantage" . . . , which are not discernible to the public, unskilled as it is in the intellectual's craft. (p. 39)

Aristophanes might happily testify, untouched by great possibilities of self-aggrandizement and public adventure.

I

An example from the *Phaedrus* of the overlapping mechanisms touching personal, educational, and political life may usefully preface a study of these issues in the *Charmides*. In the famous palinode of the *Phaedrus*, Socrates retracts the cynical views of erotic relationship spelled out in two earlier speeches, which disparaged the lover and praised the nonlover as intimate companion on prudential grounds of self-interest. In his retraction of these views, a professedly inspired Socrates describes how the desire of beauty raises the lover's winged soul above mundane preoccupations toward a supernal realm of vision beyond the sky and how the beloved, by reflection of the lover's *erōs*, can also be raised up to greater glory and happiness. In general, the glamorous philosophical ideal that Socrates paints for Phaedrus appears to be a remedy for ignorant pretension, as well as for greed of gain, petty ambition, and clever enterprise. But in a fashion typical of Socratic myth, the particulars of his vision tend to subvert this therapeutic aim by mischievously reinscribing within the remedy the very ills it would cure.

I think especially of the palinode's description of the lover's choice of beloved and his refashioning his chosen one as a sort of statue ambiguously related to Zeus, the special god in whose heavenly host the chariot of the lover's soul races:

> Now each person picks out his love from the beautiful according to temper [*pros tropous*], and as though he were his god, he frames and fashions him out like an ikon [*agalma*], to honor and worship him. (252D–E)

The confusion here among lover, beloved, image, and god is deliberate and telling. The commentary that follows this description sustains its confusion of persons and causes as the lover turns to the god, to the beloved, to the experts, and to his memory in the attempt to actualize or express the feeling for "the philosophic and authoritative character" that had supposedly drawn the lover to this beloved in the first place. The cause, the desired object, that is, seems to get pieced together after its declared effect. Imputing such progress in the arts of Zeus to the beloved,

> still more do the lovers delight [*agapōsi*], and if from Zeus they draw draughts, just like the bacchae, on the soul of the beloved pouring them out, they make him as similar as possible to their god. (253A)

The idea of the god mediates the erotic relation, glamorizes it in a way reminiscent of the old heroic genealogies, and captures this glamor in a sculptural or monumental form. We might say the lover dedicates a statue of himself to the beloved, though "himself" must then refer to lover, beloved, and their shared, supposedly divine type all at once.

This account of self-fashioning is bracketed by versions of chariot rides across the heavens that attempt to depict what Diotima in the *Symposium* characterizes as the higher mysteries (209E–212A). According to the chariot fable, Zeus leads a host of souls, including a contingent of his attending gods, spirits, and human souls, in their regular feeding on hyperuranian reality. When later embodied as a result of discord in the soul, human souls of this troop continue to share in the *ēthos* of Zeus. Lover finds beloved under the influence of this god and as much as possible re-creates a primordially lost potential in them both. But as with the lower mysteries, so with the higher: The linearity of the narrative and the invocation of customary hierarchies headed by Zeus imperfectly mute a subversive potential of these accounts, which threaten to collapse into what we might nowadays term a scene of "mimetic desire." Philosophical, psychological, or religious knowledge is almost wholly eclipsed by the more vivid and convincing dynamics of personal relationship.

On the one hand, there are the vaguely rendered supernal objects—"the things beyond the heaven," "colorless, formless, impalpable being that really is," "justice itself and temperance [*sōphrosunē*] and knowledge [*epistēmē*]" (247C, D). How unhelpful these specifications are the controversy among commentators might attest. On the other hand, there is the vividly depicted competition for these vague prizes among and within human souls,

> . . . all striving after the things above but unable to reach them, . . . carried around under the surface, trampling and jostling one another, one vying to pass another. Uproar, then,

> and contention and extreme sweat result, in which, because of the incompetence of charioteers, many are lamed, and many have wings shattered. . . . (248A–B)

Let the difference between descriptions of race and goal at least raise a doubt about a straightforward desire for the beautiful, which is here enmeshed in another, more emulative scenario: the desire for the desire of another (namely, Zeus) for the beautiful. This dissimulation is responsible, I believe, for the fact that Socrates in his myth valorizes Zeus, a figure of domination and control from the cultural center, rather than Apollo, Aphrodite, Dionysus, or some other divinity more in tune with his eccentric arguments for *erōs* and ecstasy.[2]

René Girard's insights into "mimetic desire" helpfully catch the danger implicit in this vision. In this view, Zeus is not only a *model* but also, and perhaps more powerfully, a *rival*.

> Rivalry does not arise because of the fortuitous convergence of two desires on a single object; rather *the subject desires the object because the rival desires it*. In desiring an object the rival alerts the subject to the desirability of the object. The rival, then, serves as a model for the subject, not only in regard to such secondary matters as style and opinions but also, and more essentially, in regard to desires. . . . Two desires converging on the same object are bound to clash. Thus, mimesis coupled with desire leads automatically to conflict.[3]

In Socrates' myth, the pious quest for a purifying vision is undercut by the soul's hubristic, socially competitive desire to be like Zeus. The violence and ambivalences of the myth (later comically reduced and exorcised in a cartoon of two adverse horses) may stem from the myth's uneasy dissembling of a rival as a model, of an enemy as a friend. The race for the holy in the *Phaedrus* recalls Euthyphro's view that one loves sublime things because the gods love them, not because they are lovable (9E, passim). The hazard of this view is clearly shown by Euthyphro's

---

2. On the puzzle of Zeus's place here, see M. Dyson, "Zeus and Philosophy in the Myth of Plato's *Phaedrus*," *Classical Quarterly* 32 (1982): 307–11.

3. *Violence and the Sacred*, trans. Patrick Gregory (Baltimore, Md.: Johns Hopkins University Press, 1977), pp. 145, 146.

identification with Zeus as he places himself on equal footing with the gods (5D–6A). So, too, the present account in the *Phaedrus*. The lover emulates the god's quest for the beautiful. Then the beloved, catching wind of this, emulates the lover's quest of this quest (255C–D).

Girard thinks that such a vicious circle of mimesis can lead in time to the misrule of "no-difference," all distinction gone, to the violence of all against all, eventually to sacrificial crisis and a scapegoating that arbitrarily restores gradation and a sense of the sacred. The comparison of lovers to Bacchae at 253A—imagining, creating, deifying, and destroying their object all at once—might offer evidence for the relevance of such a view here. It is at any rate possible and illuminating to map this scenario across Socrates' Platonic career or to imagine Socrates, in effect, reluctantly playing the Dionysian Zeus of his own fable, made the model that all competitors level at.

But I would also point out an additional moral for this digression and emphasize the structure and hazards of "mimetic rivalry" on the social scene that Socrates inhabits. The model-who-is-a-rival results from a hermeneutical ruse whereby one who purports only to experience a vibrant reality or object, perhaps simply the extraordinary beauty or excellence of another, in fact helps create or constitute that object. Plato further shows the isomorphism of this structure or mechanism in several spheres: in religion, politics, poetry, and education, as well as in erotics—wherever some desirable, exalted, philosophical and authoritative nature is elected for special, even charismatic gifts imputed to him or her. Finally, as the allusion to the Bacchae insinuates, to make desire the paradigm for institutional authority in this way is potentially to make learning, politics, and religion as fickle and unpredictable as the shifting affections of the passive-aggressive lover.

II

The *Charmides* imagines Socrates narrating his return to the scenes of philosophy after unpleasant time spent in war at the siege of Potidaea. He reports his experiences to an anonymous but not nondescript auditor. Socrates enters a palaestra, he tells this auditor, and encounters there a number of young students and their older companions, in particular Critias, evidently a former associate of Socrates (156A), who introduces

Socrates to his cousin and protégé, Charmides, the current darling of all in the palaestra and, in fact, an uncle of Plato. On the pretense of offering a cure for chronic headache, Socrates interrogates Charmides about the nature of *sōphrosunē,* a quality Charmides is thought to possess. When after several attempts Charmides is unable to satisfy Socrates, he intrigues to engage Critias in discussion with Socrates by passing on a definition Critias had taught him—"*sōphrosunē* is doing one's own business" (161B). Thus provoked, Critias tries briefly to defend this view, then abandons it in favor of the more interesting claim that *sōphrosunē* is a kind of self-knowledge. Just what kind of self-knowledge it might be— self-recognition, knowledge of itself, knowledge of one's self, knowledge of what one knows and does not know—proves elusive under Socratic questioning, which eventually closes the ambitious Critias into its refutation. At the end, Critias conspires with Charmides to pursue further Socrates' secret "charm" for inducing *sōphrosunē.*

Like the *Phaedrus,* the *Charmides* shelters interesting anxieties, tensions, and antagonisms under a benign aspect. Charmides' adolescence, his statuesque beauty (154C), his evident modesty (158C–D), his reserve—all suggest a winning naïveté. Charmides is charming. And he is charming thanks to what one might first assume to be natural gifts, since his capacity for philosophy, poetry, and virtue make league both with natural beauty and with lineage (155A).[4] All the more wonder, then, that the natural disharmony of a headache has troubled this native charmer's mornings. Probably this headache results from too much drinking rather than from too much thinking and so invites *sōphrosunē* in the more restrictive sense of moderation. But it may also then reinforce the many suggestions of Charmides' special sociability, his popularity to his own cost, whereby he has become a paragon for those around him, a focus for mimetic rivalries, therefore both cause and effect of mimetic rivalry. These courtiers ascribe to Charmides his virtue and make him embody willy-nilly an ideal of the group, upon which he confers solidarity by what seems an innocent or unknowing reciprocation. Such a Charmides—indeed, the whole group—would then be innocent or unaware of the musical processes (to allude to dynamics portrayed in the *Ion*) by which they constitute their own community. Socrates' account of the group's movements emphasizes a sense of frolicsome innocence and

---

4. For a relevant discussion of natural gifts, music, and virtue, see Warman Welliver, *Character, Plot, and Thought in Plato's "Timaeus-Critias"* (Leiden: Brill, 1977), pp. 8–38.

spontaneity (154C, 155C), especially among the youngest, but this account also includes more ominous hints of military *taxis*, or deployment, echoing Critias's earlier figure of speech ("advance guard"—154A) and the awkward exchange of war for philosophy at the narrative's outset and conclusion.

A student, struggling with Charmides' definitions of *sōphrosunē*, offered her own definition of that virtue as "knowing your place." This working definition of a term defying easy conceptualization is not so imperfect as it first appears. In fact, scholarship has anticipated this student's sense of the relevance of this rich colloquial phrase.[5] The social and psychological connotations of knowledge count for a lot in the case of *sōphrosunē*, and the colloquial flavor of "knowing one's place" follows the rooting of this knowledge in common sense and collective prudence. For one thing, the word *place* carries with it a relevant sense of hierarchic space—of contested, strategic statuses—as well as of social and political space. The colloquial definition thus captures *sōphrosunē*'s relevance to military and civic discipline.[6] At the same time, the word *knowing* answers to the derivation of *sōphrosunē*,[7] roughly "soundness of mind" (as evidenced by one's behavior).

Too much knowing, on the other hand, augments an innocent temperance with worldly wisdom or experience, with the care or curiosity of reason or prudence. An emphasis on knowing can deform or hollow out a popular, traditionalist virtue that would preferably be non-self-conscious, spontaneous, natural, innocent, *common* in the sense of *koinon*. The Athenian of the *Laws* (710), for example, expresses admiration for this natural or innocent temperance of which some children and animals partake. Continence or "moderation [becomes] necessary to those who have left this state" of nature or innocence.[8] The sophistication of the fifth century in fact seemed to prefer this view of an embattled or tested *sōphrosunē*. "This is the *sōphrosunē*," Helen North writes, "that is drama-

---

5. For instance, T. G. Tuckey, *Plato's "Charmides"* (Cambridge: Cambridge University Press, 1951), pp. 6, 10; Drew Hyland, *The Virtue of Philosophy: An Interpretation of Plato's "Charmides"* (Athens: Ohio University Press, 1981), pp. 72, 84.

6. See the survey in Helen North, *Sophrosyne: Self-Knowledge and Self-Restraint in Greek Literature* (Ithaca, N.Y.: Cornell University Press, 1966), pp. 12–31; also the remarks of Jean-Pierre Vernant, *Myth and Society in Ancient Greece*, pp. 41–42, 86–87.

7. ". . . the very etymology of *so-phro-syne* suggests a reference to 'mind' that is overlooked in the simple definition of 'doing good actions,'" Paul Friedländer, *Plato*, 2:72.

8. Christopher Bruell, "Socratic Politics and Self-Knowledge: An Interpretation of Plato's *Charmides*," *Interpretation: A Journal of Political Philosophy* 6 (1977): 149.

tized repeatedly by Euripides and constitutes one of the major themes in his tragedy. There is no anticipation in either Antiphon or Euripides of Aristotle's view that *sōphrosunē* is a habitual state requiring no effort" (p. 89). The word *anticipation* here is misleading in its implication that Aristotle's view is more modern than Euripides'; in fact, Aristotle's standpoint is more traditional in its desire to restore through non-self-conscious habit the innocence or naturalness of *sōphrosunē* as a key attribute of the well-nurtured citizen, perhaps along the lines of the utopian citizen's justice in the *Republic*.

Aristotle might urge such a view partly because the knowing inherent in *sōphrosunē* might otherwise incline toward the artificial reconstruction of nature or, worse, toward a calculation through which this virtue falls prey to hypocrisy, to superficial conformity, to knowing what your place is expected to be (according, say, to *nomos* or social decree), but not feeling this to be your destined or proper place (according to *phusis*, your talent or genius). Such duplicity is a condition of *experience*, of worldly wisdom, of the sort of disenchantment with social myths and practices made familiar to us by Antiphon or Euripides or by Socrates whenever he challenges received truth and conventional understanding.[9]

Plato's Charmides has grown into this web of uncertainties, to some extent enlightened and emboldened by Critias, his skeptical, ambitious mentor, to some extent more shrewdly holding to the inexplicit sense of "knowing your place." Although Charmides has not thought through this definition's possibilities as Critias will articulate them in the dialogue, he shows a keen practical sense of such a definition's uses in calculating social power—most effectively in his modestly acquiescing to his acclaimed supremacy. As he well knows, for instance, Charmides is

---

9. This skeptical reading of social morality, incidentally, is embodied in a comedy on *Sisyphus* often attributed to Critias. According to the fragment preserved by Sextus Empiricus in "Against the Physicists," I. 54:

> . . . as the laws did hold men back from deeds
> Of open violence, but still such deeds
> Were done in secret—then, as I maintain,
> Some shrewd man first, a man in counsel
>   wise,
> Discovered unto men the fear of Gods,
> Thereby to frighten sinners should they sin
> E'en secretly in deed, or word, or thought.
>   Trans. R. G. Bury in the Loeb
>   *Sextus Empiricus III* (Cambridge, Mass.:
>   Harvard University Press, 1960), p. 31

Critias's protégé; he has a place to know and to take right here at Critias's side as Critias's showpiece. He knows this place implicitly without being able to rationalize his performance in the manner of Critias.

In fact, all of Charmides' suggested definitions of *sōphrosunē* are evidenced by his behavior in the dialogue. Charmides modestly ventures the claim that *sōphrosunē* is a certain poise or quietness (*hēsuchistēs tis*—159B), then later blushingly that *sōphrosunē* is just *aidōs*—shame, respect, modesty (160E).[10] Both of Charmides' suggestions are finely matched to his celebrity status, incidentally a status celebrated with Socratic archness *in* Plato (157E–158B) and, only in this notably disinterested sense, *by* Plato, the nephew of Charmides. This celebrity is specifically slanted toward looking good, however, and what looks good to his throng of enthusiasts is clearly differently motivated from what conventional wisdom about *sōphrosunē* intends. Plato's Charmides has *cool* or *charm*, not *virtue*, and in the Athens of this time, Plato shows, the former passes muster for the latter.

That all these terms—*sōphrosunē, aidōs, hēsuchia*—have clearly marked social connotations aligning a Critias, a Charmides, or a Socrates with pro-Spartan or oligarchic fashions (North, 102ff.) only reinforces a sense of the superficiality of this particular *sōphrosunē*, its fashionability within current social codes. Charmides' stillness is stylish. Again and again in his narration Socrates emphasizes Charmides' reputation for virtue, his letting himself be determined by others to be virtuous in certain respects.

This emphasis on decorous *eidos,* on mien, appearance, and demeanor, on attitude and posture, sets Charmides up for a Socratic questioning that predictably aims at broaching and, if possible, distinguishing a true and false *sōphrosunē*, for instance an inward configuration or *eidos* of the virtue distinct from this superficial *sōphrosunē*. This finely plotted aim of Socratic questioning is at least partly frustrated, however, by a telling paradoxical character of the virtue first encountered by Charmides in his

---

10. In the case of the *Charmides*, we must comprehend a double line of tension. One tension spans the two levels on which the conversation is conducted. The Charmides level, where the youthfully beautiful and philosophically naive kind of *sophrosyne*, characteristic of a noble disposition and an education within the strict bounds of social conventions, is expressed in simple conceptual terms; and the Kritias level, where the perfect kind of *sophrosyne* characteristic of a philosophical attitude of mind is envisaged through all the devious, dialectical detours. And both levels open a view—though by means of ironically involved complications—upon a social order. (Friedländer, 2:79)

E. R. Dodds, "From Shame-Culture to Guilt-Culture," in *The Greeks and the Irrational*, pp. 28–63, provides a fine introduction to the social-psychological interplay in these questions of public and private performance.

charmingly perplexed response at 158C–D, where his modesty conflicts with his need to answer for his high reputation. This paradoxical character is shared among Charmides and Socrates, superficial *sōphrosunē* and deep *sōphrosunē*: In this case, if you think you have *sōphrosunē*, you need it; if you think you lack it, perhaps you do not. Like a transcendent but participatory *eidos*, or form, *sōphrosunē*, it turns out, must be both pure and compromised, both innocent and experienced, both ignorant and knowing according to whether its determinations are internal or exterior.[11] These paradoxes reflect the way *sōphrosunē* as a social virtue is suspended between inner and outer forces, between the soul's self-regulation and its ascribed or regulated place in a social order.

Socrates' narration also makes plain that he is being urged to cast his vote in this election of Charmides as paragon. While Socrates is able to resist Critias's more sophistical assaults, his narration raises doubts about his ability to deal with or distance himself from the intuitive cunning of Charmides' blandishments. And it is crucial, I think, to gauge this stratum of the conversational interplay. As with his apology, which for many reasons is pertinent to the *Charmides,* opposed to Socrates' evident innocence is his inability not to indulge in self-incriminating exchanges in such a social setting. The implicit rules of encounter compel one to defile one's innocent knowledge or *sōphrosunē* in the compromising terms of transactional game playing. The *Charmides,* in this way like the *Apology,* shows Socrates unable to escape the gravity of these forces, unable, that is, in his own terms to clear himself from his widely suspected alliance with Critias or Charmides.

III

As his last contribution to the search for a description of what is in him, Charmides offers up a bit of hearsay in words that exemplify both his detachment from the philosophic quest and his mischievous engagement with a particular bystander. "Indeed, Socrates," Charmides says, conceding Socrates' refutation of the definition of *sōphrosunē* as modesty,

---

11. This perplexed case of *sōphrosunē* parallels the perplexity of *eidos* described by Derrida in "Plato's Pharmacy," pp. 166–69.

this seems to me to be rightly said; but now look at how this claim about *sōphrosunē* seems to you. For I've just recollected—something I earlier heard someone saying—that *sōphrosunē* is the doing of one's own things [*to ta heautou prattein*]. Now then see if this speaker seems to you to speak rightly. (161B)

Charmides uses this opportunity both to hide behind and to test his teacher, knowing his own place, so to speak, in order to learn more about Critias's place (162C–D). Within a pedagogical culture oriented toward persons rather than precepts, Charmides, like Plato's Lysis, is interested in Socrates less for his philosophy than for his use as a factor in interpersonal relationships and rivalries, in this case the emulation or rivalry of student and teacher. Socrates instantly remarks upon Charmides' disingenuousness in passing off an interpersonal dig as a bona fide philosophic request and in circulating secondhand goods in place of essence of *sōphrosunē*. "Foul fellow!" he exclaims. "From Critias here you've heard this or from another of the sophists" (161B–C).

Several features of this exchange point to key lines of stress in the conversation and in the social discipline whose lack it explores. First, the ensuing dialogue makes of this apparently innocuous phrase—"the doing of one's own things," the minding of one's own business—an enigma (161C), a wonder of ambiguity and danger. What, after all, is one's own, and according to what distributive justice with what authority? Here, for example, Charmides seems to Socrates to be minding Critias's business. Later, in arguing for a virtue that is knowledge, Critias seems to be minding Socrates' business.

These examples anticipate a second, more involved line of stress. The *Charmides* comprises a tangle of personal ratios, relations, and contests that interestingly deform and erupt into its explicitly philosophical discussion of impersonal knowledge and *epistēmai*. Some of these plots, like Charmides' mischievous shift of the conversation from himself to Critias, seem to be intentional within the conversation. Others, to be seen shortly, function within the narration.

Within the conversation, Socrates becomes a cat's-paw in the relationship of Critias and Charmides. Perhaps this is Charmides' return for the way Critias, after conspiring to use Socrates against Charmides (155B), also uses Charmides against Socrates, as if to say, "look what *my* teaching has wrought." By pitting Socrates against Critias, Charmides avenges himself for Critias's high-handedness; he also converts philosophy into a spectacle that feeds his appetite for theatrical, disengaged knowledge of the famous Socrates. And if Socrates, for his part, effectively uses Charmides against Critias, it is because Charmides lets himself be used in this way as a prize over which Critias and Socrates are made to wrangle. In fact, the *Charmides* presents us with the situation of a "mimetic rivalry" with Charmides more than knowledge, truth, *sōphrosunē*, or Socrates, for that matter, as its object.[12]

An impression of personal jockeying amid the mutual servicing of interests reminiscent of *Phaedrus* charioteers is partly conveyed by the decorum and by the elliptical quality of the dialogue between Critias and Socrates.[13] Like chess players hurrying through openings, they anticipate or readily grasp one another's points and positions, generously take certain things for granted, and move the arguments along with minimal elaboration. At times their procedures are justified by the pursuit of truth in the company of friends, but this readiness to agree, to shift direction, to accommodate claims or allow hypotheticals does not very well hide an underlying rivalry, suspiciousness, sense of ulterior motive, or ambition for victory (for example, 166B–E). Socrates carries this mutual, deeply ambivalent intimacy to a fine excess when he teases Critias's weakness for

---

12. Again, one does not simply desire; one imitates the desire of an other, desires what is desired (in addition to *Violence and the Sacred*, see Girard's *Deceit, Desire, and the Novel: Self and Other in Literary Structure*, trans. Yvonne Freccero [Baltimore, Md.: Johns Hopkins University Press, 1965], pp. 1–82). The dynamics of educational emulation are in any case crossed by the scheme of mimetic desire in the *Charmides*: Pedagogically, Charmides should imitate Critias's desire to possess the erotic Socrates, but pederastically, Socrates imitates—and parodies—the desire for the erotic Charmides shared by Critias, Chaerephon, his auditor, and others. The dialogue at points mentions the first possibility as philosophically promising—though the struggles between students and teachers portrayed in the *Charmides* might cast doubt on such promise—but gets held within the second possibility, in part because Charmides contrives to stand aloof from the dynamics of emulation that depend on the engagement of the disciple. The subversion of the pedagogical system by the erotic system is very much a problem in the *Phaedrus*, too, which broadly develops the analogy between teacher, rhetor, lover, writer, on the one hand, and disciple, audience, beloved, reader, on the other. As we shall see, an argumentative or rhetorical attempt is made in the *Phaedrus* to inscribe these hierarchies in nature, and yet in committing the case to nature, the argument touches on the very problem with these hierarchies: The teacher may envy the disciple's youthful innocence and beauty more than the disciple envies the teacher's wisdom. As embodied in ephemeral human beings, destined to alter, to age, to die, abstract categories and roles also alter, succumb to experience, disperse themselves in matter.

13. Gerasimos Santas remarks how "Charmides' and Critias' answers have the required generality from the beginning; somehow they seem to know the sort of thing Socrates is after, which is rather surprising in the case of Charmides at least since he has just met Socrates for the first time," "Socrates at Work on Virtue and Knowledge in Plato's *Charmides*," in *Exegesis and Argument: Studies in Greek Philosophy Presented to Gregory Vlastos*, ed. E. N. Lee, A. P. D. Mourelatos, and R. M. Rorty (New York: Humanities Press, 1973), p. 110.

quasi-Socratic object choices with suggestions and possibilities, like the utopian republic of 173B–D or the megalomaniac *sōphrosunē* of 167A, that he then retracts. Indeed, it is Critias's sympathy for certain Socratic commonplaces, especially those that hint at philosophical power, that makes for his relatively easy refutation when Socrates somewhat unexpectedly contests those commonplaces.

Beyond these motives of the conversation, which took place "yesterday evening" or "the previous evening" (153A), there are other relations and tensions that function within the intentionality of Socrates' narration of this conversation to a weakly specified auditor. Some differences between these narrative and conversational strata are immediately broached in the crossed purposes of the soldier Socrates seeking his old philosophic places (153A) and news of philosophy (153D) and of the students and teachers of philosophy there who are eager for news of the war. This eagerness seems to show concern about casualties in the wake of a military debacle: Each person has a particular question, probably for news of a friend or relative, that demands a particular answer (153C). The language of martial heroics or distinction, which one might expect from ambitious youths in wartime, is notably absent until Socrates introduces it in his question about young men who may have "distinguished themselves" in trials of wisdom or beauty or both (153D).

Socrates' sardonic narration to this anonymous audience of these crossings of war and philosophy, of military and civic virtue, nevertheless assumes a society-page bias on his listener's part. Socrates' tale concerns news of philosophy—specifically, philosophy as pederasty—rather than of Potidaea. He reports his meeting with Charmides in his celebrated but dissembled persona of the inveterate *erastēs*, or lover, making common cause with his auditor when he emphasizes that infatuation with the likes of Charmides is "no wonder for men like us" (154C). The comic climax of this lovers' gossip, the hilarity of which the auditor doubtless does not share, comes with the dizzying glimpse inside Charmides' cloak that ignites Socrates' ardor and, in his furor, incidentally puts him in mind of Cydias, "wisest in erotics,"

> who, speaking of a beautiful boy, urges "taking care lest one come as a fawn opposite the lion and get seized as a piece of meat," for I, too, seemed to have been ravished by such a creature. (155D–E)

So Socrates lushly portrays himself for his auditor as the lion in fawn's clothing, plying Charmides for a seduction. The citation of Cydias exemplifies the transpositions of hunter and hunted at work in the seduction. In similar fashion, Socrates' discourse portrays the social mechanism whereby the fawn is lionized and the lion fawned over. These images also catch the way Socrates and Critias stalk Charmides (154D–155B), as well as the way they are charmed or stymied by his replies.

The frequently gossipy tone of Socrates' narration (indeed, its form as narration rather than as dialogue) also indicates a range of forces working beyond Socratic control. On the one hand, there is his somewhat helpless servicing of a listener's expectations of great moments in pederastic pursuit. On the other hand, it is impossible for a reader to ignore the pale anticipation of apologia in Socrates' narrated account of his relationship with Critias and Charmides, our knowledge of whom—that they are to become two prominent members of the notorious Thirty—introduces powerful structural and historical ironies into both conversation and narrative:

> "Now for myself, I am little concerned; but for you, Charmides," I said, "I am much concerned, if somebody like you, with your fine form and in addition your most temperate soul, should neither profit nor benefit from this temperance in your coming life." (175D–E)

Socrates can only guess, but we know how this turns out. Foreshadowing this ominous future, the narrated form of the episode spills the conversation's problems into a later present tense as unfinished business and second thoughts of Socrates. The pathos of unfinished business is increased by the fact of an indefinite, not very forthcoming auditor, on whom Socrates' philosophical hairsplitting is probably wasted and before whom his apologetic impulses are probably lost. Perhaps it is fair to imagine a smug zero-sum game at this audience, where what Socrates' mockery of Critias subtracts from the value of philosophy gets added to the value of pederasty, a business where one's efforts at least may be more tangibly rewarded before eventual betrayals. Against the implied auditor's sense of what business one ought to mind, at any rate, comes a sense of perplexity—Socrates', Plato's, our perplexity—about just what business Socrates was minding with Critias and Charmides and about what business he is now minding in relating this discussion to a third party.

IV

What is it to mind one's own business? What is one's own? How is one to know one's place? Let us follow Critias's case for a while to see what it is, as both example and answer, that Charmides has turned loose on Socrates. Critias makes a run at saving the commonplace—"to do one's own"—and takes his attempt to clear up this enigma "so difficult to understand" (162C) through a series of maneuvers that we are to construe as sophistical.[14] Socrates lets both his audiences know (e.g., at 163D) that he is encountering familiar tactics, just as Critias's melodramatic part in the argument (e.g., at 163A–B) implies the same sense of staginess, the telling sense of a rehearsed or pre-scripted performance.[15] As in other sophistic dialogues, Socrates must smoke a studious interlocutor out of such opening gambits, gambits that suggest recitation and catechization, as well as martial calisthenics. When refuted, Critias forthrightly (though there is sophistic art here as well) abandons his defense at 164D after denying the force of what, from Plato's retrospective standpoint, amounts to profound irony. The physician who cannot know whether his treatment of a patient will ultimately work benefit or harm, and so cannot know the good or evil of what he is doing, cannot exemplify *sōphrosunē* (164B–C).[16]

The example of the physician is one of many that mirrors at a distance and mocks the purpose of Socratic practice—here, Socrates' enactment of a physician treating the "headache" of a tyrannical soul not known to have benefited from the treatment. This retrospective irony is lessened, but only slightly, by Socrates' earlier implication that he is more Thracian shaman than true doctor (156D–157C). By contrast to this Socratic difference from the master physician, Dr. Critias moves to close out

---

14. See Friedländer, 2:72ff.

15. The definition of self-knowledge, for instance, is "obviously a formula already worked out and not produced in the course of the argument," M. Dyson, "Some Problems Concerning Knowledge in Plato's 'Charmides,' " *Phronesis* 19 (1974): 104.

16. Actually, nothing in the dialogue eliminates this objection, as Socrates' later wishful positing of "true prophets" (173C) pointedly recalls.

mischance, irrationality, and Thracian ignorance. His is certainly not the *epistēmē* of Hippocrates, for whom knowledge is more a practice than a theory or concept of practice. "Life is short and art [*technē*] long," goes the familiar Hippocratic aphorism, "and opportunity is fleeting, and experiment perilous, and judgment difficult." Critias refuses to admit exactly the manic—and tragic—component in the similarly pessimistic Socratic practice of philosophy, a practice that cannot know its ends in the terms of 164B–C and so, in an important sense, can never yet quite know what it is doing.

This persisting dramatic or structural irony of the *Charmides*' conversation, its pathetic openness to the future, is reinforced by Critias's ignorance of difficulty and his impatience with the obstacles to concluding the discussion and translating philosophy into disciplinary power. Without this pervasive irony, which epitomizes the chronic apparent failures besetting the Socratic quest, the *sōphrosunē* of Critias's hopeful definition could be mistaken for the animating virtue of the *Apology*'s evangelical Socrates, the pious servant of the Delphic god:[17]

> Then only the *sōphrōn* person will know himself and be able to examine what he happens to know and what not, and in the same fashion be able to inspect others—what someone knows and thinks he knows, whether he knows it, and again what someone thinks he knows, but does not know—but nobody else will have this power. Is this what you're saying? (167A)

This resemblance to Socratic commitment is strengthened by the fact that these attractive words—a carrot dangled before Critias—issue from Socrates. Taking up this cause, like the epigones mentioned in the *Apology* (23C), Critias aims anew at pinning down *sōphrosunē*—in fact, "the *sōphrōn* person"—as possessing a general knowledge of any person's place. To Critias, no doubt this seems to be the knowledge that informs Socrates' philosophic practice. "Is this what you're saying?" Socrates asks of Critias, ironically mirroring the way that Critias, the mimetic rival, is

---

17. This similarity is widely mentioned but not well explained. So Santas points out how "in raising questions about the possibility and benefit of knowledge of oneself, Socrates is raising questions about the presupposition and aims of his own method," though without acknowledging, except in the usual ironic terms, the centrality of these questions to his very method (p. 120). See also Santas, pp. 117–18, Hyland, p. 124, Guthrie, 4:169–70, and Gadamer, "*Logos* and *Ergon* in Plato's *Lysis*," in *Dialogue and Dialectic*, pp. 2–3.

trying to address the same question to Socrates, seeking a Socratic authorization or imprimatur for his will to epistemic power.

Anticipating the hubristic, sophistical construer of oracles and corrector of countrymen in the *Apology*, Critias had proudly introduced a Delphic injunction into the discussion as proof text at 164D.[18] Critias pivots this "Know thyself" from an intimidating command of restraint to a positive connotation that includes the possibility of positive knowledge, knowledge beyond that knowledge of one's worthlessness traditionally purveyed to humans from the transcendent standpoint of the god.

> For I would almost say this very thing to be *sōphrosunē*, to know oneself, and I go along with the one who set up [*anathenti*] such an inscription at Delphi. And so this seems to me how that inscription was laid up [*anakeisthai*], to be an address from the god to those coming in instead of "Hail"—this address, this hailing, not being right—instead it is necessary to command one another to be *sōphrōn*. Thus the god calls to those entering his temple in a way different from what men say; with such an intention, it seems to me, the dedicator [*anatheis*] set up [*anethēken*] the inscription; and he [Apollo] says [*legei*] to those entering nothing other than "Be *sōphrōn*," he [the dedicator] says [*phēsin*]. And quite enigmatically, like a prophet, he speaks [*legei*]; for "Know thyself" and "Be *sōphrōn*" are the same thing, as the words say [*phēsin*] and I, too, though indeed one might think them different, which they seem to have felt who dedicated [*anathentes*] the later inscriptions "Never excess" and "Give a pledge, get misfortune." For these thought "Know thyself" was advice, but not an address from the god to those entering; and in order to set up [*anatheien*] no less useful counsels, they inscribed and dedicated [*anethesan*] these. (164D–165A)

This laboring interpretation reprises the revisions shown earlier in the discussion of minding one's own business ("for I learned from Hesiod, who said 'Work is nothing blameworthy,' " 163B). In drawing down a commonplace or traditional wisdom—Hesiodic or Delphic wisdom—to

---

18. This appeal to Delphi is another clear structural parallel to the *Apology*, a parallel between Critias and Socrates able to darken Socrates in two ways: It makes Socrates in the *Apology* seem sophistical and the Critias in the *Charmides* seem Socratic.

serve an individual case or action, Critias conforms the rule to the particular need of his argument rather than measuring the particular by the rule.

Critias's use of the famous Delphic text, however, is much richer than his appropriation of Hesiod. Given the joy with which he speaks it, Critias seems to regard his interpretation itself as a clear example of positive knowledge, a datum turned up by applying his intelligence to its given world. But the trickier provenance of this datum is equally suggested by Critias's reiterations of *anatithēmi*, first in his disclaimer ("I will rather take back my claims . . . ," 164D), then in his account of how the inscription was "placed *ana*"—"up," "back," "behind," or the like. Critias worries the verb, and by stressing verbal action he downplays the name and occasion of the votive offering, *anathēma* (the *offering* following the *attribution* of good fortune to the god's intervention), which might give this human use of the temple a less opportunistic, more traditionally pious aspect. Critias sees discursive process, that is, rather than material product: He sees people crowding into sacred space rather than a temple full of dedicated objects; he sees people dedicating but also debating or competing with inscriptions. In particular, he focuses on what "he"—a subject sliding through Apollo, to some ancient hermeneut, to Critias himself—set up, not on what pious worshipers have since dedicated. In its literal sense of "lay upon, attribute," *anatithēmi* might designate this slide, this displacement, of intentions that Critias performs in the god's name.

Both his disclaimer of the previous argument and his set speech on the Delphic inscription illustrate Critias's use of the verb as instrument of his own knowledge in action, as it first gives to the world, behind his back, so to speak, what he claims experience to give him as fact. The verb's spatial sense also implies that Critias knows his place, with respect to which *ana-*, "up," "back," "behind," acquires its force. Thus Critias, like Ion in the *Ion*, stands in the present reinterpreting a past back there and also, with respect to its authority in common life, *up there*. Critias constitutes the past as his place, too, as "his own" or "his business," laying claim to it in a way that puts him in the place of Apollo. Critias's pseudoprophecy, in short, has him putting words in Apollo's mouth so as to make it appear that Apollo puts words in Critias's mouth.

It is probably this impersonating or voicing of authority that has Critias fussing about the difference between a greeting and a piece of advice. While the greeting may look like advice, Critias would embed it in a different set of conventions that confer on the phrase a power both more routine and greater than advice. With a greeting or address, there is always an interface, a potential confrontation, leverage, however latent, on a social stage. A greeting is situated, here perhaps as a transcendent claim of god on man, perhaps as encouragement of a potential equal.[19] This sense of situation gives rhetorical force to a piece of otherwise detachable or abstract wisdom. When directed from god to human being, such an address comes, at best, as a calling, at worst, as an accusation.[20] It is wisdom in a challenging, aggressive, interpersonal mode, not a platitude or tagline for the soul to carry inward at its leisure. This difference is analogous, I think, to the dialogue's wrestling over senses of *epistēmē:* In a more philosophical sense, *epistēmē* might be *knowledge* or *knowledge-that;* in another, more socially addressed sense, which is dominant in the *Charmides, epistēmē* is *know-how,* practical knowledge with social content and use-value.

Of course, these motives that I have laid back upon Critias might unobjectionably remain Apollo's doing of his business, since "Be *sōphrōn*" hardly makes a radical gloss on "Know thyself." But there is more at stake here, I think, since this mystification of the commonplace is a staple of sophistic rhetoric. What can be radical in such rhetorical overworking of pretexts is Critias's self-dramatizing interpretation and the claim for positive knowledge that his commentary serves.[21] In the interpretation, Critias insists on consenting to a meaning that in this case seems innocuous enough. But such consent implicitly reserves a right to decide its own meanings, to depart from common law in order to follow private understanding in some other case.

Though the gods naturally try to keep human knowledge and action to a minimum (indeed, in exemplum, legend, and myth, the divine tries

---

19. Critias' point here seems to be that gods do not give counsels (moral advice, as if to inferiors) but rather greetings (as if to equals). He implies that the author of the inscription "Know yourself" meant that gods, and the wise who understand their hints, are beyond good and evil. (Thomas G. West and Grace Starry West, trans. and eds., *Charmides* [Indianapolis, Ind.: Hackett, 1986], p. 36)

20. Hyland, pp. 89–90, argues a similar sense of the greeting in Heideggerian terms. He claims that this sense adumbrates a Socratic way of being in the world that Critias is unable to live up to. From this speculation one might hold on to the uncertainty about whose *logos* is whose. For a trenchant critique of Hyland that really assesses the hermeneutical hazards of the *Charmides*, see David L. Levine, "The Tyranny of Scholarship," *Ancient Philosophy* 4 (1984): 65–72.

21. To Critias's "hypocritical" hermeneutics, compare Socrates' freewheeling, tongue-in-cheek interpretation of Simonides at *Protagoras* 340–347A.

to suggest the negative effects of knowledge and action), Critias's *sōphrosunē* would be a staging area for great enterprise. In terms of the emerging definition (167Aff.), Critias's *sōphrosunē* would be the science of what one knows, while Socrates' *sōphrosunē*, sensitive to divine disdain of human effort, would answer as the more perplexing science of what one does not know. For Critias, to know oneself implies knowing one's accomplishments, one's talents, one's capabilities. This is the knowledge of self that translates for an Alcibiades, a Lysandrus, or a Critias into a dare-to-be-great mentality as, with Apollo, they look down on the lesser gifts of ordinary people. And this is the architectonic knowledge that is the subject of Critias's ambitious definition of *sōphrosunē*: " 'Then I say,' he said, 'that alone of all the other *epistēmai* this both of itself and of all the other *epistēmai* is the *epistēmē*' " (166E).

V

Thereupon Socrates examines and refutes this claim. More interesting than the objective refutation, however, is the way he manages a complicated, compromising personal dilemma. The interpersonal drama worked out in the dialogue has Charmides first enacting a *logos* of Critias, then Critias enacting a *logos* of Socrates so that Socrates, as he says, can examine his own words (as defended by Critias). At 166C, as Critias astutely criticizes Socrates' argumentation from analogy, he reiterates the reflexive knowledge of *sōphrosunē* and then scolds Socrates for duplicity:

> And these things must by a long shot have escaped your notice, for, I think, what you said you would not do, this you're doing: for it's me you're attempting to refute, letting go those things about which our discussion is. (166C)

Socrates, in other words, is acting contrary to what Critias knows he knows, and he takes the argument off its explicit, bona fide paths because, Critias thinks, Socrates does not want to admit his agreement with Critias, that Critias's assertions are Socrates' own, or, put differently, that Critias's knowledge of himself entails a knowledge of Socrates' knowledge. From Critias's earlier standpoint, Socrates is not conforming to his own strictures; he is not minding his business, not knowing his place in the discussion.

After all, do not the unreconciled assertions of Critias's argument—*sōphrosunē* is knowledge of virtue and *sōphrosunē* is knowledge of knowledge—in general stem from the Socratic equation of virtue and knowledge and in this instance stem from Critias's attempt to adapt and elaborate this equation?

> . . . Critias' definitions (knowledge of oneself, and knowledge of knowledge) are at the heart of Socrates' life and method. In the second round . . . , it seems, Socrates is examining his own favorite doctrines. (Santas, pp. 117–18)

So complicit is Socrates with his interlocutor that he would, by the indirection of Critias's emulation of him, introduce or insinuate or put—maybe *anatithenai* is the right verb—his own formulas into Critias's discourse; in Critias's *logos* would be reflected an elusive theory of Socratic practice foreshadowing the Socrates of *Apology* at 167A, the technocratic Socrates of *Republic* at 171D–172A.

The tensions that result from the frustrated catechizations in the *Charmides*, Socrates says, resemble a quarrel brewing between a poet and "an actor [*hupokritēi*] badly setting forth [*diatithenti*] his poetry" (162D). Not just because of a clear verbal echo do I suppose this term *hupocritēs* to include Critias as well as Charmides, the "under-Critias" immediately referred to here. One must also, I believe, take seriously all the negative implications of the ratio between Charmides and Critias and Critias and Socrates (Charmides is to Critias as Critias is to Socrates), insofar as Charmides' developing sense of performance, of staging and upstaging, resembles Critias's own deflection of philosophy to ends that are not *sōphrōn*. The theatrical analogy implies that knowing one's place—here, mindful of sociology's useful distinction between status and role, let us say knowing one's *part*—involves an act or performance more or less deliberately pursued. One is estranged from *sōphrosunē* as an actor is detached from a role; though one is not at heart a conventional Athenian, one should act the part, be *"sōphrōn,"* not *sōphrōn*, where the virtue is always in quotation marks as something impersonated or cited so as to befit a social theater. Among its other implications, the narrative frame of the dialogue powerfully adds to Socrates' part a similar dimension of performance as he re-creates his role in the conversational drama. In fact, the layers go at least three deep: Socrates gives (1) a performed recitation of (2) a very performance-conscious conversation marked at points by (3) the pat recitations or reprises of past performances of Charmides, of Critias, and of Socrates himself.

His narration's repeated references to Critias's consciousness of performance and self-display—particularly Socrates' disparaging, ironic performing of the *aporia* at 169C, where Critias literally mirrors Socrates, like one yawner another—not only keep Critias's eagerness for public victory on the surface of the dialogue; they also import Socrates' performance consciousness as he later recalls these events for his auditor. So predictable is Critias-as-Socrates that Socrates stymies him as easily as one infringes a gentleman's agreement. When Critias accuses Socrates of proceeding in bad faith, ignoring the *logos* to refute the interlocutor, Critias also, of course, concedes his own bad faith, showing concern for himself rather than for the *logos*. But the key question his accusation immediately follows—What is that of which *sōphrosunē* is the science? (166B)—is the very question to which the dialogue finally circles back at 174B when again the Socratic elenchus, or refutation, is deployed. When Critias admits that *sōphrosunē* is the science of good and evil, Socrates responds as he responded to Charmides' plagiarized definition of *sōphrosunē* as the doing of one's own things—"Foul fellow!" (174B). Bruell sensibly wonders, "If Charmides had heard [his] definition from Critias, had not Critias in turn heard it, as he had doubtless heard of a science of the good and the bad, from Socrates? Is one a wretch [i.e., a foul or polluted fellow] for repeating what seems to be a Socratic teaching?" (Bruell, p. 155)

The Socrates of the *Charmides*, however, stubbornly resists outward acknowledgment of his part in Critias. Indeed, he voices his coolness toward an eager Critias in admonishing him for expecting too much of him:

> But, Critias . . . , you appeal to me [*prospherēi pros me*] as though I claimed to know those things about which I question, and if I were willing, I could agree with you. But that's not how it is; rather I search into every proposition [*protithemenon*] with you, because I myself do not know it (165B).

Thus Socrates, officially insisting on the proposition rather than on his person, rejects the mantle of authority that Critias ascribes to him, a mantle that Critias hopes to inherit and refashion.

Suppose we understand and sympathize with this rejection, given our deeper insight into Socrates and our detachment from the cultural type of the sage, not to mention what time has revealed to us about Critias. Still, we might pause over Socrates' rejection to note how, at the same time that it puts off, Socrates is also tacitly admitting "I'm you and you're me":

> How can you think . . . , if I most strive to refute you, I wrangle on any other account than to investigate what I say, fearful lest I suppose I know something I don't really know? And so I say this is what I am now doing, examining the argument mostly for my own sake and also perhaps for the sake of other associates. Or don't you consider it the common good for almost everybody that how things really are should be found out [*kataphanes*]? (166C–D)

The *logos* is Critias's (he is being refuted as its possessor), but it is also Socrates' ("what I say"). They make common cause, perhaps, as friends, but what sort of friend then is Critias to Socrates? Here, both "another self" and a selfish other, according to ambivalences that seem to arise in Socrates as well as in Critias, ambivalences that exemplify the instability of a wisdom dependent on *philia,* communal love or friendship, in pursuit of the good that here proves vulnerable to mimetic rivalry.

Socrates' protest of innocence, good faith, and fair meaning teeters on those equivocal platitudes that guard Socratic conversation. The pursuit of truth in the company of friends, the impersonality of the argument, the humble desire for insight and self-improvement, the pious concern lest one not mind one's proper business—each of these readily converts into (even invites, as Socrates well knows) a diabolical, Critian version (e.g., the use of truth to pursue others, the desire to make other people's business your business, etc.). It is also remarkable how barbed this reproof is in spite of its sense. Even in its explicit terms, that is, Socrates' disclaimer is tricky, perhaps even coy: As if truth actually were so close as to be about to come clearly beneath one's gaze! As if a possessive or oligarchic Critias would wish this impending truth shared in common! In this way Socrates teases and mocks Critias's ambition and snobbishness at the very instant he professes to disavow such ad hominem tactics. And so Socrates also intimates a difference, and his own enviable prepossession, when he ironically asserts common cause with Critias.

In these exchanges Socrates uses such *epistēmē* or technique of ignorance to prevent "knowledge-that *epistēmē* " (a common good, something for almost everybody) from issuing into "know-how *epistēmē* " (a specialist knowledge).[22] But we might also see how such knowledge without issue or result throws a bind around the next generation; indeed it perplexes the disciple per se. While Critias, in the manner of an avid student, is attempting to extrapolate or appropriate Socratic views, as he did a Delphic slogan, to his own uses, and while Critias looks to Socrates in the *Charmides* for some kind of approval, Socrates steadfastly refuses to offer him anything of the sort. Paradoxically, this return to the mentor would have Critias turning to Socrates rather than to *sōphrosunē* to confirm his knowledge and "his knowledge of his knowledge." For Critias, the desideratum of the virtue is exactly such authority, external confirmation of internal virtue according to the conundrum of *sōphrosunē*. Though he professes this self-knowledge, Critias's ambivalent dependence on Socrates shows he lacks it. And yet this dependence, which is reminiscent of Alcibiades' charismatic bondage to Socrates as reported in the *Symposium*, to some extent testifies to Critias's knowledge of his lack.

In the historical perspective this interaction between Socrates and Critias is uncannily public despite the illusion of private conversation and debate among as-yet-unenfranchised youths and their tutors. What is more obscure is how the fictional Socrates, too, seems to intuit and anticipate the political stakes in the plotting, whereby he manages to transpose unto Critias views Socrates advances elsewhere in Plato, views he here rejects—knowledge of knowledge and ignorance, Delphic self-knowledge, the fitness of philosophers to rule, an ambitious and intuitive sense of wholes. But in the *Charmides,* Socrates elicits and articulates utopian political and epistemological views as though these constituted Critian, not Socratic or philosophical, ideals. The apparent magnanimity with which Socrates conditionally grants Critias the possibility of a "knowledge of knowledge" and so releases him from his comical *aporia* at 169C–D climaxes the choreography that casts and then casts off the Socratic Critias in a mime of his mentor.

It is sometimes attractively argued that Plato means to exonerate

---

22. For a differently focused view of the Socratic failure here, see Richard McKim, "Socratic Self-Knowledge and Knowledge of Knowledge," *Transactions of the American Philological Association* 115 (1985): 59–77. "Plato presents Socratic self-knowledge as falling radically short of the knowledge which is virtue, and the Socratic method of inquiry as being powerless to bridge the gap," p. 60.

Socrates in the court of history by (Plato's) showing in the *Charmides* Socrates' differences from Critias, at points his antagonism toward Critias, and even, in the narrating voice, his outright disdain for Critias. But it seems to me that Plato first shows *Socrates* himself attempting to assert such differences from Critias and as a result of this attempt, first, obscuring rather than clarifying the consistency of his epistemology and its ends, and, second, apparently reestablishing bonds of interdependency with Critias and Charmides.

Though Socrates, despite his declared avoidance of ad hominem tactics, punishes Critias for his ambitious views, these other complicities and confusions are not resolved either in the conversation or in its subsequent narration. It is not entirely perverse to hear Socrates protesting too much in this narration, which uses storytelling privileges to mock, scapegoat, and exorcise Critias even more sarcastically than he had in conversation. The problem is that Socrates' assertions of difference from Critias' emulation of him carry within them clear evidence of Socrates' similarity to and complicity with Critias—in skill of plotting, in contentious argument, in jealousy of prestige, in speculative knowledge, in the dream of an aristocracy of knowers. Thanks to the auditor's interests, moreover, the narrating Socrates can make no very adequate apology in any case, since even if he succeeds in casting off his Critian persona, Socrates falls, as we have seen, into his pederastic persona, perhaps too into his eristic persona. From the auditor's standpoint, such philosophical battles must seem as pointless as Potidaea, and this overall impression is more likely to amuse than to challenge or disturb such hearers. Compared to what has gone before, the conclusion that everything depends on an *epistēmē* of good and evil (and who, once out of Socrates' earshot, does not think to have such an *epistēmē* already?) seems bland and anticlimactic and reassuring. "Do let us know, Socrates, if some new truth turns up," one might imagine the auditor bidding Socrates in farewell, "or better yet, let us know if some new beauty turns up."

Within the constraints of these stereotypes, Socrates' virtue is brought down or corrupted by those who, like Critias or Charmides or Alcibiades, would validate his charm, however coyly he tries to resist them. Here is Socrates laboring *not* to be teacher, father, or figurehead of some sort— Socrates forced to choose between betraying himself to Critias's expectations and betraying or disowning Critias, Socrates later forced to choose between submitting himself to his auditor's expectations or surrendering to misanthropy and misology. Where is the choice for Socrates in all of this? Surrendering himself on the genealogical model would condone the glib recitations in the *Charmides* and the superficial, performative sense of virtue. But disowning Critias is no more possible for Socrates than not telling his story or not making his apology, if only because this would be to abandon the citizen's commitment to the common good for almost everybody. This includes the responsibility of private correction and nurturance of fellow citizens that is embodied, however reluctantly and with howsoever many misgivings, in both the conversation and Socrates' narration of it. This responsibility falls within the traditional horizon of civic *sōphrosunē*, of mutual restraint and support. This is the *Charmides'* Potidaean heroism, the stoic valor of lost causes.

VI

The *Charmides* shows Socrates trying unsuccessfully to rise above habits, practices, and contests he views as hostile to philosophy, as well as to his own integrity. When Socrates interrogates the *hupokritēs*, or "under-Critias," who "didn't have in mind the same as he spoke when saying that *sōphrosunē* is doing one's own things" (161C–D), he not only dispossesses the interlocutor of his owness or self-mastery but also reveals that owness or self-property to be already appropriated by transpersonal mechanisms. Critias and Charmides belong to their clients, who in turn belong, as youths regularly do, to basic social myths, values, ideals, and pressures that the education of adolescents stages with unparalleled clarity. Ideally, so Socratic interrogation assumes, one should want to and be able to repossess oneself from such unknowing regulation by unexamined others.

In a familiar image of this problem, Charmides is made out to be the *agalma*, the artificial showpiece (154C). His aloofness, his winningly coy acceptance of his ascribed celebrity, his inscrutability—all match that of another *agalma* described in the *Symposium* by an Alcibiades who, himself such a celebrated *agalma*, knows whereof he speaks (215–217A): "when you open the statue [*agalma*] down the middle there are little figures of the god inside" (215B). In his questioning of Charmides, Socrates tries to open up this *agalma* as if in quest, Alcibiades-like, of its transcendent charm. "Why then," says Socrates, playing back Critias's violent suggestion, "shouldn't we strip that very part of him and see it before his figure [*tou eidous*]?" (154E). Shortly thereafter, Socrates' questioning places a distinctive emphasis on Charmides' interiority, both on the *sōphrosunē* in Charmides and on the inward direction that Charmides' search for an answer should take: " 'Once more, Charmides,' I said, 'rather apply your mind and look into yourself . . .'" (160D). As with Ion, this quest leads Socrates outward and downward, not upward and inward. At the end of this abortive midwifery, Socrates only brings forth a nugget of conventional wisdom that he sees to be the image of Critias.

This encrypting of the self behind an internalized mentor epitomizes a particular relation to *nomos*. Charmides shelters the saying of Critias as his prize, but with no personal commitment to its truth;[23] he values it because Critias values it, and he demonstrates its use-value in his calculated embarrassment of his mentor. Charmides' self-examination climaxes in his showing his value as an object of mimetic desire; he is precisely worth the striving of his admirers or the rivalry of Critias and Socrates. Similarly, Critias values the saying that Charmides exhumes, and others like it, because those he would influence value it, and they in turn value it because such sayings have been valued through the circuitous action of tradition, authority, chance, or linguistic usage; they amount to a kind of cultural or linguistic capital awaiting the Critian entrepreneur. In opening the Charmides *agalma* and in seeking there the gold standard, Socrates finds instead a floating monetary standard for virtue dispersed through an economy of interrelations. This means that Charmides does not belong to himself, but neither does he belong to Critias, whose image he harbors. It is awkward to say so, but Charmides gets suspended among his differences from these various aspects or faces of Charmides. He is not his own person, but he is not therefore somebody else's person, as he shows when dramatizing an estrangement, however jokingly, from Critias. He not only does not know his place; he does not have a stable place to know.

Under the cover of a detached, objective sense of *sōphrosunē*, Critias derives a flashy epistemological sophistication from the more fundamental, more existential self-knowledge with which Socrates intuits and interrogates an anthropological crisis. Critias would capitalize on rather than study virtue, as Euthyphro would use religion rather than worship. The paradoxically self-interested impersonality of Critias's epistemol-

---

23. On Charmides' inability to commit himself to the argument, see W. Thomas Schmid, "Socrates' Practice of Elenchus in the *Charmides*," *Ancient Philosophy* 1 (1981): 141–47.

ogy—whereby *sōphrosunē* really means (and masks) the *sōphrōn* person, where *epistēmē* really means social power, where "knowledge of knowledge" really means one person's useful knowledge of another person's useful knowledge[24]—suggests a moral evasion, an escape into theory in which, as events later in Critias's life suggest, is inscribed a latent social program.

The ability of Critias's strategic thought to shelter or secure itself in this way, to save or redeem its practical reason (*sōphrosunē* is the *sōtēria* of *phronēsis*—*Cratylus* 411E), illustrates a potential of consciousness for self-negation and self-transcendence according to pastoral, utopian, or escapist dynamics more fully exemplified in the *Phaedrus*. Such slogans of innocent *sōphrosunē* as *doing* one's own business or *knowing* one's place paradoxically appeal to disenchanting powers of action and knowledge able to subvert the possibility of more automatic social reproduction. To raise one's consciousness about traditional *sōphrosunē* jeopardizes this *sōphrosunē*, as both Socrates and his critics well know.[25] The *Charmides'* staging of the difference between a highly mediated imitation and an implicit or automatic imitation more natural in appearance I have termed a difference between experience and innocence. This difference is biased toward innocence in a familiar way: that is, experience, disenchantment, the mentality of a Critias or an Alcibiades, must live with the guilt of not being innocent and also include within its worldly wisdom the knowledge that innocence is both necessary and impossible for it. This double bind fuels a cycle of supplementations whereby one creates or projects compensatory, wish-fulfilling alter egos—a "Charmides," a "Socrates," a *Nous*, a winged psyche—innocent creatures more perfect than their creators, whose dreams of beauty or wisdom they thus might redeem.

---

24. For brief perspectives on the much discussed shifts between personal and impersonal media of knowledge (*sōphrosunē* as knowledge of *oneself* or of *itself?*), see Dyson, p. 107, Guthrie, 4:169, and Hyland, p. 125. Also in this connection, see Stanley Rosen, "*Sōphrosunē* and *Selbstbewusstsein*," *Review of Metaphysics* 26 (1973): 617–42, which touches on many of the issues raised here.

25. Critias "had largely abandoned traditional beliefs and—which troubled Plato most—this was almost certainly the result of his association with Socrates," Tuckey, p. 16.

Six / The Reproduction of Socrates in *Phaedrus*

Many of Plato's dialogues—notably the *Symposium*, the *Theaetetus*, and the *Protagoras*—take pains to remember extraordinary individuals by means of a dazzling art of literary portraiture. Having toured other parts of Plato's gallery, I would like to draw up before Plato's extraordinary portrait of Socrates in the *Phaedrus*, to contemplate some of its features, and to suggest its way of both claiming and disowning an exemplary power unmatched in ancient, or in any, literature. The *Phaedrus*'s portrait draws one to its distinctive literary texture, of course, but it also happens to memorialize a Socrates beyond the town walls in one of the districts of tombs, shrines, and monuments where such portraiture was conventionally dedicated in the ancient world.[1]

In her masterful survey of Greek portraiture, Gisela Richter reminds us that, during the lives of Socrates and Plato, the erection of statues (the

---

1. For the topography see R. E. Wycherley, "The Scene of Plato's *Phaidros*," *Phoenix* 17 (1963): 88–98. For the distribution of tomb sites around city gates, see the maps in Donna C. Kurtz and John Boardman, *Greek Burial Customs* (Ithaca, N.Y.: Cornell University Press, 1971), pp. 336–37.

principal medium of ancient portraiture) undergoes remarkable developments.[2] Such portraiture continues to render not only the head but the whole figure—"the stance, the gestures, the drapery" (p. 3). But this statuary now moves out of tomb and sanctuary districts into public places and even homes; portraits of great personages of the past are increasingly devised and erected; and the traditional idealizations of portraiture are modified by new concerns for and new knowledge of portrait realism. As with traditional cemetery monuments, which often include an epitaph, Greek portraits sometimes supplement or replace the name with "a quotation descriptive of the man" (p. 15). Plato's Socrates, Richter adds, is often cited as collateral evidence for these developments in portraiture.

The *Phaedrus* happens to refer to statuary (and, more generally, to the artistic reproduction of living being) several times in several ways. Departing from one of these references that Socrates in a sense rededicated for my use—the conventional tomb, epitaph, and monument by which King Midas, the fabled Phrygian, is remembered—I would like to snag a thread of text that runs through a number of additional themes more familiar in the scholarship on the *Phaedrus*: These concern the relationships between living and dead, divine and human, human and animal, soul and body, city and country, speech and writing, concept and symbol, whole and part, Egypt and Greece, method and madness. This select inventory suggests the many related issues that the ambitious conversation of Phaedrus and Socrates wishes to bring into the clearing made by its view of erotics and rhetoric, of private and public seduction. In a setting saturated with more or less legible literary, artistic, and cultural codes, Socrates and Phaedrus make various efforts at a new anthropology—new attempts, that is, to construct a theory of the person in its natural or cosmic setting that focuses on what Charles Griswold has recently developed as "self-knowledge."[3]

This anthropology, which Griswold well describes, generally explores nonmimetic relationships (causal, hierarchical, linguistic, or conceptual relationships) as antidotes to poisonous mimetic or imitative striving, which entails the sort of rivalry we briefly glanced at in the pursuit of Zeus in Socrates' palinode myth but more generally studied with respect to *Ion* and *Charmides*. The new anthropology tries to reconceive human

---

2. Gisela M. A. Richter, *The Portraits of the Greeks*, 3 vols. (London: Phaidon Press, 1965), I: 3–33.
3. Charles Griswold, Jr., *Self-Knowledge in Plato's "Phaedrus"* (New Haven, Conn.: Yale University Press, 1986).

existence according to new axioms of virtue independent of the baleful mimesis targeted, for example, in the *Republic*—the erotic, embodied, contentious imitation with which Athenians are so personally and socially preoccupied. But in the *Phaedrus*, as in the *Republic*, Plato shows deep contradictions in these attempts to transcend such mimesis. In the *Republic*, the antimimetic legislation of the ideal state belies its own dependence on educative mimesis for the behavioral conditioning of its own citizens. And the countermimetic ends of the *Phaedrus*'s discussion belie several of their mimetic means—for example, the mimetic basis of rhetorical narration and of rhetorical *ēthos*, as well as the mimetic basis of portraiture, including Plato's portrait of Socrates. As a result, the *Phaedrus* comprises a self-critiquing portraiture that displaces or offsets the bystander's usual privileged viewpoint. Socrates criticizes social and artistic production that depends on mimesis, or imitation, but this criticism is itself mimetically produced in Plato's likeness of Socrates.

The pursuit of Zeus and beauty in the palinode myth illustrates how accounts of conventional hierarchical relationships in the *Phaedrus*'s conversation differ from themselves, proving inconsistent in legible ways, if not in audible ways that Phaedrus will hear and remark upon. Generally, such conventionally hierarchical relationships as those between god and human, human and beast, or soul and body are upset by the interruption or feedback of perplexing mimetic relationships.[4] The hunting of a higher ideal in the company of the god presents an ambiguous face: It might show pious love of the divine or it might equally show us a Euthyphro-like emulation of the god aimed at appropriating his divine power. Though he claims to assert a strictly philosophic priority over Lysias, again, we find Socrates imitating, contending with, and parodying Lysias in a very ambivalent performance reminiscent of the *Symposium*'s resourceful, erotic, emulative Socrates. More generally, clear causal and hierarchical relationships in the dialogue are upset or contradicted by the odd relationship of Socrates and Phaedrus, who exhibit interesting, awkward reciprocal dependencies. These two certainly do not themselves embody the clear and distinct examples their various speculations might depend on. It is perhaps their restless inability to fill the being of lover

---

4. A very suggestive background for Socratic experiments in the reconstructing of language, thought, and relationship is sketched in Page duBois, *Centaurs and Amazons: Women and the Pre-History of the Great Chain of Being* (Ann Arbor: University of Michigan Press, 1982). The contest that duBois describes between analogical and hierarchic thought in classical Greece is, I believe, more problematically staged in Plato than her argument allows.

and beloved, of speaker and listener, or of teacher and pupil that both motivates and limits the search for more absolute relationships like that of an "unmoved mover" featured in an unusual Socratic proof for the immortality of the soul (245C–E). In other words, the complexity of the person in the *Phaedrus* and the overdetermination of social relations obstruct, infiltrate, or bias the project of philosophy in the dialogue; given this social context, the "unmoved mover" (perhaps a reprise of Lysias's desirable nonlover, another sort of unmoved mover) is ambiguously a personal, as well as a metaphysical, ideal.[5]

My focus on Plato's portrait of Socrates—or better, on the reproduction of Socrates in Plato—is an attempt to enlarge and more adequately suggest the problematic quality of these relationships in the *Phaedrus*. By means of this portrait, mimesis continues to enchain the philosophical project, not only in the sense elucidated by Derrida in his fine essay on the *Phaedrus*[6] but also as a more or less controlled function of fictional rendering. Plato's portrait art, that is, frames or transvalues discursive claims of the spoken conversation, claims concerning the surpassing of mimesis, in ways that demand a *reader*'s careful elucidation. Following a conventional division, my discussion will try to read the complex memorial portrait, and Plato's fiction, in three passes: first, seeing the individual subject; second, surveying the setting or depicted backdrop in relation to this subject; and third, deciphering the epitaph or inscription that supplements the image.

I

Plato's portrait of Socrates comprises fascinating asymmetries: that between image and speech, what is seen in the mind's eye, heard in the

---

5. Socrates' immortality argument intrigues scholars for many reasons summarized in Guthrie, 4:419–20; R. Hackforth, *Plato's "Phaedrus": Translated with an Introduction and Commentary* (Cambridge: Cambridge University Press, 1972), pp. 4–5; and Thomas M. Robinson, "The Argument for Immortality in Plato's *Phaedrus*," in *Essays in Ancient Greek Philosophy*, ed. John P. Anton with George L. Kustas (Albany: State University of New York Press, 1971), pp. 345–53. But the argument's *voice* also raises the considerable problem of standpoint, especially in this context of interested rhetoric, irony, and dialectic: ". . . the greater the *absolutism* of the statements, the greater the *subjectivity* and *relativity* in the position of the agent making the statements," and the less the irony, drama, or dialectic of the discourse—Kenneth Burke, "Four Master Tropes," in *A Grammar of Motives* (New York: Braziller, 1955), p. 512.

6. "Plato's Pharmacy," esp. pp. 139ff. Derrida argues here and elsewhere how the differential aspect of the copy hollows out originality, which also depends on such difference.

mind's ear; that between aesthetic object and social action or function, the beauty of the work as a self-perfected "organic whole" and its insistence on an end or effect beyond its margins. These asymmetries give the portrait its vitality, its sense of arrested motion and incompleteness rather than of conventional idealizing pose, a pose in which Socrates could rest in peace, as in Xenophon, his perplexity and controversy concluded. Speaking against such repose, Socrates himself acknowledges and channels a sense of portraiture's strangeness (*to deinon*) in his characterization of the immutable mobility of graphics:

> . . . the offspring of painting stand like living beings, but if one asks them something they keep solemnly silent. And it is the same with [written] words. . . . (275D)

The portrait's mixture of life, fixity, muteness, and radiance can be terribly disconcerting, a solemn, not a stupid silence, aggression not repose, the distinct address of the living dead that survivors and inheritors labor to neutralize and transcend.

The voice of Socrates at this very instant I cite does not, of course, escape this sense of uncanniness before portraits of the dead that he, long dead, alludes to. Among its other effects, the text of Plato evokes a solemn, not a stupid silence in the double gesture whereby it constitutes the magic, power, and conviction wrought by Socrates' voice and dispels that magic in the retrospection, absence, and difference of its graphic tissue. As with vivid portraits generally, the uncanny sense of this depiction reflects one's perception that its subject somehow comes to us on his or her own terms, not simply as a dead object lesson in *hubris* or heroism, nor simply as cultural detritus, a ruin of Ozymandias that by chance mocks human purpose with its accidents. Socrates himself, for example, keenly experiences the asymmetries conveyed by his portrait—the difference between his speech and his image, between his intention and others' reading of him, between his hope for some greater general impact and the disappointing closure of particular conversations.

Thus the beauty and power of the fit between subject and portrait in Plato draw in no small part upon the graphic, textlike qualities of Socrates' personal style—his knowing ignorance, his inaccessible omnipresence, his perpetual dissembling of his sense. To accommodate this Socratic contribution to the work of reproduction, one might hold to this paradox: that Plato both follows the stricture of the *Phaedrus*'s Socrates in conforming Platonic discourse to a living being (264C), to the being of a Socrates, but that Plato also radically departs from the directive in better conforming that living being to the textuality Socrates would deny himself when Plato places him in the book.

For a quick fleshing out of this sketch, imagine if you will the scene in the *Phaedrus* where Socrates and Phaedrus, having concluded a contest of speeches, now survey the relative merits of these speeches and, in doing so, broach the matter of the portrait. Socrates claims that his two speeches—the first disparaging love, the second a palinode or retraction in praise of love—were competently organized; at least the heads of those speeches made a regular definition and methodical division of the theme. Lysias, on the other hand, whose written speech in praise of the nonlover had provoked the contest,

> . . . not from the beginning but from the end tries to swim on his back backwards through his discourse, and he begins from what the lover in concluding would say to his beloved. (264A)

"Or do I have it wrong?" Socrates demands of Phaedrus. Phaedrus wants to disagree on behalf of Lysias, but he cannot seem to find his opening against Socrates' persistent efforts to alienate his affections. "What of the rest of the speech?" Socrates asks.

> Don't the parts of the discourse seem thrown into a heap? Or does it appear that from some necessity the second thing said needed to be put second, or any of the other things he said for that matter? For it seemed to me, who knows nothing, that whatever happened to come up was boldly expressed by the writer. Do you know any compositional necessity for his setting this part by that in such a way? (264B)

"Good of you," Phaedrus replies coolly, "to think me sufficient to distinguish his reasons accurately."

Phaedrus's reluctance to join this basting of Lysias can be felt from Socrates' pressing rejoinder:

> But I do think you will say this, that every discourse ought to be put together like a living being, having a body of its own, so

that it's not without head or foot, but has both a middle and members, drawn fittingly to one another and to the whole. (264C)

"*Pōs gar ou?*" Phaedrus replies in apparent agreement—literally, "How could it not be?"—though in his annoyance he means something like "So what?" "Here's what," says Socrates, "*toinun*," as he invites Phaedrus to measure Lysias's discourse by the stricture that such speech ought to be organized like a living being. And in the same breath Socrates biases this invitation with a teasing prediction: "You will find Lysias's discourse no different from the epigram that some say is engraved over Midas the Phrygian" (264C–D).

When Phaedrus, thus prompted, requests a definition of this epigram, Socrates reveals it. "First, here it is," he says in a way that frames these verses with a commentator's motive:

A bronze maiden am I, and on the tomb of Midas I lie.
As long as water flows and tall trees grow,
Remaining in this very place on a much-lamented tomb,
I shall announce to passersby that Midas is buried here. (264D)

"Now secondly," Socrates resumes, "that it makes no difference which of these lines is said first or last, you probably noticed, I think." But no, Phaedrus seems not to have noticed this, because he was busy perceiving how, as he says, "You mock our discourse, Socrates." "Let's let the speech [of Lysias] go then," says Socrates, "so that you won't be annoyed; and yet it seemed to me to have many examples worth looking at, if not worth trying to imitate . . ." (264E).

This passage well illustrates the *Phaedrus*'s rich and engaging conversational texture, as Phaedrus unsuccessfully resists the Socrates he had hoped in a sense to seduce with the speech of Lysias. Made glum by his inability to hold his own in such conversation, Phaedrus responds more by mutely complying than by turning his rhetorical hopes to a Socratic schooling.[7] And so both Socrates and Phaedrus end up coolly humoring

---

7. There seems a consensus about Phaedrus's limited range of interests. See, for instance, the characterizations in Ronna Burger, *Plato's "Phaedrus,"* p. 17, and G. J. DeVries, *A Commentary on the "Phaedrus" of Plato* (Amsterdam: Hakkert, 1969), pp. 5–6.

one another's peculiarities, perhaps provoking justifiable curiosity about their real view of these proceedings. The conversation, like rhetoric generally, naturally elicits second-guessing about the intentions that animate fair words.

In addition to this conversational texture, the passage I have run through offers much other food for thought, as Socrates' palinode might put it. This is not, however, the raw mind food available in the soul's heavenly pasturage of the palinode (248B–C), but food that needs interpretive and critical cooking to fit it for thinking. Consider first the passage's tailpiece, this business about Midas, his epitaph, and the *parthenos*, or maiden, who bears it—all of which makes a conspicuous irrelevance here. Its apparent irrelevance invites some wonder about its deeper pertinence. For one thing, showing his peculiar bent for mischief, Socrates makes a game not only of Phaedrus and Lysias but of Midas's much-lamented tomb. What sort of reader, one might wonder, would think to juggle the lines of an epitaph or to cavil at its style? After all, this overturning of the *mnēma* or *sēma*, of the engraving, has the form of a desecration.

Of course, the epitaph, like every other form of words, was fair game for Greek literary criticism and poetic contest. Other places where this same epitaph crops up illustrate this competitive motive and the kind of practice or tradition that Socrates, and the *Phaedrus*, engages. Diogenes Laertius accepts the attribution of Midas's epitaph to Cleobulus, one of the seven *sophoi*, or sages, "distinguished for strength and beauty . . . acquainted with Egyptian philosophy," and also famous for his riddles.[8] Diogenes quotes *six* verses of the epitaph. Now the maiden will remain not only as long as waters run and trees flourish, but also as long

> As the sun shall rise and shine, and the bright moon,
> And rivers run and the sea wash the shore.

Diogenes believes that a poem of Simonides confirms Cleobulus's authorship of this epitaph. In his contentious answer to the epitaph, Simonides demands

---

8. *Lives*, I. 89–90. I quote the translation of R. D. Hicks in the Loeb *Diogenes Laertius I* (Cambridge, Mass.: Harvard University Press, 1959), p. 93.

Who, if he trusts his wits, will praise Cleobulus the dweller at Lindus for opposing the strength of a stele to everlasting rivers, the flowers of spring, the flame of the sun, and the golden moon and the eddies of the sea? But all things fall short of the might of the gods; even mortal hands break marble in pieces; this is fool's devising. (I.90)

Simonides condemns the arrogance of Midas and maker for opposing the powers of gods and nature; he experiences the monument as a claim to power against which he marshals his own powers. "Even mortal hands break marble in pieces," Simonides threatens, as his verse makes a worded equivalent to this overturning of monuments.

Long after Simonides, but before Diogenes, another enters the ring of these verses. This is Dio Chrysostom, who in the person of Favorinus cites the epitaph—whether from the *Phaedrus* or from elsewhere is not clear—and then scoffs eloquently at its presumption:

Well, my self-announcing maiden, we hear indeed the poet's words, but, though we sought, we found not thee nor yet the tomb of Midas. And though those waters still flow and those trees still thrive, in time even they are likely to vanish with the rest, like Midas, like maiden. (37.39)[9]

Where Simonides' reply reflected a sense of powers contending for eminence in the space before him, Dio Chrysostom's reply reflects a sense of loss and change, a sense of the impermanence of such monuments in time. He pities Midas and maiden as victims of mutability. Simonides responds as if insulted, lorded over; Dio Chrysostom is condescending. The old Ceian poet seems to take the monument too seriously, the Roman-age rhetor too lightly. Perhaps we need a middle ground sketched by Emily Vermeule in her reflection on this exchange between Cleobulus and Simonides. She calls Semonides of Amorgos to witness:

9. "Thirty-Seventh Discourse: The Corinthian Oration," 38–39. I quote the translation of H. Lamar Crosby in the Loeb *Dio Chrysostom IV* (Cambridge, Mass.: Harvard University Press, 1956), p. 37.

> There is no intelligence in men, but, creatures of the day, we live like cattle, knowing nothing of how god will bring each thing to finish. (I D.3–5)

Vermeule comments in this way on such "creatures of the day"—*ephemeroi*:

> As the sun may be born fresh each day, so is the mind, infant and *nepios* [witless], unable to use the past as a guide to the future or find meaning in passing events. . . . Intelligence, if we had it, might link us to the immortal sphere, but it is normally so defective in us that we replace it with hope and delusion, as winged and weightless as the *psyche*.[10]

And so we would pass, like Midas, from the sphere of nature into the sphere of "winged and weightless" symbols that express hope but signify delusion.

These extracts from Dio Chrysostom, Diogenes, and others suggest a setting for Socrates' contentiousness in a tradition of discourse and letters, and they also indicate Socrates' expedient misreading of Midas's epitaph, which he may have edited to accommodate his point. But all these readings are also interestingly obtuse, as Vermeule points out as well,[11] about the durability of symbols. Think, that is, how Simonides, Dio Chrysostom, and Diogenes perpetuate Midas and his epitaph in the instant of criticizing its pretensions to perpetuity, and see how they thereby abet the storied immortality conferred by poets and poetry. Here is a variant of the ring-making in poetic and rhetorical tradition: the past's capture of the present at the moment the present would transcend or bury the past.

If the memorial barrow outlasts Midas and if the natural world evoked by the epitaph outlives this material monument, still the literal epitaph remains; it is still here, on the page I read from, a testimonial to Midas taking its silent exception to these various attempts to appropriate it

---

10. *Aspects of Death*, p. 24.
11. ". . . in the short time between the Greeks and ourselves, rivers have dried up and oceans shifted while many Greek *pharmaka* against death are still potent," Vermeule, p. 23.

rhetorically against itself. Thinking to escape the gravity of this circular epitaph, a poetic and rhetorical tradition paradoxically gets threaded back through the porosity of such an inscription, which cryptically defeats these various attempts at victory or last rites. So we might even imagine Midas's epitaph to constitute a genuine riddle of Cleobulus—Who is this bronze maiden? it might be asking—the solution to which might be something like fame or memory or poetry or inscription or possibly something else that might announce itself in time.

The form that Socrates carps at (and may help create)—the possibility he points out of altering the sequence of lines without deeply affecting the sense—can thus be seen as a calculated virtue of the epitaph, a ring of inscription sealing itself against the contention of appropriative, rendering, or recriminating voices. This circular capacity for substitutions happens to guard the verses from interference, their internal exchanges anticipating and to some extent precluding the aggression of juggling, topsy-turvying critics. Furthermore, the epitaph's formal indifference to first and last epitomizes its content—the cycles of physical change and natural recurrence, into which all things return. Such organic internal proportion, common in funerary representation and in much portraiture, modern as well as ancient, claims a kind of unity and permanence; no doubt its internal regularity hopes to conjure an external regularity and to win a sense of life from its symbolization of death.[12] With its words and symbols deployed like charms, the monument would influence, channel, or authorize the meaning of Midas's inevitable death. Such personifications of this monument, furthermore, are not merely fanciful. They reflect a merging and, one hopes, a repose of living and dead intentionalities in the monument; they follow the work of mourning that makes death a medium of the necessary fictions of the living.[13]

But what has Socrates to do with tombs and with these implications of verbal and symbolic magic? For one thing, as I suggested at the outset,

---

12. For discussions of this representation and its motivations, see Vermeule, Kurtz and Boardman, and also G. M. A. Richter, *The Archaic Gravestones of Attica* (London: Phaidon Press, 1961).

13. . . . bare stones marking Attic graves are *semai*, signs, and their hewing as *stelai* elaborates rather than imposes hermetic significance. A placed stone is articulate, built stone eloquent, and inscribed, its substance utters the absent signifier it frames. So far from being a "primal scene [of writing"], graven stone is discursive, contextual. And what after all is stone but *to herma*: "rock, cairn, foundation, lith," and the Greek root of "Hermes," the name of the god. Inscribed stone puts the dead in this god's realm, under his title, in a territory of interpretation. . . . (John Kerrigan, "Knowing the Dead . . . ," *Essays in Criticism* 37 [1987]: 16).

for Socrates and Phaedrus to pass out of Athens is to pass into the place of tombs and monuments, of statuary, offerings, and epitaphs, beyond the city walls. These features of the landscape are so familiar to the Athenian as barely to warrant literary remark; Phaedrus finds Socrates' attentiveness to these features remarkable (229B–230E). But more directly to the question: With the conspicuous irrelevance of his citation of Midas's epitaph, Socrates' fetches another interesting potentiality—Midas in the garden, flowing waters, luxuriating foliage, a genius of the place. Much lamentation—lamentation perhaps beyond the Greek mean[14]—seems to be all that Socrates' epitaph recalls of a mighty Oriental king, famous for his dreams of knowledge, wealth, and power. Whatever history Midas might denote gets excluded, after the fashion of a pastoral reduction or simplification, for the sake of a mortal Midas in a fabled garden.

Silenus, the story goes, was wont to frequent the garden of Midas until one day Midas mixed wine in the flowing waters and captured the drunken god, hoping to glean his wisdom. What Silenus is compelled to tell Midas is much discussed and much disputed, but Nietzsche's summary is plausible enough.

> When at last Silenus fell into his hands, King Midas asked what was best of all and most desirable for man. Fixed and immovable, the demon remained silent; till at last, forced by the king, he broke out with shrill laughter into these words: "Oh, wretched race of a day, children of chance and misery, why do you compel me to say to you what it were most expedient for you not to hear? What is best of all is for ever beyond your reach: not to be born, not to be, to be nothing. The second best for you, however, is soon to die."[15]

Maybe this wisdom explains why, according to his epitaph, Midas in the garden might evoke so much lamentation. Or, to put it another way, the riddle of his tomb encodes Midas's answer to Silenus, which in turn prefigures a Socratic answer to Semonides' view of human stupidity and ephemerality. It is worth bearing in mind that in his celebrated palinode,

---

14. "Athenians were apparently prone to extravagances in their funerary art and architecture to judge from the frequency with which legislation was leveled against it," Kurtz and Boardman, p. 122.
15. *The Birth of Tragedy*, trans. W. A. Haussmann (New York: Macmillan, 1924), p. 34.

Socrates—another Silenus, as Alcibiades thinks (*Symposium* 215)—has felt constrained to bring Phaedrus in the dialogue's garden setting a similar wisdom. The best for the soul would have been never to have fallen into the flesh; the next best, to sprout wings in the soul and flee as quickly as possible to beatitude beyond the sky. From this angle, the riddle and the tomb yield a maiden soul perched for flight on a much-lamented *soma*, or body, and the lightness in Phaedrus poorly answers the weight of Socrates, whose body is the *sēma*—a tomb and its sign.

II

From the perspective of Socrates' immediate setting it is tempting to imagine Phaedrus and Socrates as Midas and Silenus.[16] But in a larger historical setting, as Plato is well aware, a spirit of Simonides has since made Socrates out also to be the Midas, the inveterate, self-destructive questioner who sought to know too much. So one might wonder whether Plato in the *Phaedrus* is making the kind of claim on behalf of Socrates, the man for all seasons, that maiden or maker engraves on behalf of Midas. This perspective shifts from Socrates-as-Silenus to Socrates-as-Midas according to a fundamental ambiguity of memorial setting (now internally composed, now externally exposed) that the cunning portraitist tries to harness. One setting is the fiction of the ephemeral pose; another setting, the ephemeral reception or place of this fiction in actuality.

These ambiguities of internal and external portrait setting can exist in tension with the subject and involve spectators in the fate of an apparently complete figure. Perhaps Homer's depiction of Odysseus marooned on Calypso's island can help illustrate this power and ambiguity of settings. Like Socrates in the country, Odysseus is simply out of his element in Calypso's verdant wilderness. And Homer's way of rendering Odysseus further implies his living entombment, his premature arrest and burial in the static, idyllic death-in-life Elysium of Calypso's Ogygia.[17] The funereal backdrops of the Ogygian paradise counterpoint the previously

---

16. This favorable case for the magic of Socrates-as-Silenus is well argued by Elizabeth Belfiore, "*Elenchus, Epode,* and Magic: Socrates as Silenus," *Phoenix* 34 (1980): 128–37.

17. William S. Anderson, "Calypso and Elysium," in *Essays on the "Odyssey": Selected Modern Criticism*, pp. 73–86.

depicted longings of Odysseus's family on rough Ithaca, where they impatiently wait to mourn, to observe the necessary obsequies, and so to commemorate Odysseus's glory in the human way. Having sketched this situation, Homer makes his hero emerge from the backdrop of living death in two ways, at two levels. He stages a very powerful resurrection of Odysseus from the unknown dead, throwing him back into the contentious, glorious life he relishes both *then* in the tale and *now* in the telling. For the portrait of Odysseus, this is an effect in a doubled setting, one internal to the tale, one external, an effect of the telling: Odysseus is resurrected, that is, for Homer's successive audiences, for us, as well as for the old Ithaca portrayed in the epic. As with the *Phaedrus*, the art of such Homeric doubling envelops its audience in its complicated, still unfolding sense of things: The uncanny, still-moving portrait of an Odysseus neither dead nor alive unsettles one's sense of death, of glory, of domesticity, of the person in his or her natural or cosmic setting.

The Calypso episode also toys with a sentimental sense of "the hero's reward," whereby the paradise of the goddess provides for Odysseus a gratification delayed during a life of heroic struggle, like the Elysian plain that we have just been told in Book IV awaits Menelaus. Odysseus's sojourn on Ogygia thus illustrates another feature of the setting of memorial art—namely, its wish-fulfilling or consoling aspect, which in this case Homer invokes only to revoke. Perhaps this idyllic setting (recall the maiden's claim for Midas's benign natural setting) provides the euphemistically better world to which we consign the dead for our own peace of mind. Or perhaps it is a setting to flatter the shade and safely hold its interest far from us on the other side.[18]

This idyllic setting has its clear parallel in the gardenlike locale of Phaedrus's and Socrates' conversation. And here the *Phaedrus* also shows a more comical aspect—a Circean aspect, perhaps—with the suggestion of a pastoral animal farm, an aspect that blurs its avowedly clear-eyed portrayal of the human being and the human condition. The conversa-

18. These hopeful representations of death, of which the maiden is an example, are cogently analyzed in Jean-Pierre Vernant, "Feminine Figures of Death in Greece," trans. Anne Doueihi, *Diacritics* 16 (1986): 54–64. Vermeule discusses the kinship among sphinxes, sirens, harpies, storm-winds, and soul-birds—all images pertinent to the *Phaedrus*—on pp. 8, 75–76, 150, 171–75, 201–2, passim. More general studies of attitudes toward the dead can be found in Jan Bremmer, *The Early Greek Concept of the Soul* (Princeton, N.J.: Princeton University Press, 1983), and Robert Garland, *The Greek Way of Death* (Ithaca, N.Y.: Cornell University Press, 1985).

tion's estimate of human stature, it turns out, is modeled not only on statuary or on the soul in the body or the shade in the tomb but also, as the Silenus testifies, on the animal in nature. Vermeule lucidly describes how for the Greeks the human being's relationships with the animal kingdom mediate its thoughts of divine relationship and stimulate human desires to live like gods rather than die like beasts.[19] This fact encourages one to take the well-known pastoral motifs of the *Phaedrus* with an open mind to their seriousness, as well as to their comedy.

Consider in this light a second point Socrates makes in the passage with which I began. There he demands that discourse be organized like a living creature, with a body of its own, a head and feet, middle and extremities, all composed in a fitting whole. Like the painter or sculptor, the speaker would reproduce a whole figure. But unlike the uncanny statue, the speaker's reproduction would really live. Here one encounters a seemingly fantastic ambition—the possibility of an art beyond art, an art such that its product would be natural rather than artificial, original or creative rather than merely imitative. This is in fact only one among a number of similar specifications in Plato of rhetoric as the nurture or mastery of beasts, imagining the rhetor or ruler as a kind of shepherd or animal tamer who best knows the breeding and nurture of discourses and discoursers.[20]

In winning Phaedrus's assent to this stipulation of the living being of discourses, Socrates, too, illustrates his skill in taming and herding living arguments (e.g., 260E–261A). But it is a skill portrayed, as I say, against a well-delimited backdrop. It ranges over a pervasive web of language and allusion in the *Phaedrus*, where there are working various motives that might usefully be termed pastoral. This pastoral sets literary or poetic, perhaps festival, quotation marks around the conversation, and it does this to ambivalent effect, since the playfulness of the conversation is entangled both in serious issues and in the serious Phaedrus so zealous for Lysias's ambiguous composition. If in earnest about its privileged view of human affairs, on the one hand, this pastoral movement would follow the "rustic sort of wisdom" that Socrates mocks when he and Phaedrus first come into the country (229E). This is the sophistical realism that would master Boreas, Centaurs, Gorgons, and Chimaera by taming them into a kind of natural history, a project (Socrates adds) that

---

19. Vermeule, pp. 83–117.
20. For example, *Republic* 343ff., 493A–C; *Critias* 109B–C; and *Statesman* 275–76.

demands both great faith in probabilities and a lot of leisure time. If playful, on the other hand, this pastoral would infuse the conversation with a festive agenda, perhaps even with Saturnalian inversions that hark back to the Golden-Age promptings of satire.[21] The trick with this ambivalent pastoral setting is gauging Phaedrus's, Socrates', and Plato's various rapports with it—for instance, their different ways of possessing or getting possessed by pastoral codes and customs involving love, music, the animal, and the divine.

The pastoralism of the *Phaedrus* stems from the dialogue's much-remarked rural setting, from the conversation's studied opposition to values and customs of the town, from its preoccupation with love and with absent lovers, from its celebration of music in a sort of song contest of lyrical speeches, from its invocation of rural deities, from its festive ambience, its masquerades, its promise of prizes, and, more generally, from its attempt to engage and reproduce something called nature in the course of its sophisticated play.[22] The pastoral setting silently comments on Phaedrus's naturalism—his fondness for physicians, for physical science, for the artistic reproduction of nature in the personal culture of self-fashioning.[23] And this setting also comments on Socrates' cosmic

---

21. One may see in this sophisticated pastoral setting an appropriation of traditional or authentic holiday motifs, for example of the Adonia and the gardens of Adonis at 276B, which Marcel Detienne analyzes in *The Gardens of Adonis: Spices in Greek Mythology*, trans. Janet Lloyd (Atlantic Highlands, N.J.: Humanities Press, 1977). For more general background, see Barbara Babcock, ed., *The Reversible World: Symbolic Inversion in Art and Society* (Ithaca, N.Y.: Cornell University Press, 1978).

22. I intend "pastoral" here more descriptively and structurally than historically, although such use would not be anachronistic (see the recent critical survey by David M. Halperin, *Before Pastoral: Theocritus and the Ancient Tradition of Bucolic Poetry* [New Haven, Conn.: Yale University Press, 1983]). For a wonderful survey of pastoral motifs in the *Phaedrus*, see Clyde Murley, "Plato's *Phaedrus* and Theocritean Pastoral," *Transactions of the American Philological Association* 71 (1940): 281–95; also Adam Parry, "Landscape in Greek Poetry," *Yale Classical Studies* 15 (1957): 3–29; and Thomas G. Rosenmeyer, *The Green Cabinet: Theocritus and the European Pastoral Lyric* (Berkeley and Los Angeles: University of California Press, 1969), p. 42. A. Philip also discusses the unity of these motifs, though not within the conventions of pastoral: "Récurrences thématiques et topologie dans le 'Phèdre' de Platon," *Revue de Métaphysique et de Morale* 86 (1981): 452–76. The literature on "pastoral" is formidable, so let me stipulate my usage. "Pastoral" generally means and involves *escape* (into pastures, into nature, into the Golden Age, into art and song, into romantic love, etc.). But note too that this escape motive is so transparent that pastoral forms very early stimulate a "metapastoral" literature, which indulges but also distances with irony the pastoral impulse and that analyzes, works through, or criticizes the various escapist strategies of pastoral. In his disparaging appreciation for his natural surroundings, his affectionate resistance to pastoral lore, Socrates is explicitly "metapastoral" at the outset of *Phaedrus* (e.g., 230D: "Country places and trees won't teach me anything . . ."). Later the dialogue resembles metapastoral in subtler ways that it is my aim to explicate.

23. Michel Foucault has, in a sense, written a finely critical edition of Phaedrus's handbook in *L'Usage des plaisirs*.

pastoral in his palinode and in his discussion of rhetoric—his rendering of the truth, that is, in distinctly pastoral or agrarian terms.

Encountered in a book, these pastoral motives invite both indulgence and detachment, but you will also find this mix of responses to mark Socrates' demeanor in the *Phaedrus*. Furthermore, the premise of pastoral—the recasting of complex social or psychological motives into simple forms so as to make things seem more intelligible and more manageable than they actually are—demands a way of reading that mediates discursive surfaces and these suppressed or excluded complications. Again, Socrates' skeptical approach to Phaedrus's as well as to Lysias's ulterior motives anticipates a reading of this sort. In short, it is as if Socrates, unlike Phaedrus, has feet in both settings—in the festive, masquelike conversation and in a more literary or poetic pastoral fiction that knows the disingenuous masquing of motives for what it is.

It is against this backdrop that I find myself taking special note of the tameness of the living being of speeches, as well as more generally observing the preponderance of animal husbandry deployed as an image of the human mastery of nature and of human nature. Of many instances of this language of animal husbandry in the *Phaedrus*, one might recall Socrates' description of how he can be led by discourses in books the way hungry animals can be led around after leaves or fruit (230E). Or one might remember lovers and beloveds characterized as so many wolves and lambs (241D), or Socrates' concern lest he and Phaedrus show the sloth of sheep at midday (259A), or Socrates' view of political debate as ignorance of the difference between horses and asses (260B–C). Most memorable, of course, is that master paradigm of the charioteer seeking heavenly pasture for himself and his steeds. Despite the glamor and epic pretensions of the chariot race, I count horses as herd animals noteworthy for their service in transport, even, as here, in mystical transport. The place of the horse in pastoral is anyway borne out by our comic friends the half-horsed sileni. In the *Phaedrus*, this standard iconography of self-mastery as the mastery of beasts is cut with Socratic irony, but also with an ironizing pastoral setting that highlights oppositions between inside and outside, body and *polis*, city and nature, internal order and external function and that disables the easy ranking of these in a hierarchy of values. For example, this double dealing of point and counterpoint keeps constant pressure on the consoling, fictionalizing pastoral imagination that informs Socrates' palinode myth, enveloping in a question mark its claims about the one true place, person, and language of human being.

Stereotypical herdsmen share their herds' preoccupation with eating and sleeping and remaining in one place, and the *Phaedrus* shows this, too, well enough—for instance in its recurrent imagery of motion and rest or in its motif of oral gratification or pain as reflected in topics of eating and drinking, but also in speech and song generally, in its view of sexual intimacy (e.g., of wolves against lambs), or in the bridling of horsey appetites. Oral gratification takes the easiest route to pleasure, but its difference from the further possibilities of human happiness also leaves the widest gulf to bridge. This is the particular aptness of Socrates' myth, in which he sings of soaring heavenward into the light while seated comfortably in the shade. The compensatory or offsetting measures that Socrates adopts thus widen the difference between words and deeds. Even the apparent exception to herdsmen's ways bears out this pastoral system of compensations in Socrates' tale of the cicada people (259B–C). The birth of muses and music moves these ancient folk toward a higher form of life distinctly reflecting the limited pastoral imagination: Their waking and fasting in an unending chorus of song simply invert the storied herdsman's normal concerns for sleeping and eating, thus expressing a rustic emblem or fable of the superhuman.

If such pastoral tends to narrow a range of human experience, portraying it as fixed, say, at an oral stage of human development, still a Socrates can also complicate and question this reduction, even in seeming to indulge it. Remember that he is an avowedly reluctant attendant on the valetudinarian Phaedrus, drugged like Silenus into the garden quest of wisdom (230D). It is from this standpoint—half in, half out of the game's circle—that he mirrors, mocks, and patronizes Phaedrus's penchant for quick fixes and his desire to take the professions of the new science in good earnest.

Socrates' palinode well illustrates this duplicity whereby he both indulges Phaedrus's fantasy hopes and speaks over Phaedrus's head. Though Socrates advertises various getaway vehicles in his pastoral rhapsody—self-moved soul, wings, horses, chariots—what he more convincingly promotes is the vehicular aspect of language itself. Though it claims to show the truth about the soul, this palinode more cogently shows a dazzling body of language, commemorating the figuration of language (say, the making of metaphors, images, or transports) against a background sense of language's density, its appealing weight and texture, its entanglement in traditions and in the idioms of other authors, other projects, other practices. The speech lures one with promises of origin, authority, and authenticity, but it perplexes or puts one off when it comes to deciding where to place the quotation marks, what interpretive canons to apply, what conventions to use to delimit the sense. It cites Milesian speculation, Pythagorean and Orphic mysticism, Eleatic doctrine, Cratylan punning, Hippocratic physiology, erotic poetry, Aristophanic funny business, and Aesopian fable, as well, of course, as Socratic commonplaces, working them all up into something new and strange on a spur of the moment.[24] Seen from this angle, the palinode makes a great example of the palinodism or "backward singing" of intertextuality as it threads its way back through the old songs, on the one hand repeating, citing, alluding, on the other laboring at a transformation, which would here make the Socratic equivalent of the Midas touch.[25] Against the claim that discourse must resemble a living body, this voice of the Siren, as Alcibiades terms it (*Symposium* 216A), urges that real life depends on a living being's becoming *logos*, or discourse.

The Siren-like lilt of the palinode should, however, alert one to the ambivalences of such discourse, of which Socrates, elsewhere so critical of poetic and rhetorical rhapsody, is certainly well aware. So what is also illustrated here is how Socrates in the palinode, as elsewhere in the *Phaedrus* too, engages a symbolic process whereby the pastoral simplifications I have described are rendered as oversimplifications and, to that extent at least, as problematical. Again, imagine conceiving *noēsis* as grazing on heavenly commons after a spirited run. Such a representation takes Phaedrus further from, not nearer to, what it would represent. Or think of the problems entailed for the plain moral message by Socrates' comic celebration of the chariot's swart horse, with all his irrelevantly articulated differences, down to his mischievously snubbed nose (235E). Even a credulous Phaedrus, who is later easy prey for Socrates' hyperbolic claims for an art of rhetoric, tunes in the irony of overstatement in the palinode and discounts the performance accordingly.[26] In the same vein Socrates' cicada story plays as a comic deflation of the palinode myth: In the story the myth's grandiloquent emphasis on ecstatic abstinence is

---

24. The best study of this texture is Anne Lebeck's "The Central Myth of Plato's *Phaedrus*," *Greek, Roman, and Byzantine Studies* 13 (1972): 267–90.

25. I adopt this sense of intertextuality from Julia Kristeva, *Sēmeiōtikē: Recherches pour une semanalyse* (Paris: Seuil, 1969), pp. 144–46; also her *Revolution in Poetic Language*, trans. Margaret Waller (New York: Columbia University Press, 1984), pp. 59–60.

26. For this "irony of hyperbole" see Albert Cook, "Dialectic, Irony, and Myth in Plato's *Phaedrus*," *American Journal of Philology* 106 (1985): 432ff. For the snubbed nose, see Murley, p. 290, Burger, p. 65.

scaled down to the self-mockery of an Aesopian apologue, a little like Socrates' shift from holy man to horsefly in the *Apology*.

In the wake of such a performance on such a stage, at any rate, it is hard to feel toward this Socrates what one might feel toward Midas, toward Protagoras in the *Theaetetus*, or toward more conventional commemorative portraits in their settings. Between his dissembling and his self-deprecation, this body of Socrates does not allow much of a hold for emulous rivals or condescending wise men. Besides, he seems unconcerned with the monumental last word, so intent is he on the next word. No wonder he left off his father's stonecutting trade to work on the more mobile statues of Daedalus (*Euthyphro* 11C–E). To experience this Socrates is to lose one's feel for the Midas, according to Alcibiades' rueful report, in the preoccupation with the Silenus. And yet Alcibiades' portrayal of Socrates' intellectual arrogance (*Symposium* 215C–E) does not ring true. The *Phaedrus* shows a practical and emotional involvement in the topics, whether of love or rhetoric, that belies suggestions of ironic intellectual detachment. In the *Phaedrus* as in the *Symposium* or the *Ion* Socrates wades neck deep into all that stuff out of which he draws his discourse, in clear if inexplicit contrast to the immaculate thinker of either Anaxagoran (269E–270A) or mystical (249C–D) stripe.

In his breathtaking performance, Socrates indulges the pastoral imagination but also makes conspicuous his indulgence, his role-playing, his impersonating of voices. Phaedrus, meanwhile, is preoccupied with other concerns (he takes rhetorical advertisements in earnest, for one thing) and so is a little nonplussed by Socratic parody and, later, a little annoyed at being forced to play Socrates' yes-man and straight-man in a satire of rhetoricians. This difference between Socrates and Phaedrus clearly distributes the different value a pastoral setting has for the holiday philosopher, on the one hand, and the pretentious rhetorician or dialectician on the other, who takes seriously the magical possibilities for human relationship through rhetoric dissembled later in the dialogue as the rural arts of animal and plant husbandry.

Such arts of the mastery of nature, the "rustic sort of wisdom" tied to the particular persons and places it means to reinterpret and master according to its demythologizing rule, conform to what we might term the logic of the monument. Socrates implies that there is something backward and macabre in the fascination with such creatures as Chimaera and Gorgons (229D–E). In trying to turn its art on experience (especially the reality of death), this wisdom actually turns away from experience (toward consoling fictions or apotropaic magic). Beneath such projects of disenchanted wise men, moreover, there may be implied a childlike spookiness and anxiety about powers that the dismantling of these old forms might release, say, about the darker emasculating powers beyond death, "the horror of unspeakable Night" (Vernant, "Feminine Figures," p. 55), that Midas's benign maiden might wish to dispel. This fear of *nemesis*, or reprisal, which may accompany disenchanted self-assertion, fuels the magical imagination and its role in the practices of Euthyphro, Ion, and others. Perhaps, too, it underwrites Phaedrus's naturalism, his concern for his health, as well as his unrealistic hopes for self-improvement.

The *Phaedo* more directly shows this logic of the tomb when the interlocutors' demands for spellbinding personal consolations repeatedly divert the discussion from its progress toward impersonal argument, truth, or philosophy (e.g., *Phaedo* 77D–78A). Like the *Phaedo*'s consoling half-truths, the *Phaedrus*'s rustic sorts of wisdom suffer through their excessive commitment to the particularity of person and place and to the magic of the proper name. Hence the affinity of such wisdom to the tomb—the final conflation of place, person, and name. This is so even when that "tomb," according to one consoling fiction, is another body in which the soul is to be reincarnated. Reincarnation, that is, is one case of a more general rule. Not only is the body a tomb, as the mystics say, but the tomb proves to be the general form of the artificial body, "the substitute person" (Vermeule, p. 45), that other, sometimes better person, place, or story to which the personal soul aspires or gets dispatched by survivors.

Against the childlike fantasy of personal omnipotence and gratification in paradise, of a self-fashioning and self-control that emulates Zeus's "philosophic and authoritative" "unmoved moving" (252E, 245D–E), the more convincing argument of both the *Phaedrus* and the *Phaedo* is that the only chance for either body or soul is its reproduction in *logos*, or discourse. And not just any discourse, as both the *Phaedrus* and the *Phaedo* take pains to suggest against the fantasy possibilities aroused by rhetoric's claims for the magic of voice as Gorgias, for one, describes it.[27]

---

27. Notably in the *Encomium of Helen*, which characterizes persuasion as a compulsion of the soul induced "by witchcraft," by druglike *logos*, and by "sacred incantations sung with words" (trans. George Kennedy in Rosamond Sprague, ed., *The Older Sophists* [Columbia: University of South Carolina Press, 1972], pp. 52, 53). In modeling his speech on Stesichorus's palinode in behalf of Helen, Socrates' incantation also vies with Gorgias's famous speech.

Rather what is sought is a language that can reckon or economize the disappointment of rhetoric, its failure to break the circle of nature in which movers are always in turn moved, a language that can somehow permeate the constraining pressures of the body, the dead, and the tomb to make philosophy something more than mourning and melancholy for a failed voice of power. Let this, at any rate, indicate some of what is at stake in Plato's consigning Socrates to the monument of his book—a setting both more and less than the better place to which one might wish him.

III

The portrait of Socrates in the *Phaedrus* makes a convincing likeness: This is Socrates, his voice, his manner, his distinctive irony. We can say this, as others always have, even though we never knew the original. Alluding to the Delphic inscription, after all, Socrates himself confesses that even he does not know his original (230A). But the text to this portrait, its epitaph, at the same time says "This is not Socrates." Such an epitaph—"a quotation descriptive of the man"[28]—paradoxically both improves the likeness to the elusive, textlike philosopher and calls attention to its status as a likeness, an imitation that displaces rather than lays to rest the Socratic project. The Platonic portraiture bequeaths us as its truth the struggles between cultural mimesis and philosophic mastery rather than a transcript of a false resolution of these contests. The Platonic portraiture mercifully disseminates Socrates' language rather than epitomizing or monumentalizing a master's thought in the manner of Xenophon. This disseminating fate was the *logos*'s only chance, its only way out of premature burials. The intellectual conflict on the Socratic scene continues as his afterlife and in effect supplies a new epic literature we call philosophy. In this literature the hero cuts against the old grain of language shaped as personal glory. In the literature we call philosophy, the protagonist, the living being, strives for the shape of a *logos*.

The difficulty of this beauty of the text can be illustrated by Socrates' seemingly conclusive last words on the art of rhetoric, an art that has yet, he says, to be adequately elaborated. His way of discussing this

---

28. Richter, *Portraits*, I:15.

rhetoric in the *Phaedrus* claims its possibility, indeed its necessity, and yet this discussion also implies the impossibility or gross unlikelihood of such a thing. Human nature throws up one obstacle to such an art of rhetoric, since humans more readily adapt a lofty object to their powers than raise their powers to so high an object. Hence, for example, the proliferation of rustic and antiquarian sorts of wisdom that contentedly traffic in pseudoscience.

An even greater obstacle results from the scope and complexity of the art of rhetoric as Socrates specifies it. The institutor of such an art must describe the soul very precisely (271A). He must carefully determine the soul's capacity to act or to be acted upon (271A). Then he must classify the types of discourse and the types of soul, relating them to each other and to their various effects and affects (271B). And he must master the occasions for speech as well. Socrates reiterates, elaborates, and piles up these requirements so as to underscore their difficulty, making what Phaedrus terms "no small task" (272B). Then he reminds Phaedrus that, on top of all this, the master of rhetoric must also know the truth and be able to "enumerate the natures of his auditors and divide things into classes and grasp each thing under a single idea" (273D–E), else he will never please the gods rather than gratify his fellow slaves (274A).

And Socrates' skepticism about this art is not based only on its complexity or difficulty. He also implies more fundamental questions, often insufficiently remarked, about its compatibility with the philosophy it would depend on. This point is partly suggested by the way Socrates distances himself from the concept he elaborates. Quite early in this account he begins to disown the rhetoric he prescribes. At 270D he explains how "we" should address the issue expertly, but at 270E the first person shifts to an indefinite third person, then to "Thrasymachus or any other who seriously offers rhetorical art" (271A), and at 272B all this difficulty has fallen to the task of "the author." This slippage is matched by another as Socrates' list of requirements shifts from the publishing of an objective, "scientific" description of rhetoric (271A–B), an abstract knowledge of a domain, to its incarnation in the practicing rhetorician (271D–272B), a personal know-how. This shift focuses the art's use-value for a particular individual in some forensic theater rather than its more general value as a kind of knowledge in a system of philosophy.

Socrates' skepticism about this rhetoric (and the facetious tone of his recipes comes clear once you grasp this skepticism) in any case follows from the stricture that rhetoric, in order to complete itself, must first master philosophy. It must know truth before opinion. This would also strangely imply that philosophy becomes the means to such rhetorical ends as knowledgeable deception (273D) or to passing off donkeys as horses (260A–D). The rhetorician needs the truth, Socrates says with a barely straight face, to guard against fooling himself when he tries only to fool others. To suppose, incidentally, that Aristotle supplies these lacks in his *Rhetoric* is to miss Socrates' more skeptical implication that one is unlikely ever to accumulate the certain premises needed for courtroom proofs or that, if one possessed such premises, the courtroom would hold any attraction. At best, the practical reason of the rhetorician must undergo the perpetual detour of philosophy, which offers only the most fugitive hopes of one day providing the requisite knowledge.[29]

These are implications, however, that Socrates elects not to spell out or strongly impress on Phaedrus. Indeed, the manner of his exposition tends to allow rhetoric rather than philosophy preeminence here, as Socrates impersonates a rhetorical rather than a philosophical point of view. His matter-of-fact, confident projections echo a more sophistical sense of wisdom as something readily accomplished on the way to study of a more demanding and rewarding rhetorical art (see, for example, *Gorgias* 460ff). Such considerations, in short, brand his promotion of this art as another of Socrates' false or misleading elaborations of a case.

The misleading claim of philosophy's part in a rhetorical whole is paralleled by a more extensive myopia of Socrates' mischievous discussion concerning basic questions of part and whole. As in the *Ion*'s discussion of *technai* and technicians, he suppresses questions of ethical right and wrong, for example, or of the larger ends toward which the art of rhetoric and its instances work. When he does mention ethical issues, Socrates lightly passes or curiously inflects them—for example, with the perspective of the wise man, the man of accomplishment, who high-mindedly aims to please the gods rather than his fellow slaves (273E–274A). This inflection of virtue envisages the problem of wholes not in terms of the impersonal, abstract concepts we typically identify with Socratic ideation, but primarily in human, even in egoistic or selfish form. Socrates'

---

29. The best discussions of this exposition do not take the possibility of a philosophical rhetoric as a matter of course. See, for example, Ernesto Grassi, "Rhetoric and Philosophy," *Philosophy and Rhetoric* 9 (1976): 200–16; Samuel IJsseling, "Rhétorique et philosophie: Platon et les Sophistes, ou la tradition métaphysique et la tradition rhétorique," *Revue philosophique de Louvain* 74 (1976): 193–209.

specifications make the whole personal in a familiar Greek way; they make the whole physical, a matter of one's personal happiness, a source of heroic glory visible to gods, if not to men. Perhaps this sense of whole follows naturally the earlier stipulation that discourse be organized like a living creature, with coherent internal articulations. Of course, the emphasis on *internal* coherence—of a whole speech statuesquely composed of members integral to its *look*—suppresses the higher-level question that Socrates routinely pursues, as with Euthyphro, Critias, or Gorgias—the question of the speech's *external* setting and purpose. Fastening mostly on its organization and its impious insult to *Erōs*, for example, Socrates has left relatively unanalyzed the larger and darker human and social purposes to which Lysias's speech might contribute its part.

Let me make clear my view of Socrates' odd biases here, which I take to be still pastoral, still deliberately and ironically reductive. Despite this emphasis on the organic internal coherence of a humanlike discourse, Socrates is not unaware of what discourse does—its functioning according to a very different, inorganic structure that needs an antinaturalistic, unconventional analysis. Socrates shows this more inclusive, Aristotelian sense of discourse when he stipulates a rhetorical art's need of knowledge of ethos, of audience, of subject, of purpose, of occasion. But then this inventory of rhetoric's *functional* whole, a construction of concepts abstracted from human media, abruptly turns toward its part in the developing rhetorician, a *personal* whole again, rather than toward its part in a general knowledge of politics, justice, or the good. This is a dubious move to which we should not hastily subscribe Socrates. To conceive the whole in this way as personal or aesthetic—that is, culminating in the conventional excellence of the gentleman, the *kalos kai agathos anēr*—downplays more interesting questions about such conceptual or functional wholes as justice itself or virtue itself, the perplexing, unconventional questions for which Socrates is famous.

Is the whole autotelic, is it autarchic, dependent on causes internal to itself? Or is it moved by external causes elaborated in an art, knowledge, or community? Do we hold to a conventional sense of human completeness, for example, following the perceived contour or surface of the body? Or do we submit human being to a more intellectual and prudential criterion of wholeness and coherence? Is philosophical self-knowledge a mirror image of one's human form, as the pastoral-minded Phaedrus is inclined to think? Or does philosophical self-knowledge, as Griswold and others have suggested, first need to bracket out or discount the biases of perception, opinion, and received wisdom by means of philosophical criteria? As Socratic conversation repeatedly illustrates, the personal whole (and the apparent unity of our embodied, lived, unexamined experience) darkens one's insight into these more perplexing, abstract, impersonal, unconventional formulations. This slippery interplay of parts and wholes, persons and concepts, in Socrates' mischievous determinations of rhetoric and dialectic, is in its way reminiscent of the stranger's procedures in the *Sophist*. There the terminology of dialectical precision is put in the service of willful, seemingly arbitrary divisions of wholes, themselves finally subsumed under the persona of sophist, of statesman, of "stranger from Elea."[30]

In the *Phaedrus*, on the one hand, the living being to which Socrates compares speech suggests the independence and autonomy associated with personal *aretē*, or excellence. That this living creature is organized and composed, on the other hand, suggests dependence on an external process or cause organizing and composing it. The difference between these two versions of the whole—one personal, aesthetic, and autonomous, one conceptual, functional, and contingent—marks a distinction that Socrates expertly makes and mangles in the strange, remarkable example of the "natural joint" between the left and right halves of the body as illustrative of the object of correct dialectical procedure: "dividing things by classes where the natural joints are, not trying to break any part like a bad butcher" (265E). For the Zeus of the *Symposium*'s Aristophanes, the line bisecting the body may seem a "natural joint" (190C–191E), but in other respects the symmetrical division, in the light of a body's real jointing, is a forced and unnatural one (a specious division, perhaps made for appearance's sake), while natural and functional joints unsymmetrically articulate the body in a number of possible ways (cf. *Statesman* 287C). The symmetrical and specular division is easy for thought, but perhaps therefore delusive. One must turn away from this aesthetic mimesis, from the primacy of the percept, to try to grasp what the skin sometimes hides—the concept or function of the joint.

This interesting, fleeting equivocation between functional joints and the joint at the plane of the mirror is mediated, it turns out, within the symbolism already deployed in the dialogue. In particular, this prescription for division collapses the difference between animal bodies, the joints

---

30. Rosen, *Plato's Sophist*, discusses many of the problems with the stranger's seemingly cavalier divisions.

of which (living or dead) serve human needs, and the human body conceived as an aesthetic object—for example, the frontal or profile views of youths and maidens, like Midas's bronze memorial, familiar from archaic art. The inconsistency of Socrates' recipe for division—bisecting the body at the natural joint—is opportune, deliberate, but perhaps necessary given a wish-fulfilling pastoral typology that equivocates human, animal, and divine natures. The emphasis on their organized living being animates discourses only to tame them, conferring a godlike lordship on their creator and master, who directs discourses so defined to ends (like servitude, slaughter, or sacrifice) beyond themselves. To make living, serving creatures of discourse is, after a fashion, to deify their creator, the master or father for whom they live, whom they serve; there is a kind of divinity conferred by subjecting other wills. If the *logos* is a living creature, in other words, it is exactly a vehicle of the soul, the sort of living creature on whose back one might ride to immortal glory.

This seems a fantastic conceit, I know, a version of the magical wish to speak something into being, but Socrates will give a closely related conceit even fuller voice later in the dialogue, when he envisions another vehicle of human happiness and immortality—words like seeds planted in receptive souls. Such a vision conceives the master rhetorician in the image of the provident gods of the *Protagoras*'s myth or of the godlike legislators of the *Republic*, methodically working to mystify their culture as our nature. During the discussion of such ambitions in the *Phaedrus*'s second half, in a movement that I would like briefly to track, Socrates mentions a number of people caught up in this sort of process of fashioning their own afterlife, their own memorials or artificial bodies. Speaking of speech-writers, law-writers, orators, politicians, professional rhetoricians, even philosophers—in short, the literati—Socrates demonstrates their failure to escape the old categories, their failure, that is, to transcend nature with their art or to regularize the law and violence of nature into the pastoral or agrarian routines of Golden Age shepherd-kings (*Statesman* 275–76).[31] In defense of Lysias, for example, Socrates claims that legislators in general are "most fond of writing and leaving writings behind them" so that they can "attain immortality as . . . writer[s] in the state."

---

31. Pierre Vidal-Naquet illuminates this disparity between nature and history, but he misses Plato, I think, by following the Eleatic Stranger's more serious "rustic wisdom" in "Plato's Myth of the Statesman, the Ambiguities of the Golden Age and of History," *Journal of Hellenic Studies* 98 (1978): 132–41.

The immortal striving of the legislators and Socrates' mordant comments on it recall again the hazards of glory seeking and the ambiguity of portrait settings that might usefully be borne in mind here. One might see such self-portraiture—for that is what this glory seeking amounts to—as framed in a double aspect. First, there is the fiction of the pose, the aspect of self-fashioning or self-mastery for the ages, which in the manner of the immortal longings described by Diotima in the *Symposium* aims to transcend time and change by means of its idealized, perfected, enduring work (*Symposium* 207C–209E). In her enlightened view, Diotima qualifies many things as such monuments or artificial bodies: She includes children, loved ones, poems, laws, and institutions, to which we might also add statues like Midas's or like those proposed by Phaedrus (253D) or the portrait in gold of himself reportedly erected by Gorgias at Delphi.[32]

As a second aspect to such portraits, however, comes something like a palinode or playback—what happens to the glorified monument when actuality takes it in hand. This aspect would include the portrait's setting, its framing, its reception, and its transmission. The contrast between the portrait's subject and its varying settings will always arouse a sense of difference that tells on the idealization of the pose or presentation. Sometimes this difference generates admiration. Like-minded sages of after-time, like Diotima, perceive these works as challenging, artful, in a sense still-living self-assertions of a more heroic age worthy of envy and emulation. Sometimes this difference induces condescension, like Protagoras's view of the old closet-sophists (*Protagoras* 316D–317C). Sometimes these old portraits set off more complicated interaction and alternation of these views. Mindful of their jeopardy, some sophisticated memorials (tombstones, poems, constitutions) try to internalize, design, or condition the sort of change they expect to continue to undergo. And of course I have been all along trying to keep in view how Plato does this, too.[33]

Like his comments on speechwriters and legislators, Socrates' marvelous recitation of the jostling among the rhetoricians in their mutual

---

32. Pliny, XXXIII. 83.
33. Speaking of the end of the *Republic*, Bruce Rosenstock writes how "Plato sets us the task as readers of attempting to cure (*therapeuein, Charmides* 157A) ourselves of the *planē* which arises within ourselves from the conjunction of, at once, the semblance of the text's self-contained integrity and the awareness of the irretrievable absence of the origin of that semblance," "Rereading the *Republic*," *Arethusa* 16 (1983), pp. 242–43.

competition also nicely illustrates Diotima's claim that "men's great incentive is the love of glory, and their one idea is 'To win eternal mention in the deathless roll of fame.' "[34] Socrates at first suggests this motive by mentioning the contenders in rhetoric under heroic pseudonyms—Nestor, Odysseus, Palamedes (261B–D). Later he will describe their contributions in mock-heroic terms that yield an ancient battle of the books. And part of the mockery stems from the suggestion, perhaps inspired by names like Hippias or Polus, "horse" or "colt," that Socrates herds these disputants around like tame animals in the condescending show of his mastery of them. He scoffs while the rhetoricians stake claim to immortal glory in the "deathless roll" of rhetoric texts. Some of Socrates' animus in this narration must stem from the way these books come forth indifferently titled after both art and self-proclaimed practitioner, so that the book about rhetoric by Theodorus (266E) is equally the "Theodorus" (in this case, "the gift of god") or the "art of rhetoric" or simply the "art." This strikes Socrates, as Cleobulus struck Simonides, as laughably presumptuous. Where Socrates, as we have repeatedly seen, might wish to problematize differences among art, artist, and person, these rhetoricians in effect would make the art the means to their own greater glory and the books entitled arts their artificial bodies or personal monuments.

An apparently culminating instance of this concern for immortality occurs with Socrates' portrait of the fully accomplished person, an adept in dialectic and other arts, "he who has knowledge of the just and the good and the beautiful" (276C). This instance shows the inevitable instability within the assertion of a stable relationship between the accomplished person and his works, his reproductions, his accomplishments. And as with his earlier, hopefully accented specifications of rhetoric, Socrates lets this wish-fulfilling view of a productive magisterial or hierarchical relationship speak through him; but in staging this voice, in impersonating it with his customary dissembling, Socrates also means to render its instability. The passage interweaves an Ion-like sense of omnipotence with a complementary Ion-like sense of vulnerability. This difference between dialogical tones that we can read and monological tones that Phaedrus thinks he hears marks the crucial difference between Socrates and the accomplished man—a sophist, a rhetorician, a master of arts—that Phaedrus mistakes him for.

---

34. *Symposium* 208C. This is the translation of Michael Joyce in *The Collected Dialogues of Plato*, ed. Edith Hamilton and Huntington Cairns (Princeton, N.J.: Princeton University Press, 1963), p. 560.

Socrates portrays such an accomplished person in the course of his discussion of correct writing. Only under certain conditions and in a certain manner would such a person consign his wisdom to written memoranda, which so imperfectly reproduce his living truth. As with the accomplished rhetorician earlier (271A–B), Socrates now again suppresses the unlikelihood that there is or could be a person of such accomplishment. He instead lets Phaedrus revel in the possibilities of "the man who can find amusement in discourse, telling stories about justice, and the other subjects of which you speak" (276E). Phaedrus's reply already suggests his inference that Socrates, like all the other wise men, intends his own accomplishment to shine through his false modesty.

Thus what may look to Socrates like the distant ideal of the dialectical art and its use (276E) to Phaedrus takes on the aspect of what one, properly schooled by a *sophos,* or sage, might become—the aspect, that is, of a wish-fulfillment fantasy quite in tune with Phaedrus's uncritical sense of pastoral escape and natural self-expansion. The anonymity of Socrates' portrait of the accomplished man—through most of it he is not termed a philosopher or dialectician, but left an indefinite person who knows or uses these—may invite such a fantasy response by encouraging one to identify or to identify with this heroic, larger-than-life figure, the immortality of whose accomplishment may rub off on your mortality as well (277A). All the more interesting then that Socrates seeds this discussion with the counterheroism of the accomplished person's busy, careful efforts to preserve his heroic, larger-than-life being.

To minimize the hazards of transmission to his truth, the accomplished man, says Socrates, should avoid the bastard medium of vulgar letters and cultivate the legitimate "word which is written with knowledge in the mind of the student and is able to defend itself, knowing to whom one must speak and before whom one must keep quiet" (276A). A word written within Phaedrus is prompt to take up this cue, assured a friendly hearing: "You mean," he says, "the living and breathing word of him who knows, of which the written word may justly be called the image." Commentators who wonder at Phaedrus's uncharacteristic alacrity in this remark miss the likelihood that he is quoting or paraphrasing some accomplished man—Alcidamas, perhaps.[35] So prompt a Phaedrus should

---

35. See DeVries, *A Commentary on the "Phaedrus,"* pp. 254–55. Plato is also having Socrates quote commonplaces of Isocrates—see Paul Shorey, "*Phusis, Meletē, Epistēmē,*" *Transactions of the American*

put one on one's guard as to whose game is being played out in this purportedly Socratic discourse, especially when Phaedrus's remark already shows the shaping powers of reception and preconceived notions over the apparently autonomous and magisterial inscription of Socrates' speech. Indeed, these powers have already infiltrated Socrates' presentation, splitting it, as they did his palinode, into a multivoiced discourse.[36]

The difference between vulgar and spiritual writing, Socrates proceeds to suggest, perhaps resembles the difference between the genuine farmer and the holiday gardener.

> A sensible farmer, who was anxious for seeds which he wished to come to fruition—would he in all seriousness plant them in summer in a garden of Adonis and rejoice to see them becoming beautiful in eight days? Or would he do this for playful holiday amusement when he did this at all? When he was serious, using the farmer's art, wouldn't he sow the seeds in fitting soil and be content when those he sowed came to perfection in eight months? (276B)

The loaded point of reference in this comparison is nature or naturalness (forcing gardens are, in this view, unnatural), so Socrates in effect declares the naturalness of certain rhetorical kinds and educational settings. "One having knowledge of the just and the beautiful and the good"—again, remember that this is assuming a lot—will not so lack sense that he will sow his seeds through a pen.

> No, but he'll sow in literary gardens, it seems, for playful amusement and will write, when he writes, to treasure up reminders for when he approaches the forgetfulness of age and for all who follow the same track, and he will be pleased seeing the tender shoots springing up. When others employ other amuse-

---

Philological Association 40 (1909): 194–98. This possible anachronism may take a slap at Isocrates' derivative views, but, more powerfully, the circulation of these commonplaces contradicts a key difference from writing claimed for embodied *logos*—its animation, its powers of self-knowledge and self-defense, its faithfulness to its "father." It is Phaedrus's use of the term *eidōlon* for writing that is partly at issue here. This term in Homer and elsewhere denotes the shadowy soul of the dead that the living *logos* would in effect ward off.

36. Mikhail Bakhtin, *Problems of Dostoevsky's Poetics*, trans. Caryl Emerson (Minneapolis: University of Minnesota Press, 1984), pp. 181–203, elucidates various forms of this multiple voicing relevant here—dialogue, conditional speech, parody, first-person narration, quotation.

ments, refreshing themselves with symposia and other things akin to these, the former one, it seems, instead of these will pass the time playing as I've said. (276D)

The general sense of this analogy of writing and gardening is plain enough, but this view of writing also begins to reveal some chinks in the armor of the accomplished man. The gardens of letters are coextensive with autobiography: Such writing can help repair "the forgetfulness of age" and also, by keeping one from symposia and related activities, help minimize physical damage from other pleasures. This character—forgetful, dying, carefully treading the line between seriousness and play, wary of pleasure and pain—on second thought may seem neither heroic nor larger than life despite his aspirations to be so. Despite the nodding impressions of Phaedrus that Socrates speaks in earnest, these features of the description indicate Socrates' detachment from this ideal type, which actually palely reflects the type of the lawgiver earlier alluded to (257D–258C). The public legislator here gets scaled back to a sort of closet lawwriter building modest castles in the air, a closet sage who evokes Phaedrus's rather than Socrates' or Plato's milieu. This portrait shows a reproduction of the wise man dominated by the reproduction of Phaedrus.

After the earlier pastoral economies we have tracked, perhaps some additional compensations at work in the vegetable analogy of reproduction are obvious enough—for one, the upward striving that entails downward comparisons. Notice, too, the classic hobble-step frontward and back from pastoral to georgic, from herding animals to the more settled and civilized cultivation of plants. The autoeroticism that figured in various places of Socrates' palinode now also returns as the extreme "self-moving" of autogenesis, a self repairing itself by itself. And Socrates' comparison is also quite clear about its escape from human sexuality, not only in its weakly sublimated language of insemination but also in the seeds' eight months' term and in the somewhat regrettable recourses to the gardens of Adonis, which seem to have been the special delight of town prostitutes,[37] with whom it is tempting to identify them here.

Beneath what seems a sentimental appeal to the emeritus philosopher, there stirs a negative effect, like that of Midas's epitaph, to the argu-

---

37. Detienne, *Gardens of Adonis*, pp. 64–66.

ment's commitment to a merely pastoral view of natural regularity. The teleology of fruition also incorporates the seeds of degeneration; against the farmer's "perfection in the eighth month" comes the "forgetfulness of age" and the implied fragility of the natural body. The discourse that is like a body in this way would entail the body's destiny, its anxiety, its decline of the sort Diotima emphasizes in her account of the debilities of human nature (207D–E). And so the "same track" others will follow intimates the eternal recurrence of growth and decay, which the argument both valorizes in the criterion of naturalness and, in its concern with immortality through reproduction, strives to escape, a recurrence that the argument thus both accepts and resents.

This preoccupation with the physical leads to a gross miscalculation of writing's power and durability. Amid such consciousness of the physical, writing is not a durable enough body; it too much resembles those defects of actuality that threaten to overturn the accomplished man's accomplishments. Writing must be mere play, not only because it is pleasurable, but also because it is ephemeral and pathetic, because letters are doomed by their unreconstructed matter and their apparent lack of power or resistance. We must shun Adonis of Byblos, perhaps, as a prophylactic against too compromising a love of him. To secure the seed more surely,

> one employs the dialectic art, taking a heedful soul, and plants and sows by means of knowledge words [*logous*], which are capable of helping both themselves and him who planted them and are not fruitless but have seed, whence others in other characters spring up able to render this [seed? sower?] deathless for ever and make their possessor as happy as is possible for a human. (276E–277A)

Maybe the reproduction of philosophy can be thought to occur in this way according to a legislative poetics of noble lies and unwritten constitutions; but like Derrida (p. 172), I think that so peculiar a way of portraying intellectual continuities invites its Simonides to question this triumph over biology from within biology by the slender means of apotropaic figures that try to harness the power they dread. How can the critic of aftertime *not* question this rhetoric of soul, which tries to let go of corporeal nature (it must some day) but only strengthens the soul's debt to the body in the process, caught within the logic of the tomb or artificial body?

The description of soul-seeding makes it ambiguous whether the process would render the seed or its sower *athanatos*, immortal, divine—whether, that is, the fable would preserve the thinker or the thinking. But this ambiguity disappears as soon as one recollects that it is exactly the *logos* that the fable, indeed this whole scene, suppresses. Even allowing the dubious metaphor, the fable concerns discursive seed, not seminal discourse; it concerns a discourse reproducing itself in bodies, not bodies processing themselves into discourses worth saving. It concerns souls being written upon unawares, not souls questioning, talking, learning.[38] True to Diotima's rather cynical view of masculine striving, it is the individual that would be returned in the seed, hopefully arresting the flow of natural reproduction by his genetic engineering of his particular truth, a personal truth apparently needing his personal care to sustain it. Such rhetorical reinscription of nature into memorial art, says Socrates, represents "the farthest possible limit of human happiness." He neglects to point out here, as he will in the *Phaedo*, a consequence of what Vermeule calls "hope and delusion, as winged and weightless as the *psyche*": how the attempt to deify physical concepts also sets the stage for disappointment and misologic revulsion (*Phaedo* 89C–91C).

By contrast to this accomplished man with immortal longings for his

---

38. Bakhtin again offers a relevant distinction and description that illuminates some of the specifications missing from Socrates' strictures. Bakhtin contrasts "internally persuasive discourse" to discourse that is "externally authoritative":

> ... consciousness awakens to independent ideological life precisely in a world of alien discourses surrounding it, and from which it cannot initially separate itself. . . . When thought begins to work in an independent, experimenting and discriminating way, what first occurs is a separation between internally persuasive discourse and authoritarian enforced discourse . . . , the internally persuasive word is half-ours and half-someone else's. Its creativity and productiveness consist precisely in the fact that such a word awakens new and independent words, that it organizes masses of our words from within, and does not remain in an isolated and static condition. It is not so much interpreted by us as it is further, that is, freely, developed, applied to new material, new conditions; it enters into interanimating relationships with new contexts. More than that, it enters into an intense interaction, a *struggle* with other internally persuasive discourses. . . . The semantic structure of an internally persuasive discourse is *not finite*, it is *open*; in each of the new contexts that dialogize it, this discourse is able to reveal ever newer *ways to mean*. (*The Dialogic Imagination*, trans. Caryl Emerson and Michael Holquist [Austin: University of Texas Press, 1981], pp. 345–46)

While Socratic dialogue generally may aspire to the action of the internally persuasive word, Socrates' "accomplished man" in this particular context exemplifies much more the "authoritarian enforced discourse" from which Phaedrus, Plato, and we readers as well must separate our internally persuasive discourse.

discursive seed, it may be worth recalling how we have arrived here and what we are doing: You are following me, probably somewhat skeptically, as I try to read Plato closely while I am also trying to listen to a mischievous Socrates, who is deeply attuned to the pastoral of intellect and its abuses. This is a bitter harvest only if one expects real fruit for eight months' or eighty minutes' patience. Nor would I encourage, I think, an attractive possibility that also peeks out from such an ironizing of the patriarchal accomplished man, a possibility that Socrates himself labors to deflect: that we might be the children of a maternal Socrates, despite his claims of sterility; that we might be nurtured and fed by his imperfectly dissembled sufficiency, the very missing mother our accomplished man shies away from. Instead of this, I suppose, we might study what we really are, whether we are the offspring only of a natural process or also reproduced in some other way.

At the end of the *Phaedrus,* Socrates, author and praiser of the accomplished man, somewhat reluctantly defends Isocrates as the fruit of his philosophical farming. The similarity between the accomplished man and the unconvincing hero of, say, Isocrates' *Antidosis* can precisely indicate the failure of discursive insemination and the overturning of its monuments by a skeptical readership, the would-be master of beasts in his turn devoured.[39] But let this similarity also indicate that in leaving the farm to an Isocrates, Socrates makes possible a Plato in his garden of Adonis, where mourning supplies a pretext for perpetual recuperation. And if Socrates has erected the maidenly accomplished man as a kind of monument to his own Stesichoran quest of becoming his discourse, of finding a discourse worth becoming, let this memorial truly testify to what is missing: to a Socrates whose beauty is his passage through all those things that the accomplished man avoids—through *erōs,* through upstart learners, through symposia, through the main streets of the town, and yes, through books, where missing Socrates becomes the perpetual condition and the perpetual liberation of philosophy.

---

39. Isocrates' *Antidosis* or "exchange" (technically, a redress against evaders of Athenian liturgies) exemplifies many of the compensatory exchanges aimed at by Socrates' would-be accomplished man. Weakened by age, made indignant by backbiting, haunted by heroic models of virtue and valor, but still full of himself—Isocrates in his "apology" falls short of Plato's on nearly every count. For discussion of additional ways Isocrates might be implicated in the *Phaedrus,* see Malcolm Brown and James Coulter, "The Middle Speech of Plato's *Phaedrus,*" *Journal of the History of Philosophy* 9 (1971): 405–23; also Hackforth, pp. 10–12, 167–69; and deVries, pp. 15–18.

Seven / Derrida in the Prescience of Plato

*T*hough it has sometimes been the despair of scholars working in the traditional disciplines, the writing of Jacques Derrida illustrates the emergence of new perspectives that cut—some would say, slash—across what we customarily think of as philosophy, rhetoric, literary interpretation, criticism, and the history of all these enterprises. The generality of this impact, I suggested at the outset, usefully approximates ancient circumstances of the Platonic text in that Derrida's anomalous practices may be imagined in parallel with the anomalous practices of Plato's Socrates, about whom Derrida has in fact written. For the same kinds of complaints leveled at Derrida can also be leveled at Socrates, perhaps also at Plato, as I would like to suggest. I do not mean to make Derrida look good by denigrating Plato or Socrates; nevertheless, I would like to vindicate Derrida after a fashion, as well as to suggest by way of conclusion the challenge to method—to philosophy and to rhetoric both, that is—posed by a fascination for the paradoxical and the problematical within a Platonic tradition presumed to be more secure than it is.

Derrida's celebrated essay "La pharmacie de Platon"[1] strives to disclose deep inconsistencies in Platonic thought that stem from the seriocomic fact that this *logos*-loving philosopher must also write. According to Derrida, the face-to-face Socratic discourse of intention present to language is expressly betrayed by the shift of medium to Platonic writing, importing all of writing's transactions with the writer's absence, transactions therefore with death, deferral, and what Derrida terms *différance*. Derrida's explication of Plato is vigorous and, for *Tel Quel*, the radical journal where the essay first appeared, surprisingly learned and philological in its discursive style, as if to render conspicuous the traditional scholarship supplementing Plato and Platonism. In view of Derrida's thesis, this *Tel Quel* setting is perhaps more surprising than the essay's scholarly apparatus: What looks like a radical critique of Plato and of the intellectual tradition actually gives us more of the Plato we already know. Except for a few passages, Derrida's avant-garde reading is of the same old Plato, but of a Plato now viewed with a certain critical alarm rather than with donnish complacency. This alarm is aimed less at Plato's alleged political authoritarianism than at a logic of noncontradiction and excluded middles, of original and copy, that, passing under Plato's name, sanctions an authoritarianism permeating our very thinking.

Disappointed with this nonrevolution in philosophic thought about Plato, I wish in the spirit of Derrida's palinodic essay and in the name of the reader's license fostered there to reverse the inquiry. Rather than invoke the apparent "Platonism" of Derrida (and I use the quotation marks to signify my suspicion that we often strain for the *rumor* of a Platonic philosophy),[2] I intend, rather, by way of conclusion to review the Derrideanism of Plato. Let me explain. Derrida seems to deconstruct Platonism and to appropriate Plato's text to Derrida's textualist program. But many of Derrida's most interesting contentions—his most characteristic contentions—suit Plato and the puzzles raised for the dogmatist by

---

1. I cite the translation of Barbara Johnson, "Plato's Pharmacy," in *Dissemination*; I cite the French version from "La pharmacie de Platon" in *La dissémination* (Paris: Seuil, 1972).
2. More and more, Plato scholars have come to acknowledge what Werner Jaeger had stated back in 1912: namely, that in spite of everything "it will continue to remain a mere expedient when in the absence of other sources we attempt to get information concerning Plato's doctrine of ideas or number theory from his dialogues." Consequently Plato scholarship has concerned itself to an ever greater extent with didactic discussions of the academy, of which we no longer have any direct knowledge. (Gadamer, "Dialectic and Sophism in Plato's *Seventh Letter*," *Dialogue and Dialectic*, p. 94)

See also Berger's strictures against "Indirect Listeners" in "Levels of Discourse in Plato's Dialogues."

Socratic and Platonic play. In trying to appropriate Plato, in other words, Derrida is himself caught up in a play exceeding his *logos*; true to its title in an unheralded way, this essay, "La pharmacie de Platon," is Plato's, not Derrida's. But I also suspect that this assertion is too simple, both because rights and copyrights, proprieties and personae comprise interesting difficulties in Plato and because I do not think I have yet written anything Derrida would be surprised or dismayed to read. On the margins of his writings, in the traces and outlines of his grammatology, Derrida acknowledges repeatedly that he will be constantly stolen from himself by writing as he does, by writing as Plato did, by getting his fingers caught in textuality. The necessary Platonism of Derrideanism, which Derrida seems to lament, only inverts the necessary Derrideanism of Platonism, which Plato, according to Derrida, seems to lament.

In particular we find Derrida enmeshed in the memorable passage where Socrates contrives an Egyptian fable about the invention of writing and its momentous consequences for memory. Thanks to Derrida, this passage has quickly become a crux and a commonplace in contemporary interpretation and theory, as well as a reflexive fable into which Plato and Socrates for better or worse have been cast. According to Socrates, the god Theuth one day brings writing, among other recent inventions, to the great god Ammon (Thamus) for judgment. Theuth claims to have invented "an elixir [*pharmakon*] of memory and wisdom," but Thamus judges it "an elixir not of memory, but of reminding; and you offer your pupils the appearance of wisdom, not true wisdom, for they will read many things without instruction . . ." (274E, 275A).[3] Theuth, "the father of letters" (275A), apparently surrenders his children to this judgment, though there is more to say on this score later.

Derrida, for his part, offers an extensive and splendid reading of the scene, noting especially the *peripeteia* stemming from the ambivalences of the word *pharmakon*, which Fowler renders hopefully into English as "elixir," apparently taking his cue from Theuth, who tacitly solicits such a benign translation of his arts. *Pharmakon* may mean "remedy," in the light under which Theuth sees his invention, or it may mean "poison," in the light under which Thamus sees writing. Such translations as Fowler's, of which Derrida makes an issue (pp. 71–72, 97), defuse the deep ambivalences of *pharmakon*, prove uncannily complicit in an inten-

---

3. This is the translation of H. N. Fowler in the Loeb *Plato I*. Other translations of the *Phaedrus* from this edition are mine.

tion or communication that, according to the fable, never gets sent because Theuth abandons his project—or at least so much seems implied by the intention of the Socratic fable. These letters are apparently effaced at their origin, but, against this intention and in part thanks to Socrates, Theuth's Egyptian letters nevertheless arrive.

This scene between the two Egyptian deities culminates the dialogue's sometimes explicit, sometimes furtive, but at any rate pervasive concern with *pharmakon*. Socrates, Derrida points out, applies the same word to Lysias's written discourse (230D), which on this singular occasion charms the citizen beyond the walls. In this pastoral setting Socrates also imagines Orytheia's mythical death, a death occasioned by her play with Pharmaceia (229C–D). These references early in the dialogue herald the major scene about writing and memory. Theuth—for whatever, if any, reasons (he is Egypt's Hermes and Palamedes, after all, and so an unlikely ingenu)—dissimulates the evil repetition of the *pharmakon* (pp. 97–98) and, "with a humility as unsettling as a dare" (p. 94), offers it as a remedy for forgetfulness, an elixir of knowledge. In this dissimulation of the *pharmakon*, Theuth already models and mimics its potency, its capacity for deception or inversion. But the disguise is nevertheless incomplete, the *pharmakon* still a *pharmakon* (more so in Greek, of course, than in French or English). Theuth, that is, proves a foil of the potentate: He supplies an authoritarian Thamus his cue; he leaves it to Thamus to declare the poison of this *pharmakon* and to unveil Theuth's uncanny dissimulation (p. 98). As this scenario predictably unfolds, one wonders whether any look of surprise or dismay ever crosses Theuth's face (if text, or *logos*, had a face, that is).

The disguise of the ambivalent *pharmakon* as a remedy (a very imperfect disguise and thus perhaps obscuring a more profound dissimulation) sets the stage for the pronouncement of the king, for his successful warding off of a menace, and for the validation of his essence as Derrida's logocentric complex of father-sun-good-capital (pp. 81ff.). And Theuth, we are led innocently to assume by the story's abrupt conclusion, complies with the king's and Socrates' criticisms of writing by not coming to the defense of his letters. As Thamus claims,

> . . . once it is written, every word [*logos*] is spun round and round, among the heedful and the nonchalant alike, and it doesn't know to whom to speak and to whom not to; when ill-treated or unjustly reproached, it always needs its father's help, for it is unable either to defend or help itself. (275D–E)

Were Theuth less subservient to pharaonic despotism, he might sense an unjust reproach right here. The scene itself not only declares, but also actualizes, the king's criticism when Theuth leaves his alphabet in the lurch, undefended, helpless. It is interesting, however, that though letters have just been invented, Thamus already knows what to do with them, as if he recognized or remembered them. One wonders, again, whether any look of surprise or dismay ever crosses Thamus's face during this scene of judgment. In probing these multiple complicities, Derrida finds that the essence of father-sun-good-capital, the logocentric complex of preeminent value, is covertly indebted to the challenge of writing for the declaration or staging of its efficacy, as seriousness is indebted to play, workaday to holiday.

This complicity between servant and master continues to unravel in the dialogue concerning writing, education, and philosophy that follows Socrates' rendering of his myth. Writing obliquely rules the magisterial pronouncements of that discussion just as it ruled, obscurely and from the other side, the unanswerable verdicts of Thamus. Socrates and Phaedrus set about to distinguish good and bad writing, good and bad repetition, not original and copy. Platonism, Derrida rightly insists, preoccupies itself with imitations, not originals, despite the efforts in the dialogues to raise a logic above mimesis. Thus the theme of Derrida's study is the problem of repetition in Plato, who will reportedly not tolerate the problematic of repetition that Derrida marshals against him. Derrida claims that, given the reproductive operations in his ontology, Plato must insist on two distinct sorts of repetition (one good, one bad) that might make possible Platonic philosophy and, by extension, all of Western metaphysics. The catch, for Derrida and for Plato, is that these repetitions cannot be distinguished, certainly not by Socrates' cavalier appeal to "natural division" and the method of diairesis (265E–266C). "One cannot, *in the pharmacy*, distinguish the remedy from the poison" ("La pharmacie," p. 195, my translation; Johnson, p. 169).

Good repetition, as Plato (says Derrida) would like to declare it, is of *logos*, of *anamnēsis*, of Socratic presence and self-control—ultimately of father-sun-good-capital. To function successfully in the system of Platonism, *eidos* must offer itself to repetition, to reduplication, to a "legitimate" stamping out of its types, like sons faithfully presenting a living paternal truth. Hence the menace of mimesis and bad repetition, which is of writing, of *hypomnēsis*, of mythic difference and mimetic simulacra—ultimately of bastard-*pharmakon*-poison, an orphan copy that pitifully represents a dead or absent parent. As a paradigm of such bad repetition, writing too pointedly signals death, the absence of the author, that father of the discourse not there to defend his orphan. And the *pharmakon* of writing is thus a *pharmakos*, too: Asking for trouble, it is scapegoated for the sake of good repetition, which nevertheless appropriates writing in apparent bad faith at strategic moments in the Platonic text as *logos*'s own model and metaphor. Following Socrates' slander of writing in the *Phaedrus* is his curious discussion of the writing in the soul, the writing of dialectic (276A ff.) by the accomplished man we have recently met.

It is a problem for Derrida's analysis, I believe, that it makes this accomplished man out to be a Socratic and Platonic ideal, when both Socratic archness and a closely read Plato urge against this identification. Socrates' voicing of Phaedrus's desires, like his eliciting of Critias's desires, says more about pedagogical discourse and Phaedrus's hearing than about some unlikely candor from Socrates concerning sentimental hopes for his personal, substantive teachings. And if, like Derrida, we share or to a degree accredit Phaedrus's hopes for certitudes, this will only confirm the shaping power of tradition as we reproduce one venerable version of the missing Socrates that is Platonism.

But against the magnetism of this tradition, Plato, I believe, inclines us to retrace our steps, to flip back the pages, to turn back the roll, in search of another missing Socrates luring us like the Helen of Stesichorus, this one not a phantom Socrates in pastoral exile in Egypt, so to speak, but an agonizing Socrates biding his time among the heroic cognoscenti at Troy. Consider Egypt in this other light.

"One person is able to beget arts," says Thamus, lord of Egypt and philosopher-king, "and another able to judge their harmfulness and helpfulness to prospective users" (274E–275A). Apparently at stake at this meeting of gods in Naucratis is the decision whether to publish these arts or not; the great king is to decide their future. As we have heard, the problem with the letters that Theuth has just invented is that they would incapacitate people by rendering memory obsolete. With such external memorials people would "not practice their memory"; they would not "recollect on their own" (275A).

But Thamus's benevolent concern for the self-sufficiency of his subjects includes other interests as well, these more typical of the overlord, for memory supplies a form of discipline. Let writing weaken that and the real incapacities of the ruled would emerge—namely, their reluctance to be ruled. Theuth's pupils "will read many things without instruction and will therefore seem to know many things, when they are for the most part ignorant and hard to get along with, since they are not wise, but only appear wise" (275A–B). Here, I think, Thamus alludes to his real concern, otherwise muted in these and related discussions of the *Phaedrus*, which prefer one-way discourse, the authoritarian primal word that automatically inscribes value, automatically puts its receivers in their place unawares. This real problem is *reading* and the structures of plurality, election, selectivity, privacy, privilege, and autonomy that potentially attend reading, even in the ancient world. These are structures constituted by the book and its technology, structures that Thamus rightly perceives to be neither reliably privatistic nor hermetic. He already senses the unpredictable social consequences of reading. He already feels them on his horizon threatening institutional elaboration in a social revolution (like that of sixth- and fifth-century Athens, say) that will jeopardize the status of oligarchs and despots. Is it too much, then, to sense here a timeless mystification, as Thamus sees the passage from the sonorous primal word to rambunctious reading, fears for his own impending fall from power, and thereupon reframes this as his subjects' dangerous fall from innocence?

I presume that Theuth's other inventions, unlike writing, pass Ammon's inspection. Socrates, at least, lets them go without a doomsaying. These include—in a naturally ascending order—numbers, arithmetic, geometry, and astronomy, followed by draughts and dice (perhaps the contemplative sage turns to these when weary of those higher numerical mysteries) and, last and especially, writing (275D). In other words, Ammon (and Socrates) lets pass inventions that concern regularity and timelessness, on the one hand, and inventions that concern chance on the other. These are all neutral, impersonal, transparent to thought, in a sense given by nature and thus transpolitical, but in jeopardy of becoming subpolitical (cf. the analogous case of Pericles' use of Anaxagoran speculation—270A). Between the extremes of chance and absolute regularity fall the arts, like writing and memory, of most concern to the monarch as a temporal medium of authority. Hence my suspicions that Thamus's proscription of letters follows politic as well as theoretic lines. This proscription at any rate would facilitate his monopolizing of memory with certain contents—the *themis* or traditional wisdom of Thamus—at those worrisome points in human affairs that admit of controversy and variability. It is no coincidence that it is at just such points—in politics, in ethics, in war, in business—that the young, contentious, pluralistic Greeks are sometimes seen to differ most from the old Egyptians.[4]

One might imagine Thamus concerned lest his people not practice their memory of the old words and old ones, and instead, their minds freed by a new medium and its new forms, seek to find out new things. They would forget Thamus's judgments and apply the inventor's arts. And let us not forget, as Socrates well knows, how these things turn out—the Socrates who with the living memory of Ion interrogated a precisely similar structure of the portable past. Thamus's discretion is outflanked by the spread of letters, perhaps from this port called Naucratis, the famous trading center and crossroads between Egypt and Greece, the very name of which (suggesting "mastery of the sea") figures human power and art riding in triumph over the forces of nature. In the historical perspective of the opening of Egypt to Greek merchants, mercenaries, and tourists,[5] Naucratis epitomizes movement and change that is neither regular nor simply chancy. Its material and technical development tacitly argues against Thamus and against his monopoly of memory, the closure of Egyptian culture, or the finality of accomplishment assumed by Socrates' exposition. Socrates' recent definition of the rhetorical art has left everything yet to be done—true art, knowledge, and memory all yet to be provisioned—but in the fable he proceeds to indulge a Critias-like fantasy of such closure and completion whose reactionary impulses compete with its philosophical moral.

The Egyptian passage bears comparison to sections of Plato's *Meno* not only for its discussion of memory with complacent despots like Meno but also for its awakening, with graphic aids, of the potential of such enslaved or subjected intellects as Meno's novice geometer. When the overlord lacks benevolence, the lack of writing abets arbitrary rule—a fact an Athenian democrat would probably remember even if the common places of his town were not littered with the omnipresent documentation of *isonomia*, the published laws meant to ensure equality before the law. And amid much partisan talk of an unwritten "ancestral constitution," the Athenian democrat will be quite familiar with memory's more sinister note—namely, the expedient sense of memory as a medium in which it is possible to get people to remember such new things as ancestral constitutions, well-born lies, or Egyptian parables.[6]

---

4. For example, at *Timaeus* 23D–24D, or more extensively in Book II of Herodotus.
5. Hurwit, *The Art and Culture of Early Greece*, pp. 179ff.
6. On the publication of the laws, MacDowell, *The Law in Classical Athens*, pp. 41–48. M. I. Finley

So Thamus in the fable of Socrates, as well as in the *Phaedrus*, is framed by the irrelevance of his judgment or by the historical irony that took it away. Reading this futilely authoritarian Thamus out of both discourse and text, by realizing his expressed and implied fears, honors this passage as profoundly as Derrida's reading out of the *Phaedrus* a futilely authoritarian Socrates or Plato. And Derrida even suggests a useful mechanism for reckoning these differences within the fable. He attributes the differential capacity of the *pharmakon* to "Plato's anagrammatic writing"—that is, to

> the relations interwoven among different functions of the same word in different places, relations that are virtually but necessarily "citational." When a word inscribes itself as the citation of another sense of the same word, when the textual center-stage of the word *pharmakon*, even while it means *remedy*, cites, re-cites, and makes legible that which *in the same word* signifies, in another spot and on a different level of the stage, poison (for example, since that is not the only other thing *pharmakon* means), the choice of only one of these renditions by the translator has as its first effect the neutralization of the citational play, of the "anagram," and, in the end, quite simply of the very textuality of the translated text. (Johnson, p. 98)

As Derrida knows, such citationality—akin to Bakhtin's "double-voiced" or "double-directed" discourse[7]—also functions with intertextual ele-

---

discusses the vagaries of the *patrios politeia*, or "ancestral constitution," in "The Ancestral Constitution," *The Use and Abuse of History* (New York: Viking Press, 1975), pp. 34–59. We can number Critias, Cleitophon, Thrasymachus, and Isocrates among advocates of the slogan. One might nominate Critias the elder's overture in the *Timaeus*—perhaps the whole of Timaeus's discourse as well—as among works agreeable to a Thamus.

7. Bakhtin, pp. 185–86, emphasizes the split between discourse directed toward a referential object and discourse directed "toward someone else's speech." "If we do not recognize the existence of this second context of someone else's speech . . . stylization will be taken for style, parody simply for a poor work of art" (p. 185). For example, Plato's discourse: directed toward the objects of philosophy; directed toward the speech of Socrates. Another example: In the *Phaedrus*, Socrates is not only discoursing with respect to the objects "rhetoric," "writing," or "memory"; he is also discoursing with respect to the discourses of rhetoric (he names many of them—*Phaedrus* 266–67), the discourses of writing (Alcidamas and Isocrates, for example), the discourses of Egypt (of the elder Critias, Timaeus, Solon, or Herodotus), and the discourses of despotism (of Meno, of Thrasymachus, Callicles, the younger Critias, or Alcibiades, perhaps). This multiple-directedness of discourse does not take place entirely by choice, as Derrida explains; but it also does not take place without infinite chances for art, as Bakhtin explains.

ments larger than the word. In the Egyptian fable, for example, it also works with mythemes. If Thamus at center stage cites a philosophical voice concerned for the integrity of memory, at a different level of the stage he cites the voice of the Oriental despot interested in the social uses of memory. Socrates' double-voiced, anagrammatic speaking—his irony or dissembling—releases this citational play, here precisely with his quotation of Thamus, just as surely as Platonic textuality gives rein to a *pharmakon*.

Despite his respect for anagrammatic writing, Derrida finally apprehends here less a text for close reading and provisional decoding than a pretext that he reinscribes or translates so as to confirm Thamus-as-Socrates-as-Plato's fear of the bastard uses of textual authority: providing "learners apparent, not true wisdom," a sort of wisdom only too vulnerable to ordinary skepticism, let alone to deconstruction.[8] Let Derrida bear out Thamus's prediction of rambunctious readers as he marvels at the daring of Socrates' appropriation of writing, which first condemns it, then conscripts it for soul writing:

> Presenting writing as a false brother, at once a traitor, an infidel, and a simulacrum, Socrates is led for the first time to envisage the brother of this brother, the legitimate one, as *another sort of*

---

8. The byplay between Phaedrus and Socrates immediately following this story invites comparison with these Egyptian models. Departing from the pattern, Phaedrus speaks up in a challenge of Socrates' authority: "Socrates, you easily make up stories of Egypt or any country you please" (275B). In what really is a salient criticism of this parable, he accuses Socrates of a kind of new archaism, of passing off his own invention as anciently remembered and transmitted truth. Socrates retaliates to this charge less with an answer than with more of the same applied memory. Replaying the alliance of memory and personal authority in Ammon when confronted with an irreverent skepticism, Socrates needles Phaedrus into compliance:

> They used to say, my friend, that the words of the oak in the holy place of Zeus at Dodona were the first prophetic utterances. The people of that time, not being so wise as you young folks, were content in their simplicity to hear an oak or a rock, provided only it spoke the truth; but to you, perhaps, it makes a difference who the speaker is and where he comes from, for you do not consider only whether his words are true or not. (275C–D)

Overlooking the urbane disenchantment of this reproach, which is the very problem he had idly raised, Phaedrus accepts the false dichotomy between rustic credulity and modern sophistication. But even more than the validity or justice of Socrates' reproof, Phaedrus seems to obey its disciplinary force as the voice of a superior. Phaedrus will henceforth keep quiet, holding down his usual urge to answer back until, in concluding, he at last finds a chance to chide Socrates anew about a possible double standard in his treatment of Lysias and Isocrates (278E). The nice irreverence of his remarks shows Phaedrus's distance from the model pupil and from Egypt, as well as Socrates' distance from the model teacher and from Egypt.

writing: not only as a learned discourse, living and animated, but as an *inscription* of truth in the soul. No doubt one has the feeling of being before a "metaphor" here. . . . But it is not less remarkable . . . that the so-called living speech is suddenly described by a "metaphor" borrowed from the same order which it wishes to exclude from it, the order of the simulacrum. A borrowing made necessary by that which structurally binds the intelligible to its repetition in the copy, and the language describing dialectic could not fail to make appeal there.

According to a scheme which will dominate all western philosophy, a good writing (natural, living, learned, intelligible, interior, speaking) is opposed to an evil writing (artificial, moribund, ignorant, sensible, exterior, mute). And the good can be designated only within the metaphor of the evil. Metaphoricity is the logic of contamination and the contamination of logic. Evil writing is, to the good, like a model of linguistic designation and a simulacrum of essence. And if the net of oppositions of predicates which relate one writing to the other holds in its network all the conceptual oppositions of Platonism—considered here as the dominant structure of the history of metaphysics—one will be able to say that philosophy is played within the play of two writings. Even though philosophy would like to distinguish only between speech and writing. ("La pharmacie," p. 172, my translation; Johnson, p. 149)

The copy (apparent wisdom) resembles the original (wisdom), but this means that the original also resembles the copy, true learning resembling inscription—shades of the abyss opened by the *Parmenides* into which the so-called third man forever disappears. More exactly, for Derrida the economy of original and copy depends on *différance*, on writing before the letter, for its sense of resemblance and self-identity, since the copy must differ and the original must not. Plato, says Derrida, was unable to purify his philosophy of this crippling dependency.

In this long quotation, we have Derrida writing so large that even nearsighted readers like me can pretty well see what he is aiming at: first, the dominant structures of metaphysics as putatively established, with more or less violence, by Plato (whose writing follows after but also entails clearing away Socrates); but second and more particularly, that protean metaphoricity that has all these years through a succession of transformations outrun the ability of metaphysics to purify its concepts. Thought can simply not attain any stable leverage on this scene, writes Derrida, since its analysis implies the writing, the spacing, the *différance*, the metaphoricity that it would explicate at a distance from itself.[9]

The perpetual retreat or dislocation of critical standpoints in so general a writing, in an *archē*-writing before the letter, inevitably defeats intention, mastery, instruction, leaving only the chance of dissemination and in its wake the unpredictable, ungovernable fruit of dispersionary logical and literary labors. The fate of writing allies with the phenomenon of unmeant meaning and the tireless play of the signifier, the looseness, the wobble that results from stretching limited signs over limitless actuality. This play plays into the hands of readers and interpreters who inevitably write as they read, even when they intend only to read. "Dissemination" then becomes another name for what happens to signification as it fragments and flies off into different, competing, irreconcilable semes, crypts, senses, letters, orders—neither parts nor wholes. Take, for example, the disseminatory fade-out of Derrida's essay as it plays into one's hands. Derrida writes of Plato working after hours in his pharmacy trying futilely to purify his essences:

> The walled-in voice strikes against the rafters, the words come apart, bits and pieces of sentences are separated. Disarticulated parts begin to circulate through the corridors, become fixed for a round or two, translate each other, become rejoined, bounce off each other, institute an internal commerce, take themselves for a dialogue. Full of meaning. A whole story. An entire history. All of philosophy. (Johnson, p. 169)

There is much ordinary wordplay in this passage, but the last sentences also embody the disseminatory wordplay that the passage is describing: *Plein de sens. Toute une histoire. Toute la philosophie.*[10] When the "bits and pieces" of these sentences "are separated," notice how "disarticulated parts begin to circulate through the corridors" as *Plato* and *Platonist*: *Plein . . . Tou*; *Plein . . . Tou . . . une hist. . . .* Full of sound (*son*) rather

---

9. See Derrida, "White Mythology: Metaphor in the Text of Philosophy," in *Margins of Philosophy*, pp. 207–71. For an attempt to reckon with this poststructuralist critique of philosophical discourse, see Paul Ricouer, *The Rule of Metaphor: Multidisciplinary Studies of the Creation of Meaning in Language*, trans. Robert Czerny (Toronto: University of Toronto Press, 1977).
10. "La Pharmacie de Platon," p. 196.

than sense (*sens*), these fragments or "dissemes" in the Derridean manner show an encrypted Plato, buried in a textual *mnēma* or *sēma*, which provides the name of Plato as a subtext to "all of philosophy" and "all of a (hi)story" in a way not audible to the Platonizing philosopher and audible to us mostly with the sense of surplus sense, of something more than meets the eye or ear, thus of something that will escape the closed readings and determinations of our Platonizing thought.

Failing the utopian, and indeed misanthropic, ideal of insemination as archly eulogized by Socrates in the accomplished man of the *Phaedrus*, all communication involves the risk of dissemination. This word turns on several senses in the text of Derrida, but it is interestingly *not* polysemous. Empson's complex words are *poly*semous; Derrida's words are *dis*semous, exceeding the regulated economy of multiple senses that might be comprised in a lexical entry. But among the traces of this flight of sense we might glimpse these: a Latin sense, *semen*, the semen that aims to engender and reduplicate compliant readers, listeners, and soul children; and we have a Greek sense, *sēma*, a "sign" or "token," whence we get semiotics and "seme," the minimal unit of sense. But Greek *sēma* is also a gravemarker and, by metonymy, the tomb, what the parable's philosopher tries to avoid but also falls into by writing and by speech; no doubt because of *soma*, the body, our garden of Adonis—*soma sēma*, say the mystics; body is tomb. So far, perhaps, this *is* a kind of polysemy allowed in English, even though we have transgressed languages and lexical entries, even though these are not just any senses of any words, not just a random scattering among many possible examples. Rather, all these signs—and, it should be noted, how can one even get outside this complex to assert this?—all these signs are implicated in the fable of writing and speech and philosophy and a *parousia* of tradition as written by Plato and read by Derrida: signs and seeds and tombs and bodies—all implicated in insemination and seminaries and seminars.

But dissemination is an instance of *double*-writing. It denotes waste, spillage of seed, dispersion, diaspora, catachresis, masturbation, the women's forcing gardens of Adonis as opposed to the cultured insemination of farmers and fathers. If in this respect the prefix *dis*- denotes extension, in its more powerful sense the prefix *dis*- denotes negation, invalidation, sundering, division. This second sense of *dis*- cancels the whole concept, puts the whole thing "under erasure" along with its phallic thrust; "*dis*semination" both reinforces and undoes the castration anxiety. It indicates the reproduction and deconstruction of the family scene behind struggles for authority to which Greek literature (in epic, in tragedy, in philosophic dialogue) is no stranger. Dissemination finely figures the perplexed impulse to supplement ourselves so freely let to browse in the pastures of the *Phaedrus*, the impulse simultaneously to perfect and to deny nature, the impulse to construct human nature and thus, always already, to deconstruct the naturalness of human nature.

The striving for mastery, authority, and immortality depicted in the *Phaedrus* fables wishes to proscribe, but it thereby only occults such dissemination. According to the fable of the accomplished man, the teacher (or the king) claims the superior position (no doubt Plato would also include sexual practices in the series of isomorphisms implicated in this relation).[11] The speech claims that one can authorize, control, copyright one's discourse, and thereby immortalize one's proper self with all the blind, mechanical certainty of natural process. Here the possibility of intention—really of instituting and shoring up a metaphysical respect for intention—promises to confer a kind of immortality: The author is alive, if imperfectly, in his writing but on the model of sages in the oral tradition or of lawgivers of ancestral constitutions, he would be far more penetrating and alive as superego or introjected master, who has written on innocent souls as on paper.

Against this parable of first philosophers, inseminating origins, and patriarchal *logos,* semiotics raises the paradigm of language, over which no one has autonomous authority. What authority one does have is already compromised or alienated by one's yielding to the symbolic order, the community of speech—*ours* or *its,* not *mine.* And thanks to the structurality of language—this system of "meaning" constituted by traces, differences, oppositions, and relations—a reified meaning, specie, something to hold on to, to perpetuate, or to copyright is delusory. Language, according to this argument, will not stay put for copyright (it is not there to begin with) even if it made sense for somebody to own a piece of it:

11. A few references to a gathering focus of critical attention: K. J. Dover, *Greek Homosexuality* (Cambridge, Mass.: Harvard University Press, 1978); Eva Keuls, *The Reign of the Phallus: Sexual Politics in Ancient Athens* (New York: Harper and Row, 1985); David M. Halperin, "Plato and Erotic Reciprocity," *Classical Antiquity* 5 (1986): 60–80, and, more generally, "One Hundred Years of Homosexuality," *Diacritics* 16 (1986): 34–45. Of particular relevance to the *Phaedrus* and Derrida is Page duBois's "Phallocentrism and Its Subversion in Plato's *Phaedrus,*" *Arethusa* 18 (1985): 91–103; but see also her *Sowing the Body: Psychoanalysis and Ancient Representations of Women* (Chicago: University of Chicago Press, 1988).

> ... the writer writes *in* a language and *in* a logic whose proper system, laws, and life his discourse by definition cannot dominate absolutely. He uses them only by letting himself, after a fashion and up to a point, be governed by the system. And the reading must always aim at a certain relationship, unperceived by the writer, between what he commands and what he does not command of the patterns of the language that he uses.[12]

This inability to possess or make present, even while the written utterance dissembles possession and presence, produces a "blind spot":

> ... what we call production is necessarily a text, the system of a writing and of a reading which we know is ordered around its own blind spot. We know this a priori, but only now and with a knowledge that is not a knowledge at all. (*Of Grammatology*, p. 164)

Both now and *a priori,* both with knowledge and with no knowledge at all—not only is there code or system to chasten the pride of individual intention; this system also harbors a heart of darkness to perpetually displace structuralist or semiotic systematicity.

Written language, the language of a dead or absent author and of ephemeral, situated reader, typifies this pathos of blind and errant intention, but speech is also shot through with it, as Socratic conversation might well attest in its breakdowns, absences, and ironies, its pathos, blindness, and errancy. To be sure, one might object that our speech usually offers only a trivial case of Derrida's *archē*-writing, *textual* in these ways only by a quibble or by a monstrous eruption of the sense of textuality into conversation and into ordinary language situations where disseminatory accidents are usually negligible.[13] But despite colloquial

---

12. Derrida, *Of Grammatology,* trans. Spivak, p. 158.
13. Generally deconstructive criticism confronts traditional . . . texts with a maximum demand of truth and reliability, that by far exceeds the degree of truth these texts claim for themselves, and only by means of this confrontation can it finally bracket truth itself. Operating with the logical concepts of truth or falsehood, its semantic ideal ignores the whole tradition of a consensus-oriented concept of truth and the fact that philosophical texts often are content with the assent of a given audience. (Michael Cahn, "Subversive Mimesis: T. W. Adorno and the Modern Impasse of Critique," in *Mimesis in Contemporary Theory,* Vol. I, ed. Mihai Spariosu [Philadelphia: Benjamins, 1984], p. 58)
Because Socrates never reaches or is never happy with "the assent of a given audience" that he

appearances, the language of Socrates is not ordinary, and the text of Plato is no conversation.

Under the extraordinary pressure of Socratic critique, speech shows and suffers its textuality in the extraordinary causes of philosophy that Socrates claims should be one's ordinary concern. Socrates in a sense dies for this architextural quibble, since his uncompromising purpose in Plato's *Apology* is that he be *read* justly, not that he fully transpose his truth into our common speech; the responsibility for defense, for answering the *graphē*, is placed firmly on receiver or interpreter, not on sender or originator of discourse. And this problematical and virtually modern view of the production of meaning is entangled in the *Apology* in all the disputes about critical protocols that Socrates brings up but cannot resolve in his self-defense. The condition of oral textuality dramatized at its worst in Plato's *Apology* is, of course, aggravated by Socrates' refusal or inability to write. Having been Socrates, he cannot suddenly become Plato—this is his symptomatic inability, to be imprisoned within a celebrity that is at once physical and cultural.

Enter this claim, at least, opposite more hopeful views of Socratic dialogue that imagine how its animating dialectic of desire might yoke respect for persons with respect for transhuman realities.[14] This more hopeful result might follow from dialogue in a more perfect world, but in Plato's world we do not see this happen. However much we might wish to make Socrates a champion of a new philosophic community, we do not encounter a dialogue of *two* Socratic worthies that might crystallize a new community and make good the romance of dialogue.[15] Hopeful speculation about Euthyphro's eventual conversion to virtue or philosophy, about Ion's amendment, or about Phaedrus's enlightenment—and

---

disingenuously seems to seek, one might conceive of him as collapsing Cahn's distinction: One imagines that Socrates might be "content with the assent of a given audience" to "a maximum demand of truth and reliability." Other critiques of Derrida relevant here can be found in Jasper Neel, *Plato, Derrida, and Writing*, pp. 187–93; Stanley Rosen, *Hermeneutics as Politics* (New York: Oxford University Press, 1987), pp. 50–86; and Robert Scholes, *Protocols of Reading*, pp. 50–104.

14. This desire might be tracked in the *Lysis*, for example, as Socrates' passion for friendship, his *erōs* for *philia* (211E), that somehow gets lost in the infinitely regressive circulation of exchangeable goods, a sublime wish undone by ordinary language's equivocation of *philos*—both "loved one" and "valuable thing."

15. Griswold bravely faces this anomaly of the dialogical ideal in *Self-Knowledge in Plato's "Phaedrus,"* pp. 225ff., and "Plato's Metaphilosophy," in *Platonic Investigations*, ed. D. J. O'Meara (Washington, D.C.: Catholic University Press, 1985), pp. 1–33, esp. 24ff. For a more generally skeptical discussion, see David Roochnik, "The Impossibility of Philosophical Dialogue," *Philosophy and Rhetoric* 19 (1986): 147–65.

evidence for these possibilities is conspicuously, brutally lacking—do no more than testify to the power of storytelling, as well as to the dialogues' arousing of wish-fulfillment possibilities that are subsequently frustrated by breakdowns in communication and community. It is hard to resist the conclusion that authentic Socratic dialogue among authentic persons is missing from Plato for structural or inherent rather than happenstance reasons—in other words, that such philosophy with Socrates is impossible, paradoxically that the desideratum for philosophy is a lack of Socrates. To philosophize, one needs a certain way of missing Socrates.

The Platonic program is premised on dialectical failure in a way that Socrates' own conversational vocation could not have been. Though *philia* or *erōs* or *to hosion*, for example, at best afford terms for an exploration and articulation of a problematic of self-transcendence and self-limitation, Socrates must try to make such terms constitutive of a new common sense. As is sometimes said of Derrida, Socrates must try to improvise metaphysics out of semantics, as well as to force the linguistic means of his peculiar *logos* to effect political ends. And he must do this in a conversational language that, weighed down by its embeddedness and embodiment, repeatedly reasserts its own sense, the sense of its language community. Though Socrates sometimes tries to make terms dependent on transcendences, the effect of this effort, alas, more often is to make transcendences depend on the happenstance conversations that Crito, Phaedo, and the others so keenly miss. The Socratic approach to philosophy, supposing this could be detached from Socrates, is doomed to founder on its inability to reckon its own precious failures, on its inability to economize, to think or represent in its practice the systematic difficulty of philosophy, which Socrates at times makes seem so easy, as easy as idle talk.[16] Socrates must always start from scratch, often from idle talk, though in always starting from scratch he misrepresents or dissembles the integrity, continuity, and sophistication of his project. This is his charm, I know, but it is a very mixed blessing. Plato's writing, on the other hand, does economize, affording Socratic improvisations the standpoint of a more coherent Platonic project—a literary project. The particular text economy I have sought to describe supplies a

---

16. Rosen, "*Sōphrosunē* and *Selbstbewusstsein*," pp. 639–42, describes this inability in a Hegelian perspective as a liability of the Socratic school, including Plato; Griswold, "Plato's Metaphilosophy," tries to pay off these Socratic liabilities through an exploration of Plato's "metaphilosophical" differences from Socrates.

precious recourse, or *poros,* to the philosopher closed into the *aporia* of endless conversation with persons who too much fear or reverence, hate or love him to know better.

In this light, only the differences between Socrates and his discourse might herald what Derrida has sometimes tracked as the "blind spot."[17] The differences between Socratic discourse and Platonic writing, by contrast, do not seem at all blind and so do not amount to a productive turn, visible only to a deconstruction, a turn whereby Plato's writing pairs and repairs Plato's thinking. This would be to task Plato for being insufficiently dialogical after, like Derrida, one had apparently ignored not only the dialogue format of Socratic philosophy and the indeterminacies of Socratic irony but also the much more complex and open exchanges of which Plato's writing is so mindful, exchanges across time and media between an embodied, oral, face-to-face Socratic philosophy and the Platonic text that, apparently lacking an author, exhibits that disconcerting openness of texts that Barthes termed "writable." Platonic textuality is structured with layers of uncertainty, some described by Derrida, that later disappear from translation and commentary, including Derrida's translation and commentary. He writes as though Plato wishes or intends hierarchic determinations cited in the dialogues to be faits accomplis. It would be more accurate, I think, to say that Plato, with Socrates, explores the problematical personal and cultural conditions of such determinations; such literary and philosophical experiment inevitably opens his texts to interpretation that takes a part for a whole, a problematic for a faulty solution. But if Plato is *not* a whole, what we then face is a remarkable textual structure—Plato's anagrammatic writing in tandem with Socrates' anagrammatic discourse—that through this interplay both invites and defeats attempts to translate, appropriate, and finalize its game. The *pharmakon* is a power, like the charm about which Socrates teases Charmides (157A–C), and so it invites possession. But it is the power to be legislated rather than to legislate; one must play in its terms, and so it really dispossesses.

This openness is the structural condition of the Platonic dialogue of Socrates, even though a normative philosophical reading would like to restrict such openness to early, Socratic, or aporetic dialogues so as to set

---

17. *Of Grammatology,* pp. 141–64; see also Paul de Man, "The Rhetoric of Blindness: Jacques Derrida's Reading of Rousseau," in *Blindness and Insight: Essays in the Rhetoric of Contemporary Criticism* (New York: Oxford University Press, 1971), pp. 102–41.

apart and enshrine as positive philosophy serious dialogues with epistemological content genuinely authorized by Plato, dialogues assigned to the middle and late periods of Plato's reconstructed career. But such a chronological reading of the closure of Plato's career, attractive as it is, still depends on Socratic openness. Partly this is because we are more readily persuaded by certainty after doubt; more generally this is because what enables the supposedly positive content of some dialogues is the general possibility of refutation. The claims of these dialogues can be positive only because they might also have been refuted or perplexed. But our reading of Plato does not usually acknowledge or practice this general possibility of Socratic negation, instead assuming that Plato's style evolved away from Socratic examination as he developed positive philosophical doctrines, for example concerning the immortality of the soul.

The possibility of refutation, which invites a reader's intrusion at numerous points throughout even these late dialogues, is thus narratively dispelled so as to temporize contradiction: One lets late Plato correct early Plato, or one lets the history of philosophy correct Platonism, and so these *histoires* acquire more or less resolved endings. Such reading determines Socratic and Platonic seriousness and decides where Socrates, Plato, and other interlocutors properly differ. And such reading (begging the question, unguardedly abstracting from the dialogues its rules for reading the dialogues) aims such decisions at a text like the *Phaedrus*, where all such certainties are jeopardized, as Derrida has written, by the general possibility of writing, of play, of impersonation, of citation, of quotation, of grafting.

The *Phaedrus*, like all Platonic texts, is marked with conspicuous oversimplifications, with one-sided resolutions and conclusions, with expressed as well as displaced fantasies. Action within text, as well as within the imaginary staging of persons in conflict, defeats the effort to rein a *Phaedrus* into the traces of a philosophical common sense. The strife between the reductiveness of will, intention, or prudence and the inventiveness of interpretation, reception, or criticism is evident, for example, in Theuth's wish to see writing as the remedy for forgetfulness and as a shortcut to wisdom. Thamus, revising Theuth's intention, expands its domain and significance in interpreting Theuth's claim, but then he in turn falls to the delusion of limited context and self-present intention when he supposes that his decree banishes rather than borrows writing, when he supposes that he has the last word. Faced with these reductive assertions in the dialogue, with a will to power dissembling itself as a will to truth, Derrida's text is fascinated by the display of the irreducible *pharmakon*, the semiotic fluidity of which seems to underwrite philosophic assertion and authority. Like Thamus, Derrida thinks, Plato overconfidently invests in the economy of *pharmakon* and so becomes helplessly entangled in his own web, unable to rescue his own discourse.

But such reductive urges are not unique to this scene; they can, for example, be seen as pastoral urges that try by limiting context or environment to tame the difficulty of human being and human meaning. The entire dialogue addresses the ambivalance of *pharmakon* under the opposition of method (conceived as remedy) to madness (conceived as poison), and a more ambitious exploration of the Platonic repetition in this dialogue would need, for instance, to construe the apparently purposeful, or at least legible, oscillation between madness and method: from Socrates' first singing the praises of frenzy as he exits the city into the vibrant realm of myths and muses (228A–C) to his practicing the lover's methodical dissimulation as nonlover; from the apologetic praise of madness (in the frantic chariot race away from earthly *nomos*-as-law to heavenly *nomos*-as-fodder, 248B) and back again to method—the sophistic husbanding of education and discourse (as reflected, for instance, in the peculiar proximate ranking of husbandmen and sophists at 248E). Socrates' inhabiting of such contraries is hard to describe, though he regularly demonstrates such fluency, as if by sorcery, always supplementing the argument where arrest threatens. Such circling of a *logos*, like the spinning of chariot wheels, is probably not quite the compulsive repetition that Derrida suggests it is; indeed it may be, like Derrida's, a writerly repetition, a matter of style, a Socratic play that does not, because it cannot, say just what it means. It can only play between two writings. It is, perhaps, the mania or madness of interpretation, a kind of "reading-writing" that continually overturns the determinations of method prompted by the attempt of the speaker in Lysias's speech to master *erōs* with an art of self-fashioning. Thus as an interpreter of Lysias's discourse, a writing reader, Socrates already foreshadows the sort of openness, the critical *différance,* that implicates Thamus, Plato, Derrida, and others in this ludic subtext underwriting official tradition.

Yet if Derrida seems not to appreciate Plato's Derridean play with contradictions and oppositions within his text, we must still let Derrida off the hook for an analysis that tries to mitigate the reductive "effect of analysis" (p. 99). His 126 pages, after all, are offered as a kind of

Stesichoran afterthought to the first paragraph of his essay, as an apology or palinode to critical blindness, a musing on what Theuth, father of letters, *might have said* in their defense to Thamus, were not letters, by Socratic definition, defenseless. So Derrida does not even write of himself; he speaks for, he impersonates, Theuth. Or rather, his writing takes the place of the speaking that disappears into the alphabet. Such a self-effacing Derridean move away from the authorial center can help us acknowledge or appreciate similar Socratic and Platonic moves away from an omniscient center (say, at Delphi, whence the apologizing Socrates ironically claims to draw his authority). In particular, Derrida can and should help us transvalue the frustrations of the Platonism often taught in schools, the serious Platonism of forms and unity and vision and oneness, the Platonism not well documented by Platonic *literature,* the Platonism that is sometimes in some ways a rumor of a Platonic philosophy that has obscured the texts of a writer named Plato.

The texts of a writer named Plato do not disappear, like signifiers into their signifieds, into forms or ideas or transcendences. From the Derridean standpoint—and this point often proves relevant to Platonic textuality and to Socratic aporetics—neither philosophy nor literature can finally be about anything; there is no presence there for it to be about except grammatology, the study of failing-to-be-about, the study of frustrations of presence stemming from misplaced or overeager trust in transcendent signifieds and in their institutional adequations. Could this skeptical prospect of philosophy, now identified with Derrida, have escaped Socrates? Or the author of the *Parmenides?*

Despite appearances, this study of perplexity I hope involves more than literary ingenuity displayed in close reading, since the concept of transcendence in our tradition, in both its classical and Judeo-Christian tributaries, has proven to be the concept of authority par excellence. The perplexities heralded under such slogans as "the death of god" or "the death of the author" indicate a recurrent theme of Western civilization in its long struggle to cultivate and renew in depleted soil workable structures—poems, laws, institutions—of authority. Derrida's deconstructions, by working to advance a demythologizing, try to liberate Western thought from a tradition of Platonizing transcendentalism. By restoring, for instance, the ambivalences of *pharmakon* (which are lost to translation and tradition as they are not lost to Socrates, Plato, or text), Derrida aims to retrieve an "outside" impossibly outside the closure of Western metaphysics, an "outside" also sensed in the Platonic inside by

Nietzsche, Heidegger, and Freud—three other masterless men or antiauthors revitalized by Derrida's critical discourse. To bring this "outside" inside is of course to lose it in the translation or the metaphor, so instead of presenting it, one indicates the failure of closure of metaphysics proper, indicates the gaps in its inventory of all existents/existence.

Finally, Derrida's Plato would cut a finer figure if Greek tricksters, inventors, and innovators, not to mention philosophic epigones, behaved as it is implied that their Egyptian counterparts behaved—if they had sat down and shut up as Theuth does in the fable. But this tractable spirit of Stesichorus, which preserves a benign Helen in Egypt, a pastoral Socrates resting in peace beyond the wall, did not, alas, prevail. Fact or chance or wind, weather, or war, that is, defeats magisterial opinion and majestical verdict: Neither Thamus nor Zeus had the last word in the ancient world, and Plato suggests that it is a rustic sort of wisdom that would fancy that he did. Theuth's alphabetic children defy the prolecide, run away from him, find defenders. The art of writing, like all such arts in this respect, is current and finding regulation beyond the utter prohibition; and if, in the face of Derrida, it is the *archē*-art, it will always be there anyway, hidden but traceable in its own proscription. Such art, after all, cannot itself be culpable—the fact that makes possible Theuth's, Ammon's, Socrates' and Plato's very different uses of the same art. Perhaps the more important and interesting problem exemplified by Greek experience, in contradistinction to Egyptian, is the sociology of *epistēmē* and *technē*:[18] the human and cultural dependence on arts, and the consequent independence and *hubris* arising from their mastery, a *hubris* that jeopardizes, as well as furthers, the cultural order, the *hubris* that plays between two writings. In germinal form this is a modern predicament anticipated in the modernism of ancient Athens, where religious transcendentalism placed a relatively ineffective restraint on technical enterprise.[19] According to this predicament, the technology that is our creature makes us its creature, and Plato gives this paradox particular expression in his gallery of epistemocrats and technocrats whose method becomes their madness, who are obsessed with method as a more becoming shelter for their obsessions.

---

18. If Prometheus introduces letters to the Greeks, as some say, the Greek equivalent to the Ammon-Theuth fable might be *Prometheus Bound*—for example, lines 436–71.

19. One might, for example, see Sophocles' *Oedipus Tyrannus* as offsetting Oedipus's "technical enterprise" with a remote, inscrutable, transcendental divinity.

In Socrates' commentary on his own myth, we hear a danger claimed for writing greater even than its threat to memory: "they will learn without instruction and so seem to be knowledgeable when for the most part ignorant and difficult to deal with" (275A–B). Here is the danger: that people, formerly written upon, their souls inscribed by sages accomplished in the legislative arts, will become readers; that as readers they will presume to strive to know or influence meanings; and that the presumption conferred by the power of interpretation will disrupt the usual expectations of downward flux from the head to the feet, from the father to the child, from the teacher to the student, from the past to the present. Whether we know it or not, reading and interpretation engage erotic and creative powers of invention and revision, and now that we know it—in part thanks to Ammon, Socrates, and Plato—we must reckon with those powers. Can we suppose that Socrates and Plato share a single view and a single anxiety, given this problematical model of succession? Is Socrates to dread the revisionary hand of Plato? Is Plato to resent or feel anxious before the original legislative influence of Socrates?

Socrates, thankfully, is a missing person in Plato; but first he is a displaced person. He is displaced by *logos* and by culture that make him, even to himself, "Socrates," not Socrates. He is unable to speak himself except as a repetition and performance. He is also displaced by the self-parody, whether deliberate or not, with which he routinely responds to the constraints of performance, misquoting himself in quoting himself. The *Apology*, though extreme, in this respect is also typical of the *Euthyphro, Ion, Charmides,* and *Phaedrus*. Socrates is also displaced by Plato, resurrected into the dreamless sleep of the dead letter, endlessly conversing in this afterlife, suspended between the wish and the fear with which he signs off in the *Apology* (40C–41C).

Socrates is read, and doubtless misread, in Plato's soul; but there can be little suspicion that a magisterial Socrates wrote there in the style of the *Phaedrus*'s anxious accomplished man. Missing Socrates, Plato reads a Socrates more beautiful and made new:

> ... the writing is a presentation that loves its own textuality as much as it loves and longs for, laments and mourns for, the speech it lovingly reconstructs and deconstructs. Socratic speech emerges in the dialogues as the fallen and secondary pre-text which contains hidden within itself, inscribed in the pervasive irony which Socrates' interlocutors never hear, the textuality of

Platonic discourse. But if Plato's text presents itself as primary and immediate, it remains a structure of mediations proclaiming the absence of Plato no less than that of Socrates.[20]

The "fallen and secondary pre-text" is paradoxically still prior, etched by experience that we can only reckon as its absence. More beautiful than whom? Made new from what? To suppose that Plato coolly makes Socrates his mouthpiece stretches psychological plausibility concerning Plato's debt to Socrates—concerning, perhaps, Plato's introjection of a real, remembered, or fantasized Socrates that, without the externalizing power of his writing, may indeed have threatened to render Plato a mere mouthpiece, like Aristodemus or Apollodorus of the *Symposium*. It may be enough to point out that what in Plato gets accomplished (I need the middle voice here) with, to, and for Socrates is not even remotely matched in the history of literature or philosophy, and so it is very hard to reckon many of the commentaries' frequent appeals to common experience or common sense in deciding the innumerable intricacies of this utterly uncommon case.

What a man named Plato might have wished to do with a Socratic legacy in this view disappears into what he did or, rather, into what results from this symbiosis of Platonic text and the Socratic pre-text. Plato has not simply overcome or transcended Socrates, becoming his teacher's teacher, by incorporating the Socratic *archē*-text into his "own" work. Nor has a "late Plato," I think, factored Socrates out of the philosophical equation by displacing him with a philosophical system, a kind of ontological *langue,* or grammar, of Platonism purified of the troublesome Socrates. Nor has Plato pursued a subtler reduction by exalting a heroic Socrates, owner of an untranslatable *parole,* or speech, and authenticator of a unique existential instant. Instead, as we now well know, the standoff occasioned by the paradoxical Plato-Socrates relation very imperfectly orients philosophy toward its future and subjects its fortunes to Hellenic time, Hellenic tradition, Hellenic human nature, and a Hellenic actuality—all of which resist direct attempts to smuggle into Egypt and secure there philosophy's *eidōlon*.

Platonic philosophy, as I have tried to describe it, faces these problems in the translation or transmission of human thought, but does not find—has not yet found—their solution. So I write of a paradoxical Plato-

---

20. Berger, "Facing Sophists," pp. 66–67.

Socrates relation as helpfully descriptive of Platonic philosophy's *problematic*. Like the *problēmata* cited in my epigraph, the problems of Plato's writing constitute defenses and projections, shelters and figures—constructions, really, against perplexity. They enable movement in the *aporia;* they allow something, perhaps philosophy, to proceed; they allow exploration, experiment, study, inquiry. And of course they allow new souls, new settings, new voices, readers, and interlocutors to intervene. Such a problematic follows the track of a Socratic traveler who, in fact, never did or never could renew the inquiry from the beginning, but in his own defense could only project or reorient questioning within certain horizons or foregone conclusions.

I am aware that Plato emerges from so sympathetic a reading as a can't-lose language machine productive of both Platonism and its subversion by the spirit of Socratic (and other) critique, a Plato that I may have further made out as an epitome of a "tragical-comical-historical-pastoral" literature. But since this is the fact of the case, it is impossible to describe a weaker Plato. The real challenge set by Plato—of course I refer not to the person but to the text, the *problēma,* as I have sought to describe it—is to understand and account for this productivity, to articulate internal proportions as convincingly as possible across external functions. This is less to render a true and final reading of the text (unlikely at this or any hour), or to sanction one Platonism rather than another, than to see all these consequences as indications of the particular form of Plato's text and as functions of its institutional pertinency throughout our tradition.

Let us leave it, in lieu of conclusion, as a question of isolated moments (Thamus rejoining Theuth) within larger movements (the dispersion of letters). By way of an inventory of the pharmacy, we might add up some themes, some gifts and antidotes passed back and forth: of a holiday garden against the seasonal farm, of repetition as indeterminate and ephemeral play (at most a moment plucked) against good, orderly repetition (history as Egyptian routine, best intelligible to the Greek in utopian lights), of rhetorical *kairos* against sophistical theory, ultimately of the Socratic career against its Platonic revision and appropriation in the present tense of the dialogues. This is to say, the consignment of Socratic corpus to its Platonic monument.

If I may hunt puns in Plato, flashing reader's license, a suggestive symbol of all these for me is the Plato-tree (*platanos*—"plane tree") that shades the *Phaedrus*'s Socratic holiday from the sun (and father-good-capital). This tree, an image of long time focused on short time, the unexpected fruit of Socratic dissemination, mocks the pretensions of the dialectical farmer (patient through all of eight months—276B), but also makes Adonis, his gardens, and his mother Myrrha (Adonis, the tree-born god whose ritual center was Byblos, "papyrus," "the book") a more relevant symbol than the too-careful *georgos* for this Socratic moment. While Derrida explicates the problematic of misplaced mail—for example, a serious Plato's Second Letter, which, by arriving despite its sender's intentions, behaved too much like writing, not enough like speech—another Plato here celebrates in a zany way the ridiculous possibility that the letter Socrates never sent might arrive. The Plato-tree, that unheard-of letter in this inadvertent garden, suggests the permanence of Platonic textual music trying to mediate the impasses of culture in *krisis* and to stage a *kairos* for all history, *toute une histoire*. Philosophy is so unpredictable: From some flowers, Phaedrus-flowers, soon fades the promise of their beauty or their passion; and some trees give words, now that Zeus's oak at Dodona is silent and unheeded (275B–C).

Index

The index does not discriminate between such historical personages as Protagoras, Alcibiades, or Socrates and their fictional representations in Plato.

Academy, 1, 21
Achilles, 42, 43, 94
Adonis, 21, 150 n. 21, 167, 196
  gardens of, 165, 166, 183, 196
Aeschylus
  Eumenides, 70 n. 25
  Oresteia, 11
  Prometheus Bound, 192 n. 18
Agamemnon, 4
agōn (stuggle), 34
aidōs (shame, respect), 114
Alcestis, 3
Alcibiades, 19, 27, 50, 52, 56 n. 2, 125, 129, 130, 131, 133, 147, 153, 154, 179 n. 7
Alcidamas, 35, 179 n. 7
Allen, R. E., 62 n. 13
Ammon. *See* Thamus

Anaxagoras, 43, 98, 154, 177
ancestral constitution, 178, 179 n. 6, 184
Anderson, A., 62 n. 13
Anderson, D. E., 61 n. 12
Anderson, W. S., 102 n. 25, 147 n. 17
Antigone, 3
Antiphon, 113
Anytus, 27, 37, 38
Aphrodite, 109
Apollo, 109, 122–25
Apollodorus, 56 n. 2, 194
aporia (perplex), 2, 13, 17, 29, 37, 40 n. 13, 102, 188, 195
  of Critias in the *Charmides*, 127, 129
Archilochus, 87
Aristodemus, 194
Aristophanes, 43, 107, 160

Aristotle, 7, 8, 9–10
  Metaphysics, 7–8, 90–91 n. 13
  Poetics, 8
  Rhetoric, 158, 159
  and *sōphrosunē*, 113
art. See *technē*
Asclepiads, 90
Asclepius, 88
ascription, 49
  and Socratic identity, 43
Athena, 63 n. 16
Athenian, the, 112
Auerbach, E., 12–13 n. 15
Austin, J. L., 56 n. 3

Babcock, B., 150 n. 21
Bacchants and Corybants, 100, 110
bad faith, 38–39, 42, 61, 73–74, 86, 98, 106
  in the *Charmides*, 127
Bakhtin, M., 165, 168 n. 38
  and double-directed discourse, 179 n. 7
Barilli, R., 9 n. 10
Barthes, R.
  on protocols, 3–6
  on readable and writable, 56 n. 2, 188
Belfiore, E., 147 n. 16
Benardete, S., 28 n. 28
Benveniste, E., 76
Berger, Harry, Jr., 9 n. 11, 26 n. 27, 38, 57 n. 5, 72 n. 29, 78 n. 34, 172 n. 2, 193–94
Blits, J., 62 n. 13, 65 n. 18, 76 n. 32
Bloom, A., 80 n. 2, 86 n. 8, 88, 95, 95 n. 17
Boardman, J., 135 n. 1, 145 n. 12, 146 n. 14
Bolgar, R. R., 13 n. 15
Boreas, 68, 149
Brann, E., 33, 34, 34 n. 5
Bremmer, J., 148 n. 18
Breull, C., 112 n. 8, 127
Brown, M., 169 n. 39
Burger, R., 21 n. 24, 141 n. 7, 153 n. 26
Burke, K., 138 n. 5
Burkert, W., 69 n. 23, 76 n. 33
Burnet, J., 60 n. 12, 65 n. 18, 69 n. 22, 72 n. 28, 74
Byblos, 196

Cahn, M., 185 n. 13
Callicles, 27, 40 n. 13, 179 n. 7
Calypso, 147–48
Campbell, B., 106 n. 1
care, 59 n. 7
  and carelessness, 69–71
  and Meletus, 59
Cebes, 2, 13, 33
Centaurs, 149
Chaerephon, 43, 117 n. 12

charisma
  of the person, 90–91, 110
  of the text, 18–20
  and tradition, 86, 98
Charmides, 188
  character of, 111, 131–32
  as showpiece (*agalma*), 114, 131–32
  and *sōphrosunē*, 114–15
Charrue, J.-M., 24 n. 25
Chimaera, 149, 154
Circe, 148
Cleitophon, 179 n. 6
Cleobulus, 142, 163
Clytemnestra, 3
coding of discourse, 4–7
  and decoding, 6
common sense
  and intellectualization, 106
  and sense of the *Apology*, 33, 34, 45
  tyranny of, 18–19
  and *sōphrosunē*, 112
communication. *See also* discourse
  and common sense, 50
  and dissemination, 183
  and ordinary language, 55–56, 56 n. 3, 75, 185
community
  and ascriptions, 43–45, 111
  and authority, 19–20
  in the *Charmides*, 111
  interpretive, 20
  and language, 59–60
  perversion of, 61, 78
  and philosophy, 60–61
Connor, W. R., 101 n. 24
Cook, A., 153 n. 26
Coulter, J., 169 n. 39
Critias, 5, 17, 26, 106, 159, 176, 178, 179 n. 6, 179 n. 7
  as imitator of Socrates, 121–22, 125–31
  as mentor of Charmides, 110–11, 126, 132
  and the *Sisyphus*, 113 n. 9
Critias the elder, 179 n. 6, 179 n. 7
Crito, 2, 27, 34, 41, 187
Culler, J., 95 n. 20
Cyclops, 60 n. 8
Cydias, 118–19

Daedalus, 87, 90
  statues of, 73–74, 154
Daumas, F., 21 n. 24
deconstruction, 25, 180, 188
  critique of, 185 n. 13
  of Socratic-Platonic charisma, 20
Delphi, oracle of, 33 n. 3, 43, 122–23, 156, 162, 191

de Man, Paul, 188 n. 17
democracy, Athenian, 38, 42, 101
  and "democratic man," 43–46
  and written law, 178
dēmos (the people), 5, 77
de Romilly, J., 9 n. 10, 97 n. 22
Derrida, J., 16 n. 18, 18, 24 n. 26, 60 n. 8, 95 n. 17, 95 n. 20, 115 n. 11, 171–76, 179–85, 187–92
  and the "blind spot," 185, 188
  and citationality, 179–80, 182
  critique of Platonism, 172, 175–76, 180–83, 188, 190
  and deconstruction, 16–17, 185, 191–92
  and dissemination, 71 n. 26, 182–84
  grammatology of, 46, 48, 191
  like Plato, 24–25, 171
  and mail, 16–17, 196
  and metaphysics of presence, 25, 180–82, 191–92
  and ordinary language philosophy, 56 n. 3
  Phaedrus, interpretation of, 138, 167, 173–82, 189–91
  "La pharmacie de Platon," 172–73
  on Socrates-Plato relation, 45–48, 51, 179–80, 181, 188
  as Theuth, 191
Descombes, V., 49 n. 29
Detienne, M., 150 n. 21
DeVries, G. J., 141 n. 7, 164 n. 35, 169 n. 39
dialogue, 98–99, 188
  and commonplace examples, 75
  and community, 60–61, 73–74, 78, 186–87
  as conversation in the *Phaedrus*, 140–42
  dialectical art of, 164, 167, 175
  dialogical and monological, 163, 168 n. 38
  as documentary history, 10
  drama of, 22, 98
  impersonal, 48–49, 60, 125, 132–33, 155
  impossibility of, 74, 186–87
  object of, 48–50, 60–61, 78, 117
  philosophical, 7, 159–60, 189
différance, 16, 47, 51, 172, 181, 182, 190
Dimock, G. E., Jr., 60 n. 8
Dio Chrysostom, 143–44
Diogenes Laertius, 10, 142, 144
Dionysus, 4, 109
Diotima, 108, 162, 163, 168
discourse. *See also* logos
  authoritarian, 99, 168 n. 38, 177, 184, 189–90, 193
  compared to text, 22–24, 57, 156, 185
  doubled in the *Euthyphro*, 61, 71–76
  fractured in the *Charmides*, 116, 126–27
  as function, 158–59

  as living being, 139–41, 149, 151, 153, 159, 161, 164, 165 n. 35, 168–69
  as medium of institutions, 28, 97–98, 101, 105–7, 187, 191
  mimetic and diegetic, 4
  multivoiced, 165, 179–80
  natural vs. artificial, 57 n. 5, 117 n. 12, 155–56, 160–61, 165–69, 184
  oral, 9–10
  of the rhapsode, 84–85, 99–101
  shaped by auditor, 27, 36, 41–45, 98, 119, 130, 164–65, 166, 176
disenchantment, 97–98, 154–55
  of Athenian society, 26–27, 105–6
  and Critias, 132–33
  and rhapsodic enthusiasm, 81–86
  and Socratic charisma, 26–27, 187–88
dissemination, 16, 25, 59, 71 n. 26, 196
  described, 182–84
  of Zeus, 71
Dodds, E. R., 63 n. 17, 114 n. 10
Dorter, K., 21 n. 24, 80 n. 2, 94 n. 16
Dover, K. J., 184 n. 11
drama, 99
  in the *Charmides*, 116–17, 120, 126–27
  in the *Ion*, 102–3, 103 n. 26
  protocols of, 3–6
  and rhapsode's theater, 85–86, 94
  and spectacle, 8
  and theater in the *Apology*, 37–38, 41–42, 47–48
duBois, P., 137 n. 4, 184 n. 11
Durkheim, E., 19 n. 21
Dyson, M., 109 n. 2, 120 n. 15, 133 n. 24

Edelstein, L., 2 n. 1, 3 n. 2
Egypt, 136, 173, 176
  contrasted to Greece, 178, 179 n. 8, 192, 195
eidōlon (shade), 2, 13, 165 n. 35, 194
eidos (idea, figure), 71, 115 n. 11, 175. *See also* idea
  and *sōphrosunē*, 114
eimi (go) and Ion, 58
Eleatic stranger, 13, 28, 29, 52, 160, 161 n. 31
Electra, 3
Empson, W., 183
enunciation and enunciating, 49
Epeius, 87, 88
epistēmē (knowledge), 93, 121, 125, 129, 130, 192
  know-how vs. knowledge-that, 124
erōs (desire), 19, 26, 106, 159, 186 n. 14, 187
  for Charmides, 118–19
  of lover in the *Phaedrus*, 107–10, 138
  as model of authority, 110

Index / 199

Euripides, 82, 113
  Bacchae, 83 n. 6
Euthyphro, 17, 26, 27, 55, 59, 60, 61–78, 81, 105, 106, 109–10, 132, 137, 155, 159, 186
  like Meletus, 62, 70, 77
  like Socrates, 64–66
  rhetorical consciousness of, 67–68

family, Greek
  and the hearth (*hestia*), 64–65
  justice in, 69–70, 183–84
  and piety, 62–63, 75
Favorinus, 143
Ferrari, G., 19 n. 20
Festugiere, A.-J., 76 n. 32
Ficino, M., 21
Finley, M. I., 178–79 n. 6
Foucault, M., 11 n. 13, 20 n. 22, 150 n. 23
Fowler, H. N., 173
Freud, S., 192
Friedländer, P., 21, 31–32, 32 n. 1, 35, 83 n. 7, 90, 112 n. 7, 114 n. 10, 120 n. 14
Furies, 70 n. 25
Fustel de Coulanges, N. P., 63 n. 15

Gadamer, H.-G., 12 n. 14, 21, 48, 60, 60 n. 10, 61, 72 n. 29, 73, 121 n. 17, 172 n. 2
Gaia, 73
Garland, R., 148 n. 18
Geach, P. T., 61 n. 12
Geertz, C., 6–7
Girard, R., and "mimetic desire," 109–10, 117 n. 12
Glaucon, 88
gods, Greek, 62, 63 n. 17
  as benefactors, 66, 72
  contrasted to humans, 67–68
  dependent on humans, 75–76, 81 n. 3, 99, 107–8
  and the family, 75
  intimidating human effort, 122–25
  nurture of (*therapeia*), 63, 77
  service of (*hupēretikē*), 77
  and *technē*, 90
  theogonic war of, 68, 73
Gorgias, 92, 98, 155, 159, 162
  Encomium of Helen, 97 n. 22, 155 n. 27
Gorgons, 149, 154
graphē (indictment, writing), 43, 48
Grassi, E., 158 n. 29
Griswold, C., 136, 159, 186 n. 15, 187 n. 16
Guthrie, W. K. C., 36, 62 n. 13, 79–80, 95, 100, 121 n. 17, 133 n. 24, 138 n. 5

Habermas, J., 48 n. 26
Hackforth, R., 138 n. 5, 169 n. 39

Halliday, M. A. K., 3 n. 4
Halperin, D., 150 n. 22, 184 n. 11
Harris, W. V., 9 n. 9, 19 n. 19
Hartman, G., 70 n. 25, 71 n. 26
Havelock, E., 8, 9 n. 9, 19 n. 19, 95
Heidegger, M., 18, 51–53, 59 n. 7, 60, 87, 124 n. 20, 192
Helen, 102–3, 155 n. 27, 192
Heraclitus, 92
hermeneutics. *See* interpretation
Herodotus, 178 n. 4, 179 n. 7
  Histories, 88
Hesiod, 87, 122–23
  Theogony, 6
Hippias, 17, 98, 163
Hippocrates, 121
Hoerber, R. G., 61 n. 12, 68 n. 20, 69 n. 21
holy, the (*to hosion*), 63, 74, 76–77, 187
  definitions of, 76 n. 33
  problematic of, 76 n. 32
  reciprocating piety, 66, 73, 75–77
  and traditional piety, 77
Homer, 6, 27, 56, 58, 60 n. 8, 80, 87, 92, 101
  distorted citation of, 84, 85–86, 94–96, 98, 99–100
  Iliad, 42, 94
  meter of, 83–84
  Odyssey, 102–3, 147–48
  protocols of, 3–5, 7
Homeridae, 88, 90
Hoopes, J. P., 63 n. 15, 69 n. 21, 69 n. 22
Hurwit, J., 91 n. 14
Hyland, D., 112 n. 5, 121 n. 17, 124 n. 20, 133 n. 24

ideas (forms)
  and participation, 47, 115
  and signification, 45–46, 180–82
  theory of, 45–47, 62–63, 175–76
ideology of Athens, 11
IJsseling, S., 9 n. 10, 158 n. 29
immortality, arguments for, 33, 138 n. 5
intentionality (of discourse), 11, 12, 14–16, 29, 182, 184–85, 189–90
interpretation (hermeneutics), 12–13, 18, 21–22, 25, 95–96, 142, 182, 188, 190, 192, 193
  and dialogue, 49
  hermeneutic circle, 7, 189
  and the *Ion*, 56–57, 79–80
  and regulation of uncertainty, 44 n. 20
  sophistical, 67, 68–69, 122–25, 124 n. 21, 149–50, 154–55
  and repressed textuality, 57 n. 5
  and textual complexity, 2–3, 60
intertextuality, 102, 153

Ion, 5, 8, 27, 36, 55, 56–59, 60, 67, 79–103, 105–6, 123, 132, 155, 163, 178, 186
Ionia, 58
irony
  Socratic, 41, 44, 75–76, 78 n. 34, 151, 153–54, 163, 180, 190
  structural (dramatic, historical), 22, 36–37, 65–66, 119, 120–21, 179
Isocrates, 164–65 n. 35, 179 nn. 6, 7, 180 n. 8
  Antidosis, 169, 169 n. 39
isonomia (equality before the law), 178
inspiration, 58, 80
  and Ion, 81–86, 89–90, 100

Jauss, H. R., 12 n. 14
justice
  absent at Socrates' trial, 38–39
  poetic, 37

kairos (opportunity), 98, 195
  and *krisis* (judgment, trial), 196
Kerrigan, J., 145 n. 13
Keuls, E., 184 n. 11
Klein, J., 80 n. 2
Kristeva, J., 153 n. 25
Kurtz, D. C., 135 n. 1, 145 n. 12, 146 n. 14

Lacan, J., 16 n. 18, 48 n. 26
La Driere, C., 101 n. 23
Lebeck, A., 153 n. 24
Levine, D. L., 124 n. 20
Lévi-Strauss, C., 24 n. 26
literacy, 19
  Greek, 8
literary features, 22–23
logical relations
  active and passive, 62–63, 74–76
  author and works, 163
  and genealogy, 89
  and deconstruction, 172, 174–75, 180–82
  function vs. person, 159–60
  genus and species, 62–63, 72
  hierarchy, 92, 98–99, 117 n. 12, 151
  in the *Phaedrus*, 136–38
  type and individual, 29, 89
  unmoved mover, 138, 159
  whole and part, 62, 87–89, 91, 99–100, 158–61, 182, 188
logographos (speechwriter), 5
logos (discourse), 10, 17. *See also* discourse
  as impersonal discussion, 48–49, 155
  and the person, 80, 153, 155–56, 159–61, 168
Lord, A. B., 7 n. 6
love. See *erōs* and *philia*
Lyceum, 64

Lysandrus, 125
Lysias, 5, 19, 137, 138, 142, 161, 180 n. 8
  discourse of, in the *Phaedrus*, 140–41, 149, 151, 159, 174
Lysis, 116
Lysistrata, 3

MacDowell, D. M., 68 n. 20, 178 n. 6
Machaon, 94
McKim, R., 129 n. 22
magic, 145
  and rhetoric, 97 n. 22, 154–56
  and texts, 19
  and tradition, 87, 97 n. 22
Marsyas, 56 n. 2, 100
Medea, 3
Melampodidae, 90
Melampus, 88
meletē (practice), 59 n. 7
Meletus, 27, 33 n. 3, 37, 38, 43, 59, 62, 64, 66, 70, 75, 77
memory, 176–78, 179 n. 7
Menelaus, 100, 102–3, 148
Meno, 17, 26, 178, 179 n. 7
Merlan, P., 10 n. 12
method
  argumentation, 10, 72 n. 29, 92
  and deconstruction, 171, 175
  and madness, 97–98, 190
  of Plato's writing, 14
Metrodorus, 88
miasma (pollution), 68 n. 20, 70 n. 24
Midas, 136, 141–47, 148, 153, 154, 155, 161, 162, 166
mimesis, 45, 160
  and ideas, 175–76, 181–82
  "mimetic desire," 108–10
  mimetic rivalry, 109–10, 111, 117, 117 n. 12, 121, 136–37
  and non-mimetic relations, 136–38, 175
  in *The Republic*, 137
  and temporality, 86
misology and misanthropy, 36, 97 n. 21, 168
monument (*mnēma, sēma*), 183
  as aesthetic whole, 160–61, 162
  cemetery, 136, 145 n. 13
  and epitaph, 145
  logic of, 154–55, 167–68
  of Midas, 142–45
  Platonic text as, 48, 183, 193, 195
Moore, J. D., 80 n. 2, 88 n. 12
mormolukeion (bugbear), 2
Murley, C., 150 n. 22, 153 n. 26
Muses, 6, 82–83, 86, 152
Myrrha, 196
myth, 3 n. 2, 4

names, proper
  catalogues of, in the *Ion*, 87–93
  individualism of, 91 n. 14
  meaning of, 58–60
  mirror of subject, 70
  and tomb, 155
narration, 147–48, 189
  and auditor in the *Charmides*, 110, 118–20, 130
  in the *Charmides*, 126–27
  narrational devices, 4–5
  narrative situation and nonlinguistic factors, 3–4
  of Phaedo, 32–33
  and Socrates' intention in the *Charmides*, 115, 118–20, 130–31
Naucratis, 176, 178
Neel, J., 9 n. 10, 186 n. 13
Neoplatonism, 21
Neumann, H., 61 n. 12, 62 n. 13
New Criticism
  in America, 22, 25
  in France, 23–25
Nietzsche, F., 18, 46, 46–47 n. 23, 146, 192
Nilsson, M., 76 n. 32
noēsis (thought), 153
nominalism, 26
nomos (custom, common law), 34, 95, 106 n. 1, 124, 132, 190
  and *phusis* (nature), 113
North, H., 112–13, 114

O'Brien, M. J., 78 n. 34
Odysseus, 60 n. 8, 147–48
Oedipus, 93 n. 15, 192 n. 19
Oliver, J. H., 70 n. 24
Olympus, 58, 87
Ong, W., 9 n. 9, 19 n. 19
opinion, 45
  philodoxos and *philosophos*, 47 n. 23
oral tradition, 8, 20
  Serbian, 7
ordinary language. *See* communication
Orpheus, 58, 87, 90, 100
Orytheia, 174

Parker, R., 70 n. 24
Parmenides, 92
Parry, A., 150 n. 22
Parry, M., 7 n. 6, 8
Partee, M. H., 80 n. 2
pastoral, 133
  defined, 150 n. 22
  and georgic, 166
  in the *Ion*, 85, 90, 96
  motifs of, 150

and oral gratification, 152
and simplification, 146, 151, 190
in the *Phaedrus*, 29, 148–56, 159, 161, 164, 169
and satire, 150
in the *Statesman*, 29
Patroclus, 94
pedagogy, 13, 105
  teacher-student relations in the *Charmides*, 116–17, 117 n. 12, 125–31, 132–33
pederasty, 27, 117 n. 12, 118–19
pelatēs (client), 69, 69 n. 22
Peloponnesian War, 26
Pentheus, 83, 100
performance, 97
  consciousness of, in the *Charmides*, 126–27
  in court, 41, 42
  embodied, 8–9, 99–100
  in the *Phaedrus*, 153–54
  public and private, 114 n. 10, 129
  of the rhapsode, 85–86, 99–100
Pericles, 26, 27, 96, 101, 177
personality cults, Greek, 20, 90–92
  and personal style, 27
persuasion (*peithō*), 106
  as perversion of justice, 40, 41, 42
Phaedo, 13, 32–33, 187
Phaedra, 3
Phaedrus, 19, 68, 107, 136–66, 176, 180 n. 8, 186, 196
  character of, 140–41, 150, 152
Pharmaceia, 174
pharmakon (poison, remedy), 19, 173–76, 188, 190, 191
Phemius, 58, 87, 100
philia (friendly or family love), 66, 69, 76 n. 32, 128, 186 n. 14, 187
Philip, A., 150 n. 22
philosophy (*philosophia*)
  embodied in Socrates, 50, 156, 187
  as interpretive criterion, 29
  and poetry, 79
  purpose of, 92, 194–95
  and rhetoric, 157–60
  and social power, 121–22
  as transhistorical project, 12
phronēsis (calculating wisdom), 77–78, 133
piety. *See* holy
Pindar, 101 n. 23
Plass, P., 106 n. 1
Plato
  anonymity of, 2, 20, 29–30, 188, 194
  as apologist for Socrates, 129–30, 147
  Apology of Socrates, 12, 15, 21–22, 23, 28, 31–53, 55, 92, 93, 95, 102, 105, 115, 121–22, 122 n. 18, 126, 154, 186, 193

as author, 20, 29–30, 48, 49–50, 187–88, 191, 193–96
Charmides, 5, 23, 60 n. 11, 92, 95, 106, 110–33, 136, 193
Cratylus, 71 n. 27, 133
Critias, 149 n. 20
Crito, 27, 31, 34, 35, 50
Derrideanism of, 172–73, 190–91
early vs. late dialogues, 28–29, 188–89, 194
Euthyphro, 27–28, 59, 61–78, 154, 193
and fiction of the *Phaedrus*, 138, 156, 162
Gorgias, 7, 23, 40, 40 n. 13, 65, 95, 158
Ion, 27–28, 56–59, 79–103, 111, 123, 136, 154, 158, 193
and language, 55–56, 58–60, 96–97
Laws, 112
Lysis, 69, 186 n. 14
Meno, 89, 178
nephew of Charmides, 111, 115
and the "noble lie," 56 n. 1, 178
Parmenides, 181, 191
Phaedo, 1–2, 12, 13, 14, 23, 31, 32–33, 35, 36, 50, 52, 60 n. 11, 97 n. 21, 155, 168
Phaedrus, 5, 7, 15, 18, 19, 21, 29, 32, 47, 57 n. 5, 84, 98, 103, 106, 107–10, 117, 117 n. 12, 133, 135–69, 173–80, 184, 189–90, 192–93, 195–96
philosophy of, 10, 20 n. 22, 22, 28–29, 180–83, 189, 194–95
Plato-tree (*platanos*), 21, 195–96
poetics of, 20 n. 22
Protagoras, 60 n. 11, 71 n. 27, 78 n. 34, 124 n. 21, 135, 161, 162
Republic, 4, 28, 43–44, 47 n. 23, 98, 113, 126, 137, 149 n. 20, 161
"Second Epistle," 14–18, 20, 30
at Socrates' trial, 51
Sophist, 28–29, 160
Statesman, 13, 28–29, 149 n. 20, 160, 161
as subject, 11–12, 29–30
Symposium, 4, 17, 19, 46, 50, 56 n. 2, 100, 108, 129, 131, 135, 137, 147, 153, 154, 160, 162, 163, 194
Theatetus, 4, 13, 17, 49, 60, 135, 154
Timaeus, 178 n. 4, 179 n. 6
as writer, 9–15, 23–24, 56–57, 78, 179 n. 7, 188, 190
Platonism, 37, 45–48, 53, 172, 175, 176, 189, 191–92, 194
polis (city), 36
as Meletus's mother, 59
Polugnotus, 58, 87, 88
Polus, 90–91 n. 13, 163
portraiture
funerary, 145
internal vs. external setting of, 147–48, 162

literary, 135–36
in the *Phaedrus*, 137–40
sculptural, 135–36
strangeness of, 139
poststructuralism and structuralism, 24–25, 56 n. 3
Potidaea, 110, 130
Praxagora, 3
problem
as construction, 13–14
and the problematic, 76 n. 32
as textual strategy, 14, 187–88, 194–95
Prometheus, 192 n. 18
proper, the, 60 n. 8
Protagoras, 26, 78 n. 34, 92, 98, 106, 154, 162
Proteus, 36, 100, 102–3
protocols. *See* reading
prōtokollon, 3 n. 3
Pythagoras, 92

Rabinowitz, W. G., 62 n. 13
Ranta, J., 80 n. 2, 103 n. 26
reading
against common sense, 17–19
against the dialogues, 28–29, 72 n. 29
critical, in the *Phaedrus*, 142, 145, 151, 176–77, 180, 193
historicist protocols of, 10–12
humanistic protocols of, 11–13
philological protocols of, 10
philosophical protocols of, 7–8, 9–10, 188–89
and Platonism, 25, 52–53
privileged situation of, 24
protocols of, 3–13
protocols in Plato, 7
as revision, 88–89, 95–96, 98, 122–24, 182, 189–90, 193
and social innovation, 177–78
of Socrates, 40, 186, 193–94
relativism, 26
representation, 45–47
of nature against death, 145
and presentation, 41–42
rhapsode, art of, 80, 84–86, 88, 97, 153
Rhea, 73
rhetoric, 9, 20, 25, 40, 55, 99, 124, 141–42, 154, 155–56, 162–63, 165, 167–68, 195
art of, 156–59, 163, 178
ethics of, 158–59
as mastery of beasts, 149, 151, 160–61, 166, 169
and *peithō* (persuasion, seduction), 106
and rhetoricians, 157, 159, 163, 179 n. 7
of Socrates' apology, 33–38, 33 n. 3, 42–45
texts, 163

rhetorical culture, 5
  and demagoguery, 26–27, 101
Richter, G., 135–36, 145 n. 12
Ricoeur, P., 49 n. 27, 95 n. 20, 182 n. 9
Robinson, R., 63 n. 14
Robinson, T. M., 138 n. 5
Roochnik, D., 186 n. 15
Rosen, S., 28 n. 28, 133 n. 24, 160 n. 30, 186 n. 13, 187 n. 16
Rosenmeyer, T. G., 150 n. 22
Rosenstock, B., 162 n. 33
Rousseau, J.-J., 24 n. 26

Sallis, J., 43 n. 18
Santas, G., 117 n. 13, 121 n. 17
Sartre, J.-P., 73
de Saussure, F., 24 n. 26
Schein, S., 7 n. 6
Schmid, W. T., 132 n. 23
Scholes, R., 3 n. 2, 186 n. 13
Seeskin, K. R., 9 n. 11
Segal, C., 24 n. 25
self. *See* subject
Semonides, 143–44, 146, 147, 163
Sextus Empiricus, 113 n. 9
Shakespeare
  Desdemona and Iago in *Othello*, 42
Shorey, P., 164 n. 35
signification
  breakdown of, 57–58, 185, 191
  and communication, 6, 16–18, 50
  and copyright, 184–85
  and gravestones, 145 n. 13, 183
  and metaphoric language, 152–53, 181–83
  mytheme, 180
  naturalized signs, 4–5, 183–84
  and Platonism, 45–47, 52–53, 180–81, 191
  play of signifier, 182–83
  social ground of, 6–7, 12–13, 114 n. 10
  structures of, 6–7, 12–13, 184–85
Silenus, 146–47, 149, 151
Simmias, 2, 13, 33
Simonides, 124 n. 21, 142–44
Siren, 153
skutalē (code baton), 6
Socrates
  and "accomplished man" of the *Phaedrus*, 163–69, 176, 183, 184, 186, 193
  and argumentation, 92, 117, 120, 125–26, 127–30
  audacity of, 36
  as Critias's associate, 110–11, 115, 125–31, 133 n. 25
  daimonion of, 50, 64
  as demagogue, 27, 45
  and diatribe, 64

  discourse (or *logos*) of, 22–23, 32, 33, 37–38, 47–48, 49–51, 72 n. 29, 75–76, 78 n. 34, 93–94, 128–29, 139, 152–56, 158–60, 164–66, 169, 176, 179–80, 185–88, 190–96
  fable of Ammon and Theuth of, 173–80, 189, 191
  fable of magnetic rings of, 56–57, 81–85, 89–90
  as father figure, 71, 130
  as gadfly, 31–32, 43
  as go-between of Critias and Charmides, 116–17, 126
  guilt or innocence of, 33, 51, 115
  as heroic, 42, 43, 194
  indictment of, 62
  as intimidating questioner, 66, 83, 102, 140–41
  lack of self-knowledge of, 50, 96–97, 120–21, 127–28, 156, 193
  as magician, 2, 47, 120
  mistaken identity of, 42–43, 78 n. 34, 128–30, 163–64, 193
  as model of piety, 76, 76 n. 32, 78
  as model of refutation, 28–29, 189
  as mother, 169
  myths told by, as self-subverting, 84–85, 86, 107
  as narrator, 115, 118–20, 130–31, 179–80
  novel inquiry of, 27, 158, 159–60
  openness of, 35, 46, 76, 103, 180, 188–89, 190
  palinode chariot myth of, 107–10, 136, 137, 146–47, 151, 152–56, 190
  as pastoralist, 151–52, 154
  as pederast, 118–19, 129
  perplexed, 34–38, 40–41, 49, 50–51, 186
  personae of, in the *Apology*, 36, 42–45
  as philosophical authority, 127–31
  philosohy of, compared to Critias's, 120–22, 125, 126, 129–30
  as physician, 120–21
  Platonic biography of, 23, 28, 195
  as Plato's mouthpiece, 30, 48, 194
  as rhapsode, 83, 84–85, 89–90, 94, 96, 97–98, 153
  role-playing of, 154, 158–59, 163–64, 166, 193
  as savior, 45
  as scapegoat, 43, 45, 51, 77, 110
  self-incrimination of, 33, 38–39, 115, 129–30
  self-presentation of, 42–45, 46, 193
  as Silenus, 147, 147 n. 16
  as sophist, 97, 130
  as teacher, 127–31

as technocrat, 92, 121–22, 126
as writer, 52, 186, 190
as writing, 46–48, 103, 139, 147, 156, 186, 193–94
Solon, 179 n. 7
sophistry, 9, 124–25, 158, 195
　in the *Charmides*, 120
　and *paideia* (education), 97–98, 190
　and poets, 101 n. 23
　and sophists, 74, 116, 154–55, 162, 164
Sophocles
　Antigone, 11, 35 n. 9
　Oedipus Tyrranus, 41, 93 n. 15, 192 n. 19
sōphrosunē (temperance, discipline), 111–33
　and Charmides, 111–12
　as doing one's own business, 111, 116, 120, 128, 133
　and experience (disenchantment) 113
　as innocence, 112
　internal and external, 114–15, 131–32
　as knowing one's place, 112, 121, 132–33
　as knowledge of knowledge, 125, 129, 133
　as moderation, 111, 112
　paradox of, 114–15, 129
　and personal bearing, 114–15
　and power, 118, 121–22, 132–33
　as science of good and evil, 127, 130
　as self-knowledge, 121–25, 131–33
　and the *sōphrōn* person, 132–33
　Spartan fashion of, 114
　and war, 112, 118
sparagmos (dismemberment), 99
Stasinus, 71–72, 75
Stesichorus, 155 n. 27, 176, 192
Stesimbrotus, 88
Strauss, L., 21, 41 n. 15
subject (self), 48
　artificial body of, 155, 161, 162, 168, 184
　and language community, 59–60, 132, 184
　and personal whole, 158–59
　self-advancement, 105–7, 124–25
　self-fashioning, 92–93, 107–8, 114, 150, 161, 162, 166, 190
　and self-knowledge, 49–50, 52–53, 131–33, 136, 159–60
　and society, 113, 131–33
　written, 78, 80–81, 166, 184
Swearingen, C. J., 9 n. 10

Taylor, A. E., 60 n. 12, 68 n. 20, 69 n. 21
technē (art), 81, 83, 149
　and authority, 89–90, 98, 163, 177–78, 192
　and ethical and political value, 95–96, 192
　and experience, 90–91 n. 13
　Hippocratic description of, 121
　and *hubris*, 93, 99, 192

　in Homer, 94–98
　and magic, 97–98
　as model of philosophical knowledge, 89–93
　and the person, 90–93, 98, 99, 101, 163
　poetics, 87, 89
　sociology of, 192
Tel Quel, 172
text transmission, 5
　and classical studies, 8
textuality, 173
　and Plato's writing, 15–16, 23–25
　relation to Socrates' discourse, 47–48, 50, 72 n. 29, 98–99, 185–86, 189–91, 193–96
　repressed, 57
Thamus (Ammon), 173–80
　as despot, 177–80, 189, 190, 191, 192, 193, 195
　as monarch, 176–77
Thamyrus, 58, 87, 100
theater. *See* drama
themis (law and order), 177
Theoclymenus, 94
Theodorus, 13, 52, 163
　the metalworker, 87–88
thesmophoriazousai, 3
thētes, 77
Thetis, 94
Theuth, 173–80, 189, 191, 192, 195
Thirty, the, 119
Thrasymachus, 26, 27, 157, 179 n. 6, 179 n. 7
Thucydides, 26
Timaeus, 179 n. 6, 179 n. 7
Tiresias, 41
tradition, 12–13, 79–80, 96–99, 102–3, 144–45, 152–53, 190, 191
　and canonical texts, 12–13, 18–19
　Greek cultural, 27, 90–91
　musical, 8, 57, 86–93, 97–98
　and Platonism, 48, 51, 176, 194–95
　as temporal, 84–87, 98–99
transcendence
　and authority, 26, 89–90, 123, 187, 191–92
　critique of, 25–28, 191
　and demystification, 66, 81 n. 3, 82
Tuckey, T. G., 112 n. 5, 133 n. 25
Tynnichus, 89, 91

Vermeule, E., 69 n. 23, 143–44, 144 n. 11, 145 n. 12, 148 n. 18, 149, 155, 168
Vernant, J.-P., 76 n. 33, 148 n. 18, 155
Vidal-Naquet, P., 161 n. 31
voice, 138 n. 5
　and famous names, 58
　Greek middle, 26, 74
　of the text, 19

Index / 205

Weber, M., 19 n. 21
Welliver, W., 111 n. 4
West, G. S., 124 n. 19
West, T. G., 33, 34, 41, 41 n. 16, 43 n. 18, 51 n. 30, 124 n. 19
Wilcox, J. F., 80 n. 2, 97 nn. 21, 22
Wolz, H. G., 62 n. 13
wordplay, 21–23, 182–83
   daktulos and *daktulios*, 56–57, 83–84
   katechetai and *echetai*, 81 n. 3
   melos and *meli*, 57, 100
   and proper names, 58–60, 70
   Zeus, *dei*, *deos*, *deon*, *aidōs*, and *deinos*, 71–72
writing
   anagrammatic, 179–80, 188
   as art, 192
   compared to embodied discourse, 47–48, 139–40, 188
   deceptiveness of, 45, 139
   double writing, 183–84, 190
   general writing, 46, 181–82, 185, 192
   and memory, 173, 175, 176–78, 193
   permanence of, 144–45, 167
   as *pharmakon*, 173–76
   as *pharmakos* (scapegoat), 176
   power of, 19
   proper and improper, 164–69, 175, 180–81
Wycherley, R. E., 135 n. 1

Xenophon, 34–35, 41, 139, 156
   "Apology of Socrates," 34 n. 7

Yeats, W. B., 49

Zeus, 62, 66, 68, 71–72, 73, 76 n. 32, 160, 192, 196
   leader of erotic host, 107–10, 155

www.ingramcontent.com/pod-product-compliance
Lightning Source LLC
Chambersburg PA
CBHW031550300426
44111CB00006BA/253